KUMON

Skills for success in school and beyond!

Ace First Grade

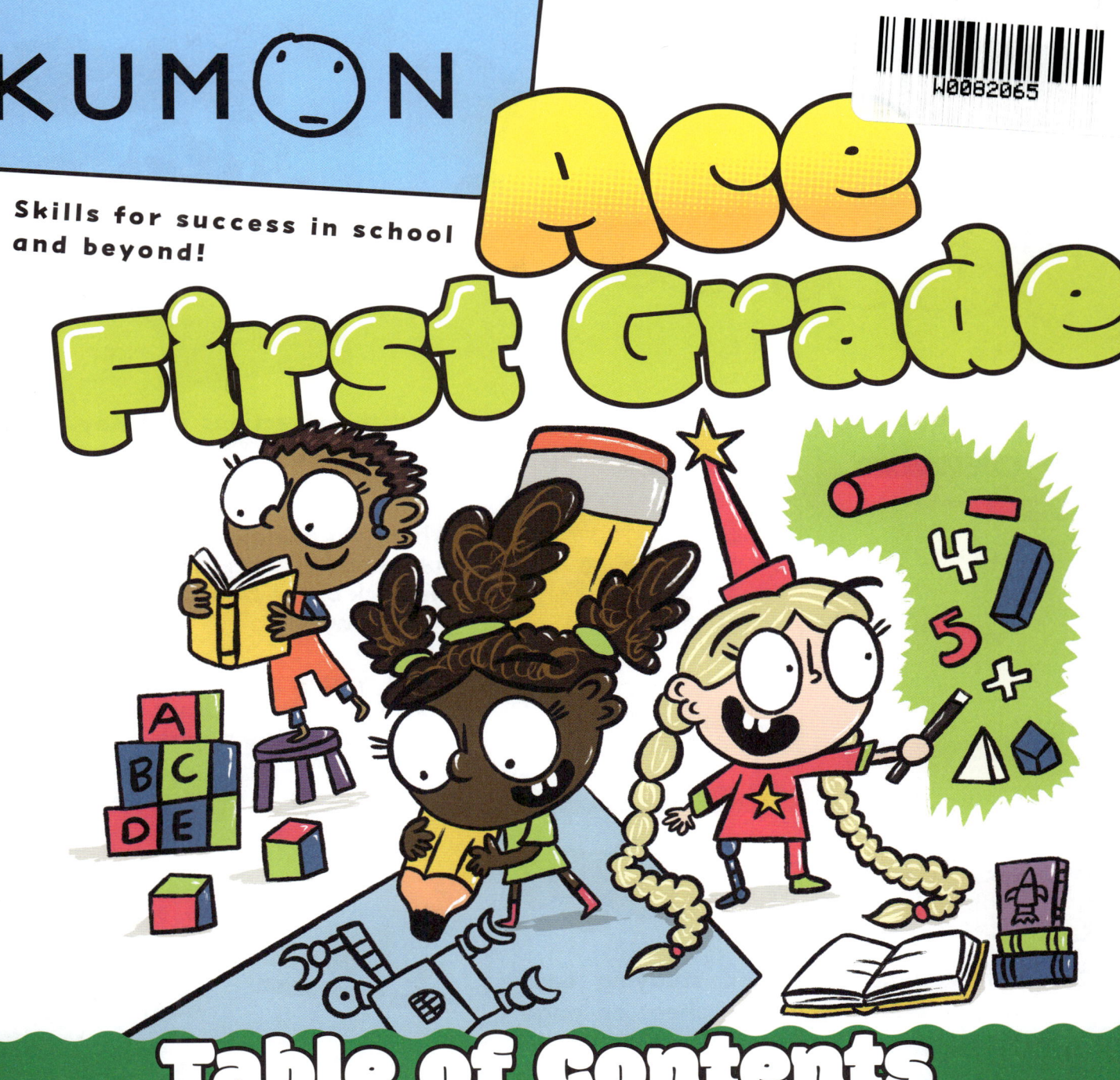

Table of Contents

Welcome to Kumon Ace First Grade ... 2

Unit 1 ... 3

Unit 2 ... 65

Unit 3 ... 127

Unit 4 ... 189

Unit 5 ... 251

Answer Key ... 313

Certificate of Achievement ... 319

W0082065

Welcome to Kumon Ace First Grade

① Write the date at the top of each page.

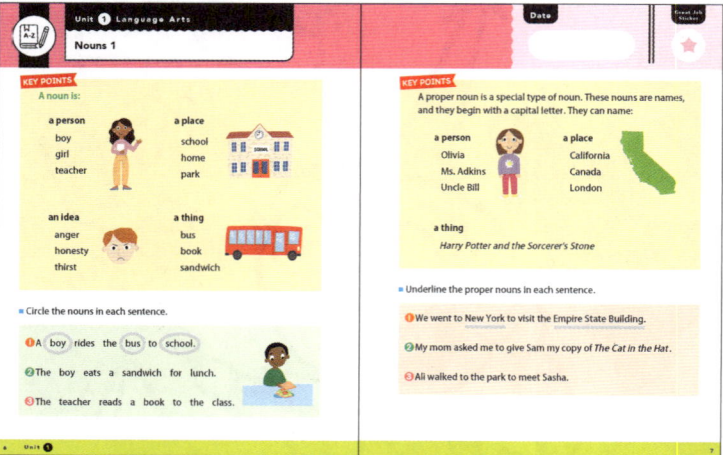

Let's study!

⭐ When you have finished studying each unit, put a sticker on the sheet on page 319.

⭐ When you have finished all of the units, place the largest sticker at the bottom of the same sheet.

⭐ Then have your parent or guardian sign the Certificate of Achievement and present it to you!

② Read the directions and Key Points on each page. Then complete each activity.

③ When you complete a section, check your answers with the Answer Key in the back of the book. Try again if you got any wrong.

④ When you are done checking your answers, place a "Great Job" sticker on the top of the page!

Cut out the study posters and hang them up for further study!

Unit ❶ Table of Contents

Use this page to keep track of your progress throughout the book. Place a check mark in the box when you have completed a section.

📖 Language Arts

- ☐ Uppercase and Lowercase Letters ---- 004
- ☐ Nouns 1 ---- 006
- ☐ Nouns 2 ---- 008
- ☐ Verbs ---- 010
- Brain Break ---- 012
- Mindfulness Break! ---- 013

📖 Reading

- ☐ Short Vowels ---- 014
- ☐ Long Vowels ---- 016
- ☐ Consonant Blends ---- 018
- ☐ Digraphs ---- 020
- Brain Break ---- 022
- Mindfulness Break! ---- 023

📊 Math

- ☐ Numbers 1–10 ---- 024
- ☐ Numbers 1–30 ---- 026
- ☐ Numbers 1–120 ---- 028
- ☐ Place Value ---- 030
- ☐ Greater Than or Less Than ---- 032
- Brain Break ---- 034
- Maze Break! ---- 035

💡 Science

- ☐ Living Things: Plants ---- 036
- ☐ Parts of a Plant ---- 038
- ☐ Plants and the Environment ---- 040
- ☐ Plant Adaptations ---- 042
- Brain Break ---- 044
- Art Break! ---- 045

🌐 Social Studies

- ☐ The United States ---- 046
- ☐ Famous Historical People of the United States ---- 048
- ☐ US Holidays ---- 050
- ☐ US National Symbols ---- 052
- Brain Break ---- 054
- Mindfulness Break! ---- 055

🖥 Technology

- ☐ Modern Technology ---- 056
- ☐ Computer Parts ---- 058
- ☐ Keyboard Skills ---- 060
- ☐ Secret Code ---- 062
- Physical Education Break! ---- 064

Uppercase and Lowercase Letters

■ Trace the letters A to Z.

A   A   B   B   C   C   D   D

E   E   F   F   G   G   H   H

I   I   J   J   K   K   L   L

M   M   N   N   O   O   P   P

Q   Q   R   R   S   S   T   T

U   U   V   V   W   W   X   X

Y   Y   Z   Z

Date

Great Job Sticker

■ Trace the letters a to z.

a	a	b	b	c	c	d	d
e	e	f	f	g	g	h	h
i	i	j	j	k	k	l	l
m	m	n	n	o	o	p	p
q	q	r	r	s	s	t	t
u	u	v	v	w	w	x	x
y	y	z	z				

Nouns 1

A noun is:

a person

boy

girl

teacher

a place

school

home

park

an idea

anger

honesty

thirst

a thing

bus

book

sandwich

■ Circle the nouns in each sentence.

❶ A ⬭boy⬭ rides the ⬭bus⬭ to ⬭school.⬭

❷ The boy eats a sandwich for lunch.

❸ The teacher reads a book to the class.

KEY POINTS

A proper noun is a special type of noun. These nouns are names, and they begin with a capital letter. They can name:

a person

Olivia

Ms. Adkins

Uncle Bill

a place

California

Canada

London

a thing

Harry Potter and the Sorcerer's Stone

■ Underline the proper nouns in each sentence.

❶ We went to New York to visit the Empire State Building.

❷ My mom asked me to give Sam my copy of *The Cat in the Hat*.

❸ Ali walked to the park to meet Sasha.

Nouns 2

KEY POINTS

A possessive noun is a noun that is owned by someone or something. "Josh's book" is a possessive noun because it is a book that belongs to Josh. Here are some more examples:

Carlos's pencil

the cat's toy

Dena's house

■ Rewrite the nouns as possessive nouns.

1 backpack, Katie — Katie's backpack

_____

2 apple, Tony

_____

3 computer, mouse

_____

■ Read the story. Circle the nouns, underline the proper nouns, and highlight the possessive nouns.

Lila was nervous. She held her dad's hand.

"Hi, I'm Ms. Francis," the teacher said.

"Welcome to Pine Grove Elementary School!"

Lila took off her backpack and sat down at

a desk. She saw her friend Quincy. Quincy

waved and Lila smiled. So far this school

wasn't so bad.

Verbs

KEY POINTS

A verb is an action word.

Some verbs are: swim

draw

listen

yell

dance

whisper

■ Fill in the blanks with the correct verb.

| play | paint | sing |

1 I ___paint___ a picture.

2 We _____ a song.

3 They _____ a game.

KEY POINTS

When one person does the action, use a singular verb. If more than one person does the action, use a plural verb. A singular verb usually has an 's' on the end.

Singular verbs: She runs.

He jumps.

For 'you' and 'I', use a singular verb.

I run. I jump.

You run. You jump.

Plural verbs: They run.

They jump.

■ Circle the correct verb.

① Wendy like / (likes) pizza.

② Mr. Gonzalez drive / drives to work.

③ Karla and Mike ride / rides the bus.

Brain Break
Noun Word Search

■ Circle the words in the Word Search.

boy	girl	teacher	school	park
anger	honesty	thirst	bus	book

S	T	Q	R	Z	W	E	R	B	U	S	T	Y	U
C	R	A	B	O	Y	C	Y	W	F	U	Y	O	B
H	F	Z	F	X	S	D	V	E	A	I	J	A	O
O	H	X	V	E	D	H	T	R	M	O	K	V	O
O	J	S	G	T	F	O	T	H	O	P	A	R	K
L	K	W	B	Y	S	N	O	J	I	R	K	C	P
S	M	G	T	U	D	E	I	C	Y	T	L	F	P
E	D	I	Y	O	F	S	U	V	B	N	M	G	O
F	E	R	U	L	G	T	H	I	R	S	T	H	I
G	R	L	J	K	H	Y	N	E	C	V	B	J	K
H	T	H	M	K	U	S	D	V	T	Y	U	I	O
U	I	L	K	N	M	C	T	E	A	C	H	E	R
A	N	G	E	R	B	N	M	R	E	W	Q	A	S

Mindfulness Break!

- Use your finger to trace the path.
  Take a deep breath in at each circle and exhale out at each square.

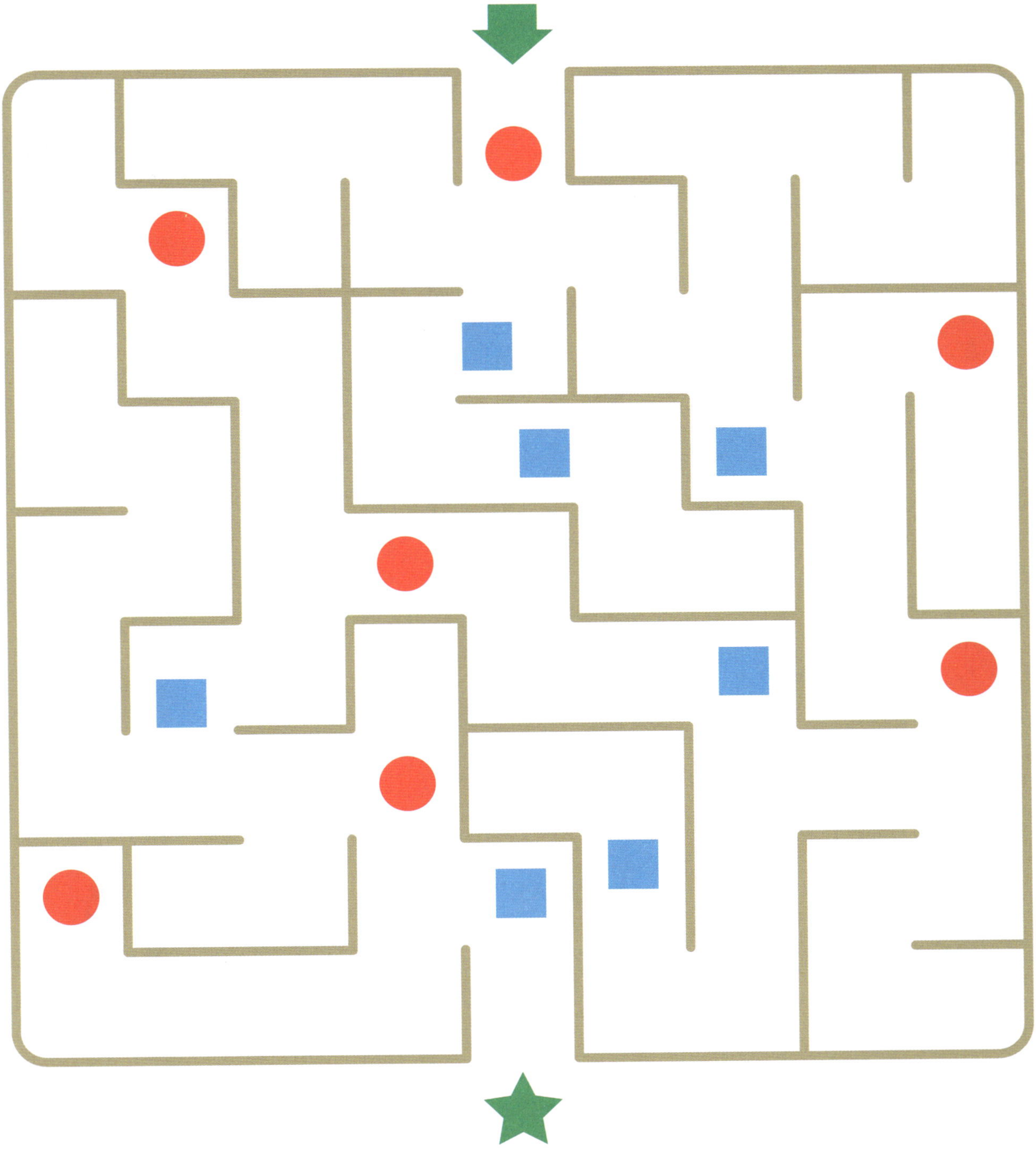

Short Vowels

Vowels are the letters A, E, I, O, and U. Vowels can be long or short. Here are the short vowels:

Short A bag

fan

Short O pot

log

Short E red

wet

Short U sun

rub

Short I rip

lid

■ Circle the short vowel in each word.

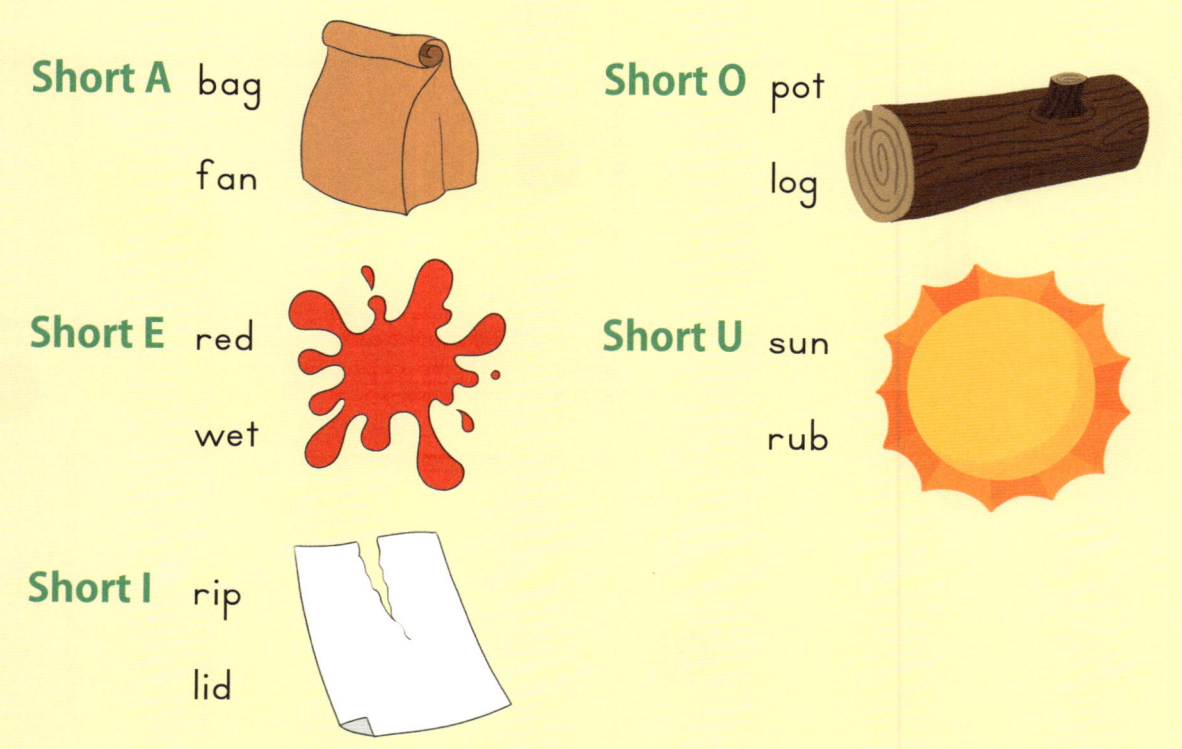

s⬭ing   lot   bun

well   rat

■ Match the words to the short vowel.

tin

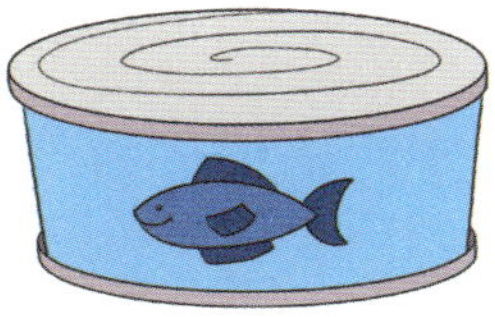

sat

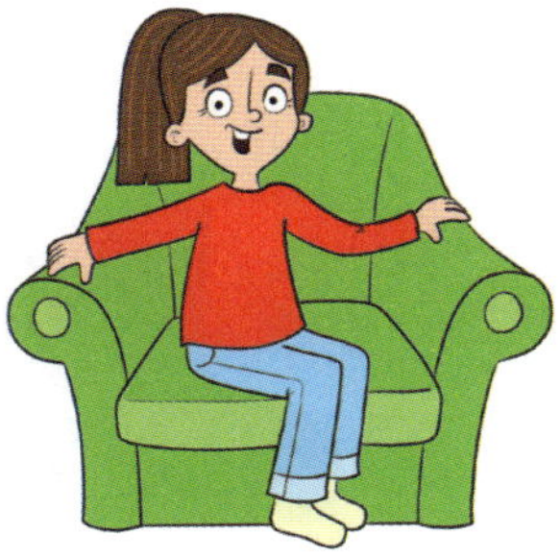

mug

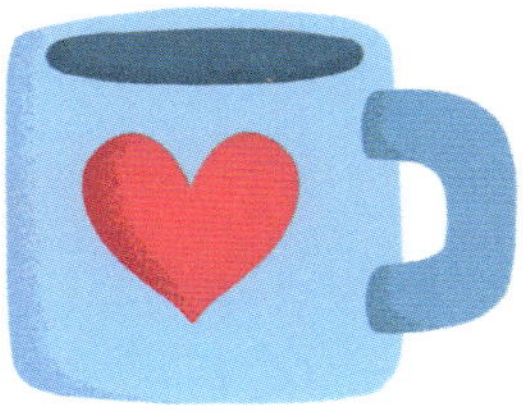

cot

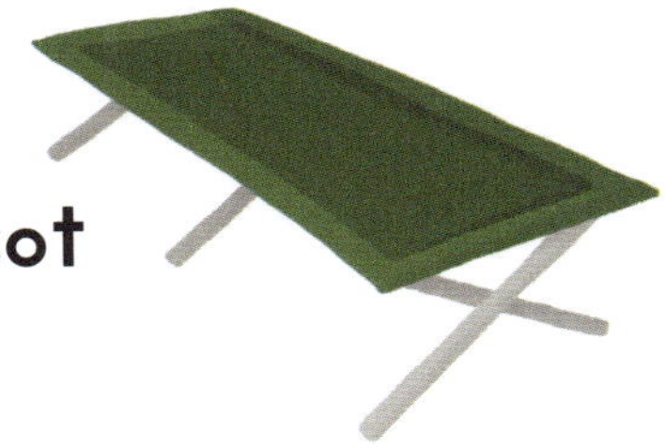

leg

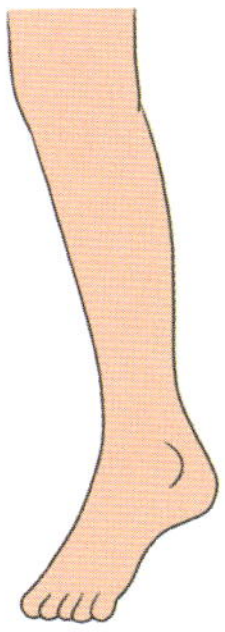

a

e

i

o

u

Long Vowels

KEY POINTS

Vowels can also be long. Here are the long vowels:

Long A face
rain

Long O goat
phone

Long E teeth
wheel

Long U truth
boot

Long I light
rice

■ Circle the long vowel in each word.

s(a)le   bone   root

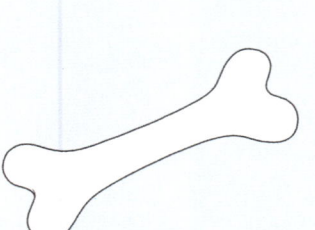

bean   fire

■ Match the words to the long vowel.

pole   ●   ●   **a**

bear   ●   ●   **e**

peel   ●   ●   **i**

pool   ●   ●   **o**

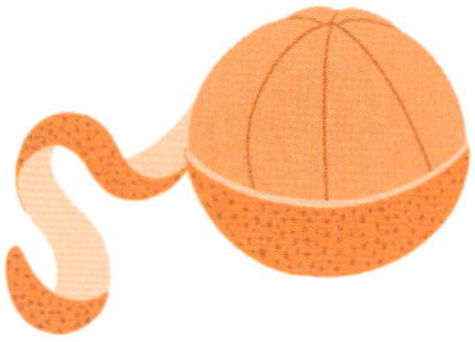

sign   ●   ●   **u**

Consonant Blends

A consonant blend is when two consonants' sounds blend together when you say them out loud.

bl	blur	**dr**	drive	**gr**	grape	**sm**	small
br	broom	**fl**	fly	**pl**	play	**sp**	spy
cl	claw	**fr**	frame	**pr**	proud	**st**	stop
cr	creek	**gl**	glitter	**sl**	slip	**tr**	try

■ Say each word out loud. Circle the blend.

break   spot

greet   flame

plop   clip

■ Match the words to the correct consonant blend.

blue

smile

speak

train

grill

plant

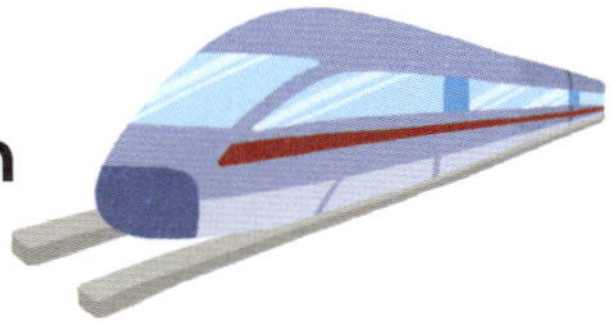

crown

sm

cr

bl

pl

sp

gr

tr

KEY POINTS

A digraph also has two consonants. These letters come together to make a new sound.

ch cheek

sh shark

ph photo

th think

■ Circle the digraphs in each word.

(ch)in   shine

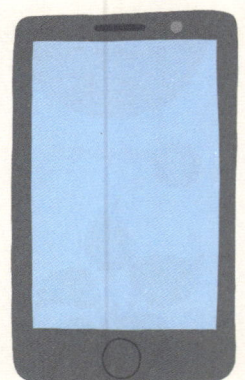

phone   this

Date

Great Job Sticker

Fill in the blank with the correct digraph.

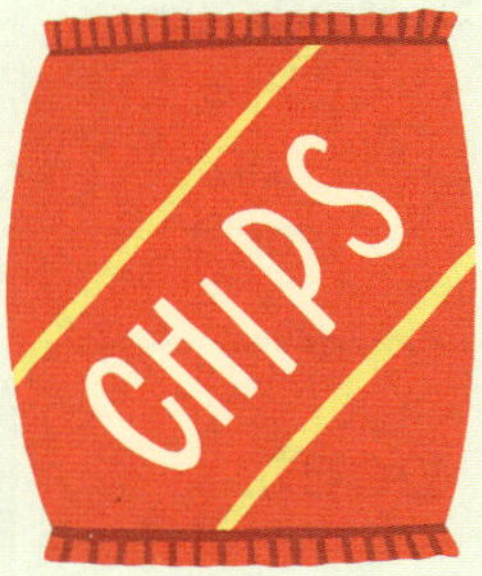

c h ips

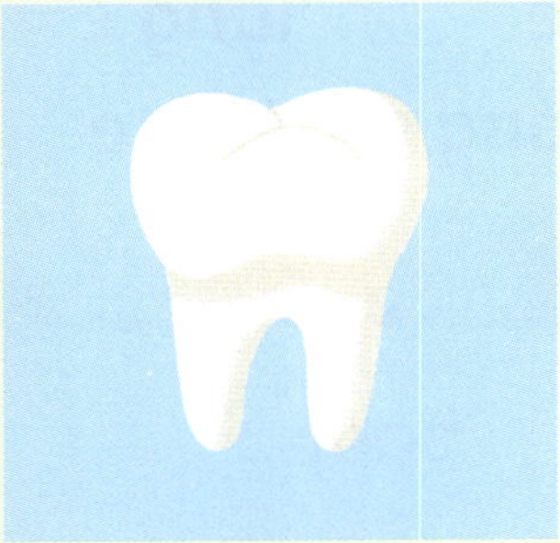

too __ __

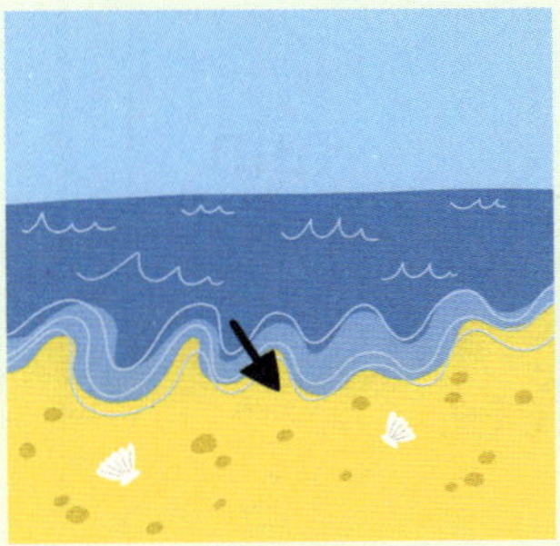

__ __ ore

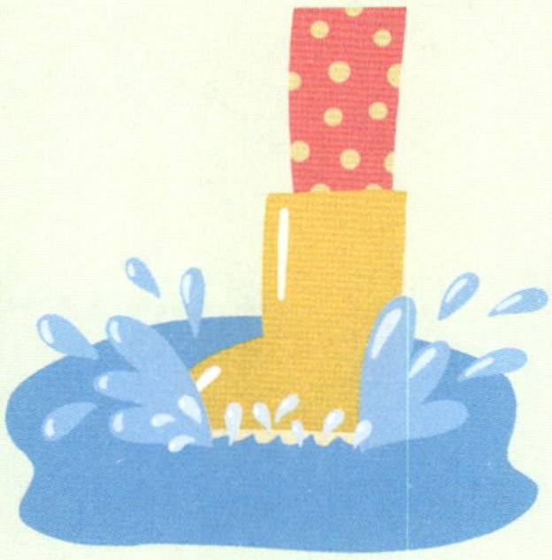

spla __ __

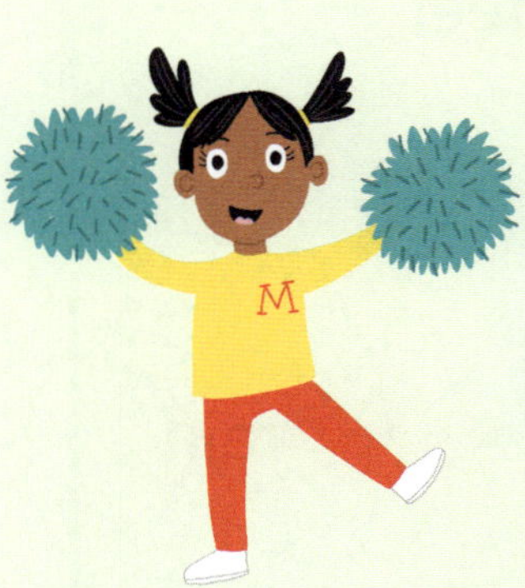

__ __ eer

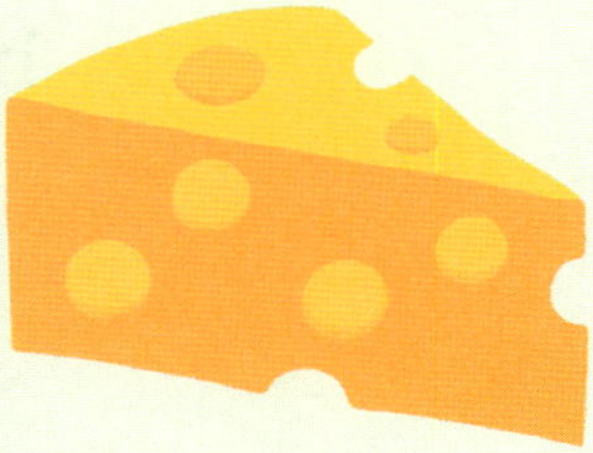

__ __ eese

Brain Break
Color by letter: Long Vowels

■ Use the key below to color by letter.

long a = blue	long e = orange	long i = yellow
long o = white	long u = gray	

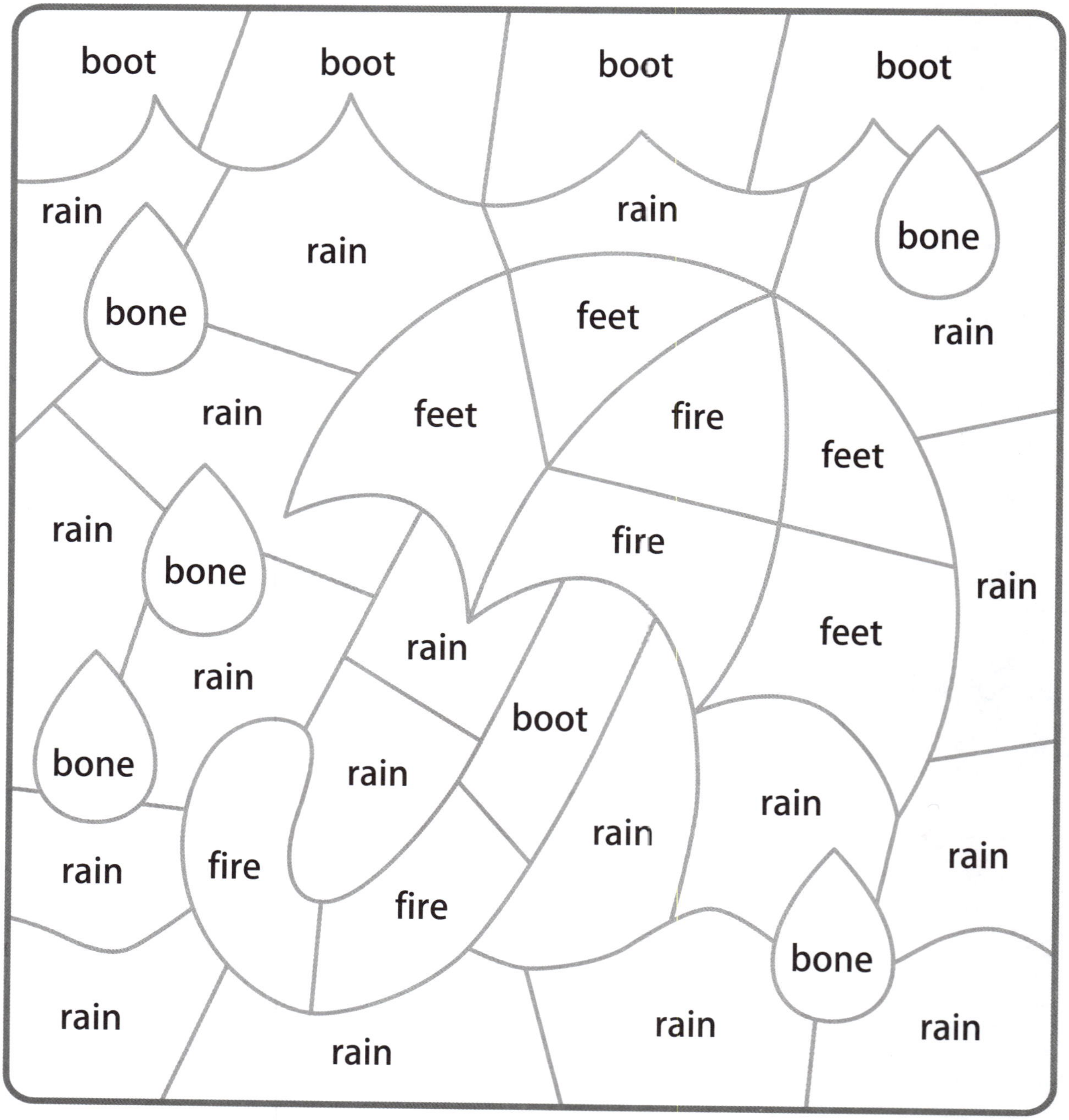

boot   boot   boot   boot

rain   rain

rain   rain   bone

bone   feet   rain

rain   feet   fire   feet

rain
bone   fire

feet

rain

boot

rain   rain

bone   rain   rain

rain   fire   fire   rain

bone

rain

rain   rain   rain

Mindfulness Break!

■ Use your finger to trace the rainbow and breathe in and out.

Breathe in ···、

Breathe in ···、

Breathe in ···、

Breathe out ···、

Breathe out ···、

Breathe out ···、

Start

Hold

Hold

Numbers 1–10

■ How many are there? Draw a line to the correct answer.

 ●

 ●

 ●

 ●

 ●

●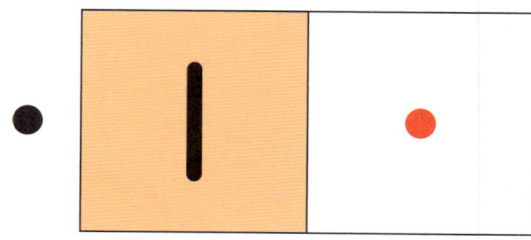

●

●

●

●

•

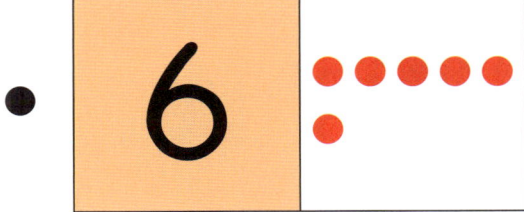

•

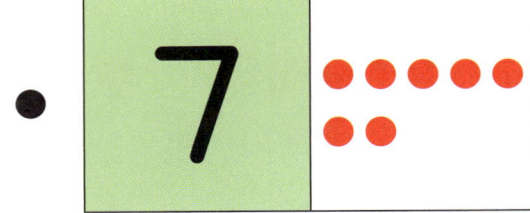

•

•

9

•

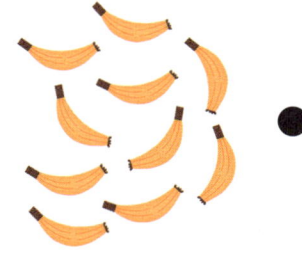

•

Numbers 1–30

■ Write the numbers and say them aloud.

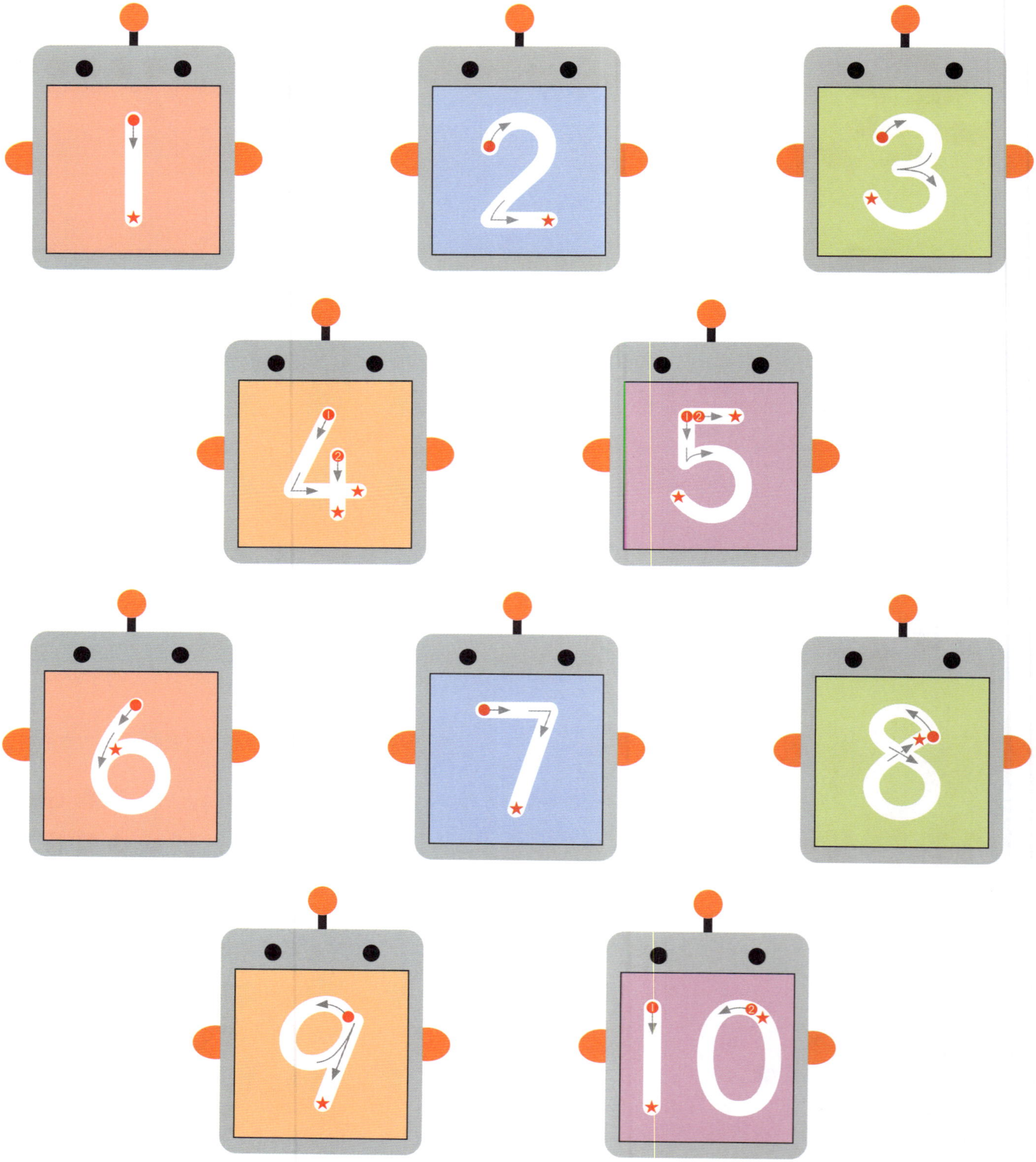

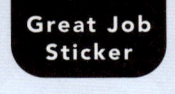

■ Fill in the missing numbers. Say each number aloud.

1	2	3	4	5
6	7	8	9	10
11	12	13	14	15
16	17	18	19	20
21	22	23	24	25
26	27	28	29	30

Numbers 1–120

■ Draw a line from 1 to 120 in order while saying each number.

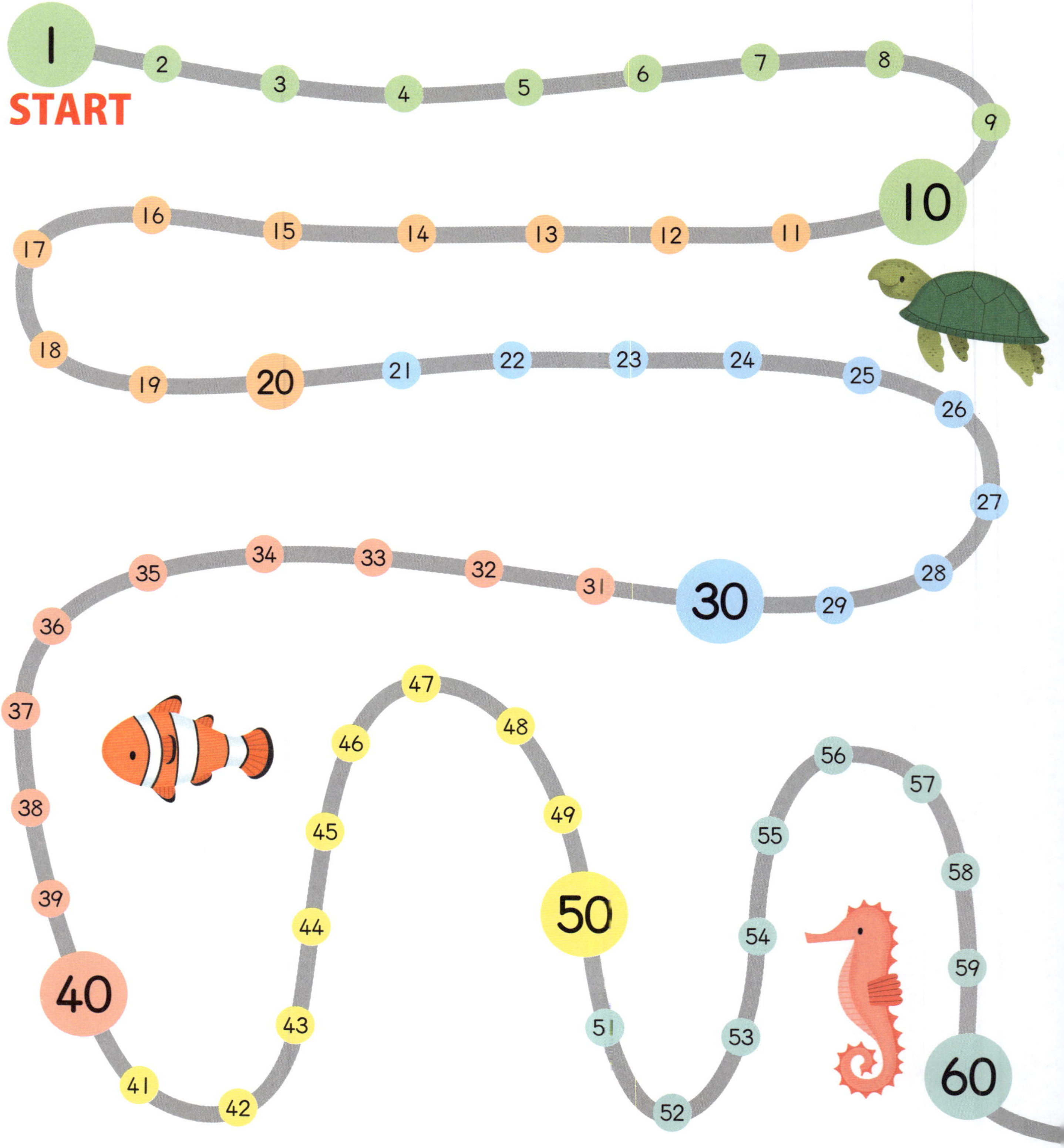

1 **START**

2 3 4 5 6 7 8 9 10

16 15 14 13 12 11

17 18 19 20 21 22 23 24 25 26

27 28 29 30 31 32 33 34 35 36 37 38 39 40 41 42 43 44 45 46 47 48 49 50 51 52 53 54 55 56 57 58 59 60

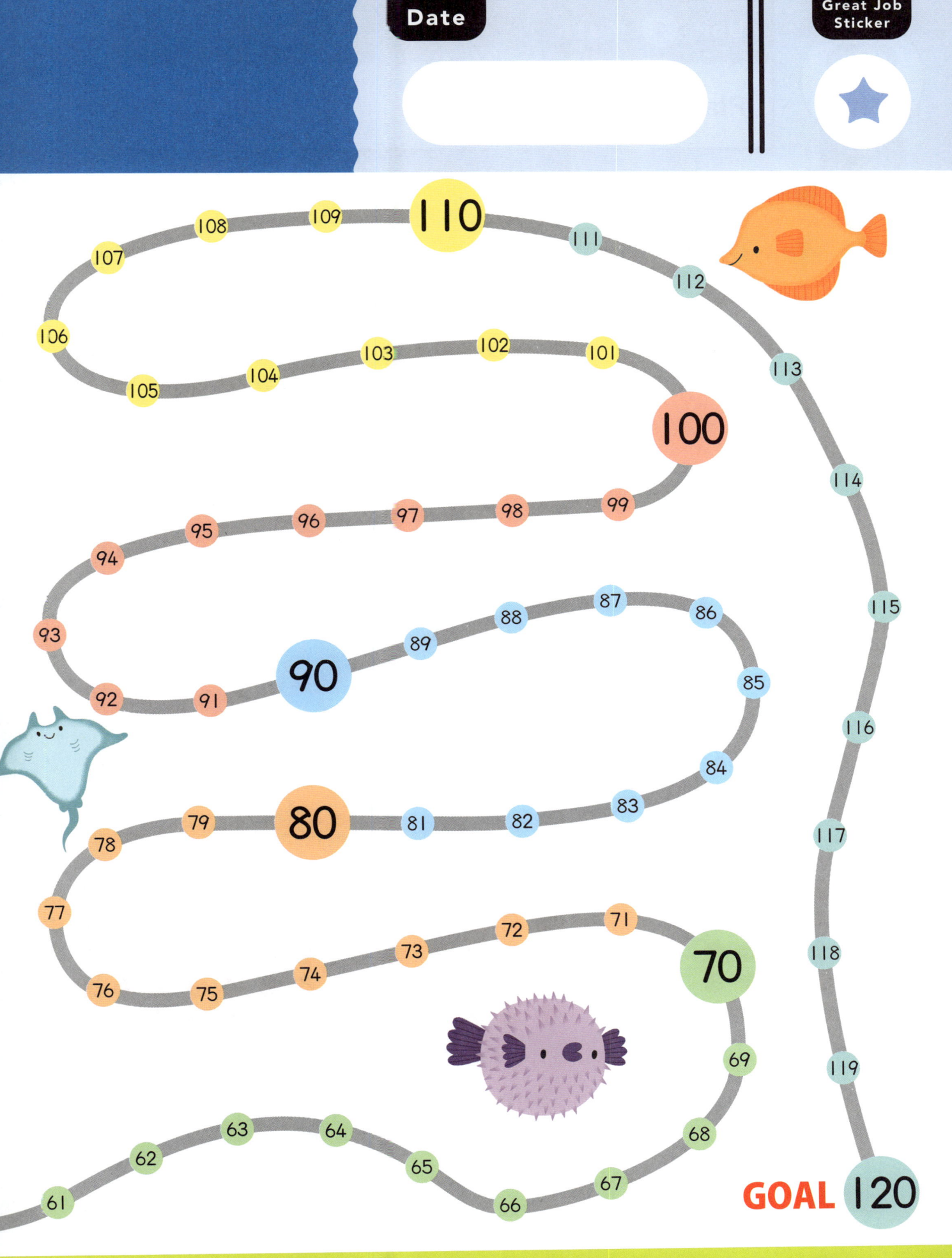

GOAL 120

Place Value

Tens (place value) tells us how many groups of ten we have.

Ones (place value) tells us how many single ones we have.

Tens	Ones
1	2

Tens	Ones
2	6

Tens	Ones
3	0

■ Circle the objects below in groups of ten. Then write the number of tens and ones in the box.

1

2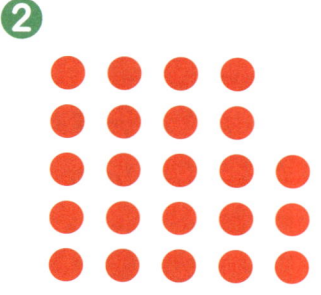

3

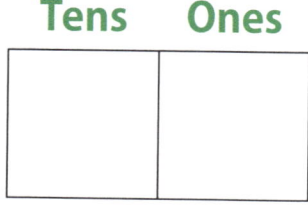

Tens	Ones

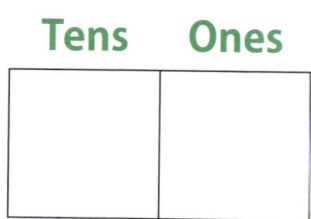

Tens	Ones

Tens	Ones

■ **Fill in the number of tens and ones.**

1 17 has [1] tens and [7] ones

2 21 has [ ] tens and [ ] ones

3 45 has [ ] tens and [ ] ones

4 33 has [ ] tens and [ ] ones

5 96 has [ ] tens and [ ] ones

6 52 has [ ] tens and [ ] ones

Greater Than or Less Than

KEY POINTS

Greater Than   **>**   **Less Than** **<**   **Equal To** **=**

■ Count the objects. Then write the symbol >, <, or = in the box.

1

4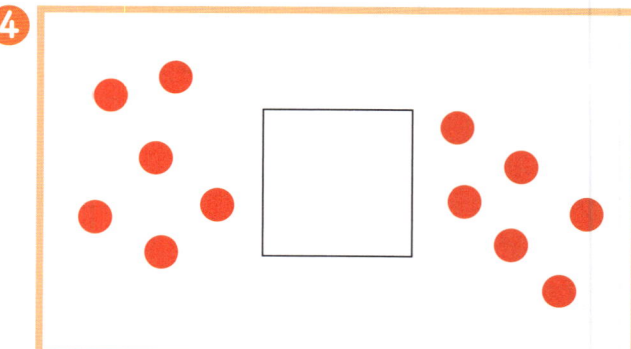

2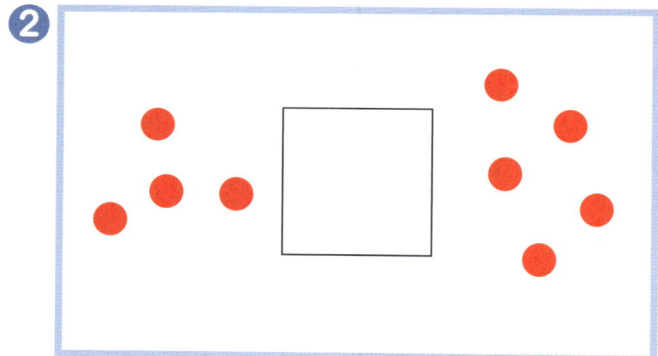

5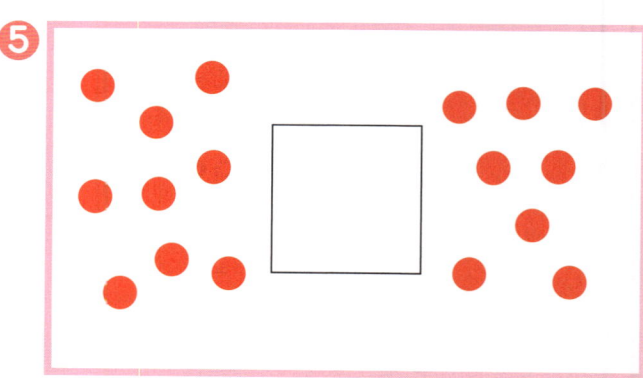

3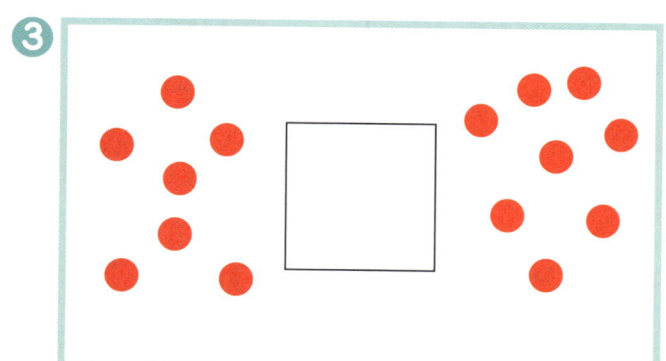

6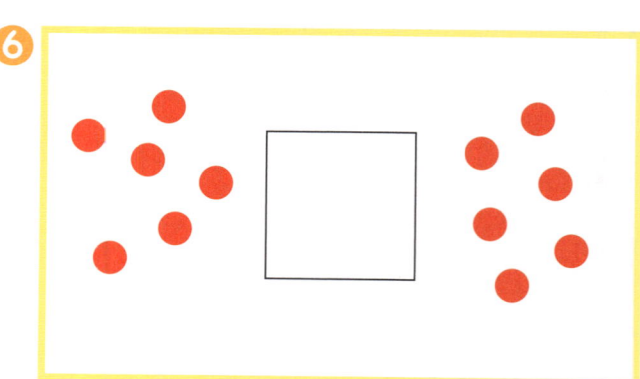

Date

Great Job Sticker

Write the symbol >, <, or = in the box.

1. 3 ☐ 5
2. 24 ☐ 14
3. 40 ☐ 41
4. 90 ☐ 90
5. 7 ☐ 6
6. 12 ☐ 12
7. 87 ☐ 76
8. 36 ☐ 63

Unit 1

Brain Break
Dot to Dot Game

■ Draw a line from 1 to 120 in order. What picture will appear?

Maze Break!

■ Trace the path from start to finish!

Living Things: Plants

KEY POINTS

Plants are living things. All living things take in food and water, grow, breathe, move, and reproduce. Plants take in water from their leaves and roots. They make their own food. They breathe in carbon dioxide from the air. They grow. They even move, by growing towards sunlight. And plants make seeds that can grow new plants. This makes them living things.

■ Answer the questions.

1 What things do all living things have in common?

_____

2 How do plants eat food?

_____

3 How do plants get water?

_____

■ Circle what plants need to live and grow.

①

②

③

Parts of a Plant

Each part of a plant helps it live and grow.

1. The leaves of a plant help it take in sunlight to make food.

2. Plants can have flowers. Flowers help plants reproduce, or make new plants.

3. The stem helps move water and food to the leaves and flowers.

4. The roots of a plant help it take water and other things it needs from the soil.

■ Label the parts of the plant.

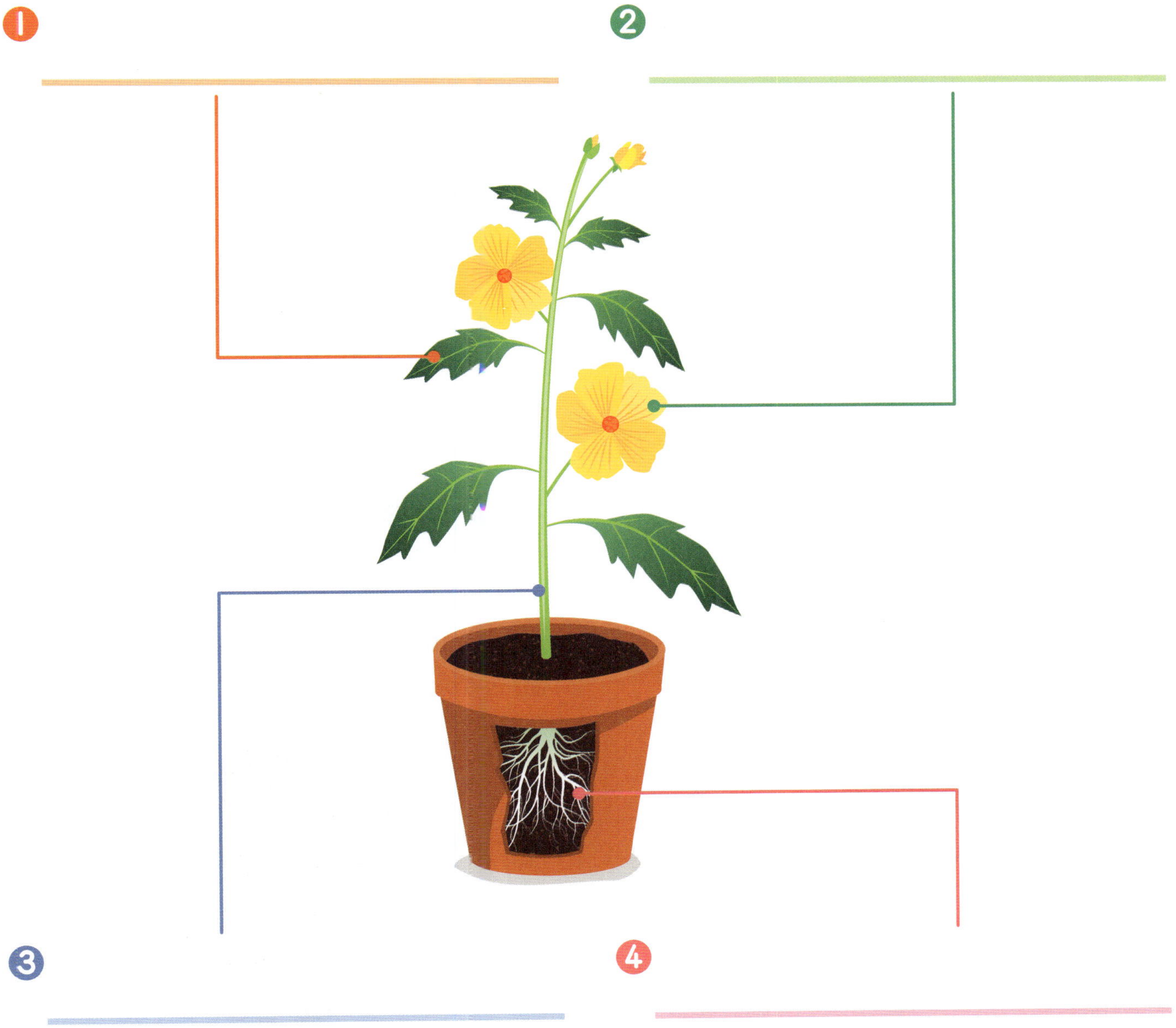

① _____

② _____

③ _____

④ _____

Did you know?

Not all plants have flowers.

39

KEY POINTS

There are many types of places around the world. They all have different kinds of plants that grow there.

Deserts are very hot. They don't get a lot of rain. Cacti grow in deserts. Their thick stems help them store a lot of water. They don't need much rain to survive.

Pine trees can survive in cold areas, like on mountain sides. Their leaves are waxy and shaped like needles. This helps them hold water during the winter, when the air is dry.

Rain forests are warm, wet forests. Kapok trees grow in rain forests. They can grow to over 200 feet tall. This helps them get sunlight, because they are taller than other plants.

Seaweed is a plant that grows in the water. There are many types of seaweed, like kelp and algae. Some types of seaweed live in salt water and others grow in fresh water.

Date

Great Job Sticker

■ Match the plants to their home.

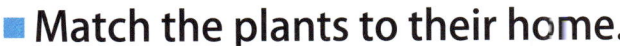

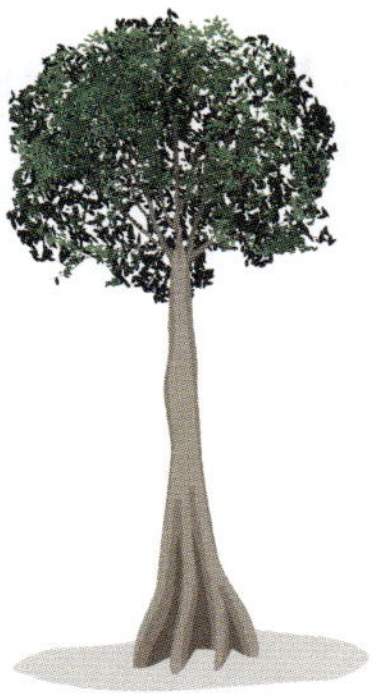

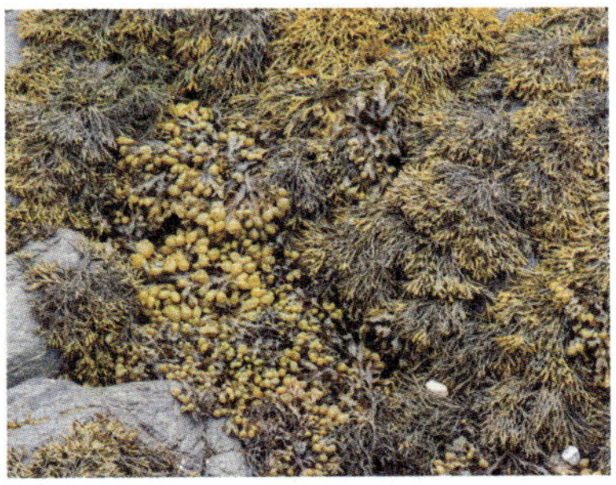

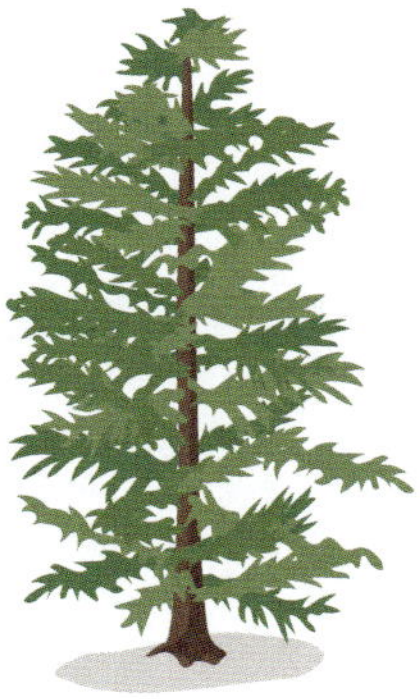

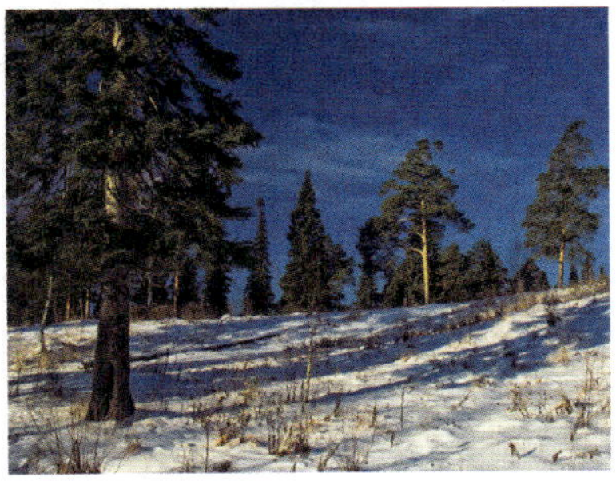

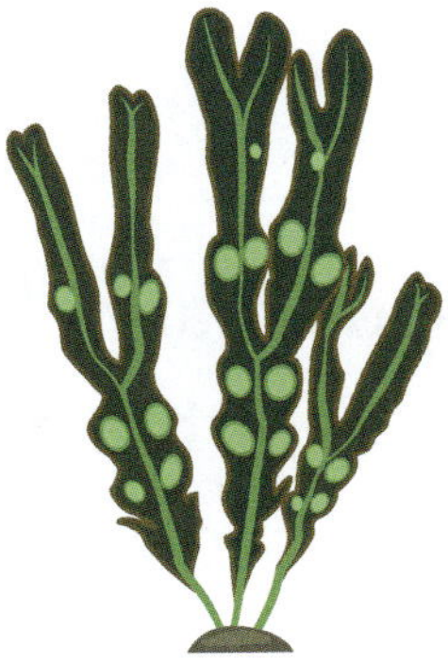

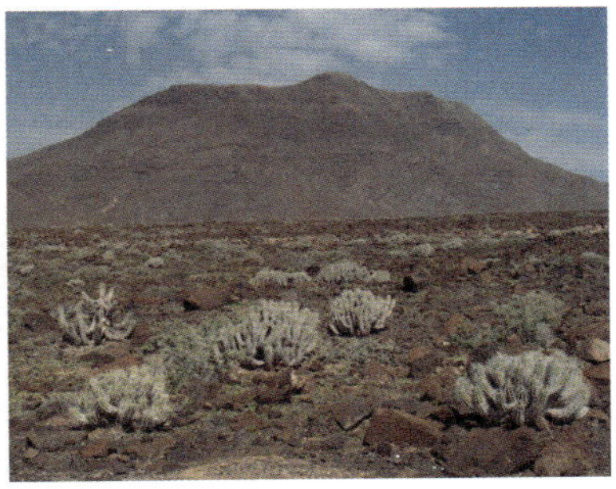

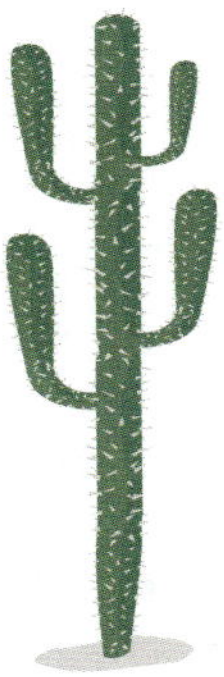

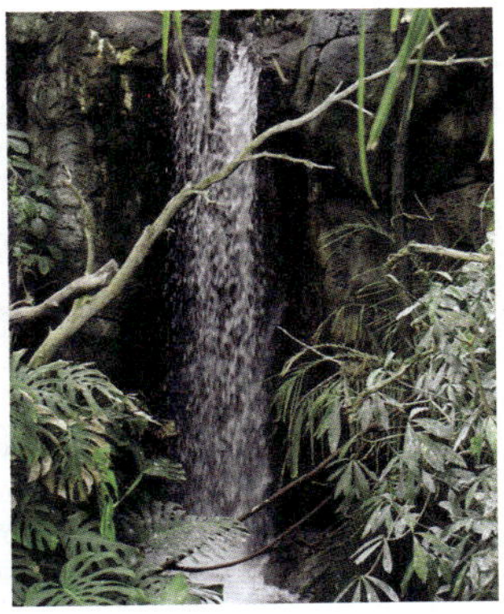

Plant Adaptations

Plants have learned to live in different places. They do this by adapting, or changing to fit their home. Adaptations help a plant survive.

A cactus has spines along its stem that protect it from being eaten.

Some plants have special seeds that help them reproduce. Dandelion seeds have fluff to help the seeds travel on the wind.

Water lilies have wide leaves that float on the water to help them take in more sunlight.

■ Fill in the blanks by choosing from the word box below.

| sunlight | protection | reproduce |

❶  A cactus has spines for

_____.

❷  Waterlilies have wide leaves to collect _____.

❸  Dandelion seeds have fluff to help it travel by wind and

_____.

Brain Break
Science Journal 1

Collect some leaves or small plants from outside your home. Have your parent or guardian help tape them to this page. Describe them below.

Art Break!

■ Imagine what plants will grow from the seeds. What adaptations would they have? Draw each below.

The United States

KEY POINTS

We live in the United States. The United States is a country. Every country has a culture. Culture can include the food, language, holidays, art, and the history of a place.

American Flag

Fireworks for the 4th of July

Apple Pie

The Statue of Liberty

George Washington

■ **Write or draw an example of each object below.**

An American holiday:

An American hero:

An American food:

A famous place in America:

Famous Historical People of the United States

The United States has many famous historical people. Read about some below.

George Washington

was the first president of the United States. He helped develop the laws and rules of the United States after the American Revolution.

Frederick Douglass

was born into slavery and escaped to freedom. He became a powerful speaker and writer, sharing his story to inspire change.

Clara Barton

was a nurse during the Civil War. Later, she founded the American Red Cross to help care for other people during bad times.

■ Answer the questions using the Key Points.

❶ Who was the first president of the United States?

❷ Who founded the American Red Cross?

❸ Who was a former enslaved person who become a powerful speaker and writer?

❹ Can you think of another famous American?

US Holidays

KEY POINTS

In the United States, there are special days that celebrate important dates or events in the country's history.

The Fourth of July (also called Independence Day) - Celebrates the Declaration of Independence on July 4th, 1776. The Declaration of Independence declared the United States a separate nation from England. It is celebrated with fireworks as a symbol of patriotism.

Juneteenth - Celebrates the end of slavery in the United States. President Abraham Lincoln said that all enslaved people should be freed on January 1, 1863, but it took until June 19, 1865 for all enslaved people to be freed.

Presidents' Day - Celebrates the accomplishments of past US presidents. It takes place in February near the birthdays of two famous presidents: George Washington and Abraham Lincoln.

Memorial Day - Celebrates the memory of the American people who have died in military service like the Army, Navy, or Air Force. It is important to remember the people who gave their lives to keep the US safe and free.

■ **Answer the questions using the Key Points.**

❶What does July 4th celebrate?

_____

❷Who does Presidents' Day celebrate?

_____

❸What does Juneteenth celebrate?

_____

❹Who does Memorial Day celebrate?

_____

US National Symbols

KEY POINTS

In the United States, there are many famous monuments. A monument is a statue, building, or structure that is made to remember an event or person who did something important in history.

The Lincoln Memorial in Washington, D.C. is a monument to Abraham Lincoln's deeds as President of the United States.

The Statue of Liberty in New York is a symbol of freedom.

Mount Rushmore in South Dakota is a monument to four of the most famous US presidents: George Washington, Thomas Jefferson, Abraham Lincoln, and Theodore Roosevelt.

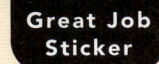

■ **Answer the questions using the Key Points.**

❶ What does the Statue of Liberty stand for?

_____

❷ How many American presidents are on Mount Rushmore?

_____

❸ Where is the Lincoln Memorial?

_____

■ **Write or draw about a different United States monument you have visited.**

Brain Break
History Vocabulary Crossword Puzzle

■ Complete the activity.

United States	monument	Washington
Douglass	July	Juneteenth	Memorial	flag

Across

① Former enslaved person known for his writing and public speaking.

③ The United States has one that is red, white, and blue.

⑤ A country in North America.

⑦ Holiday celebrating the end of slavery in the United States.

⑨ A building or statue that is built to remember a historical event.

Down

② The month the United States celebrates its freedom.

④ A day that celebrates members of the US armed forces who have died.

⑥ The first president of the United States.

Mindfulness Break!

■ Write or draw something you are grateful for in each jar.

A person

A food

A place

Modern Technology

Technology is the use of knowledge to create new machines or tools. These machines and tools are used to make work easier. Modern examples of technology are TVs and cellphones.

■ Name each machine below. Use the word bank for help.

Washing machine	Airplane	TV
Cell phone	Calculator	Refrigerator

①

②

③

④

⑤

⑥

■ Circle the machines.

Computer Parts

KEY POINTS

A computer is a machine used for working with information. Computers help us access the internet, write papers, research subjects, shop online, and play games. Computers have different parts that help us use them to do work.

■ Draw a line to match each computer item.

 ●   ● Printer

 ●   ● Mouse

 ●   ● Screen

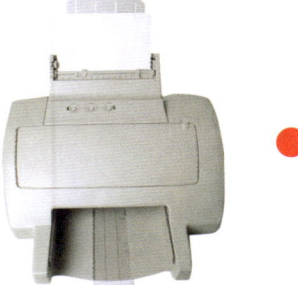 ●   ● Keyboard

■ Name each computer part below. Use the word bank for help.

Speaker	Headphones	Printer	Web camera

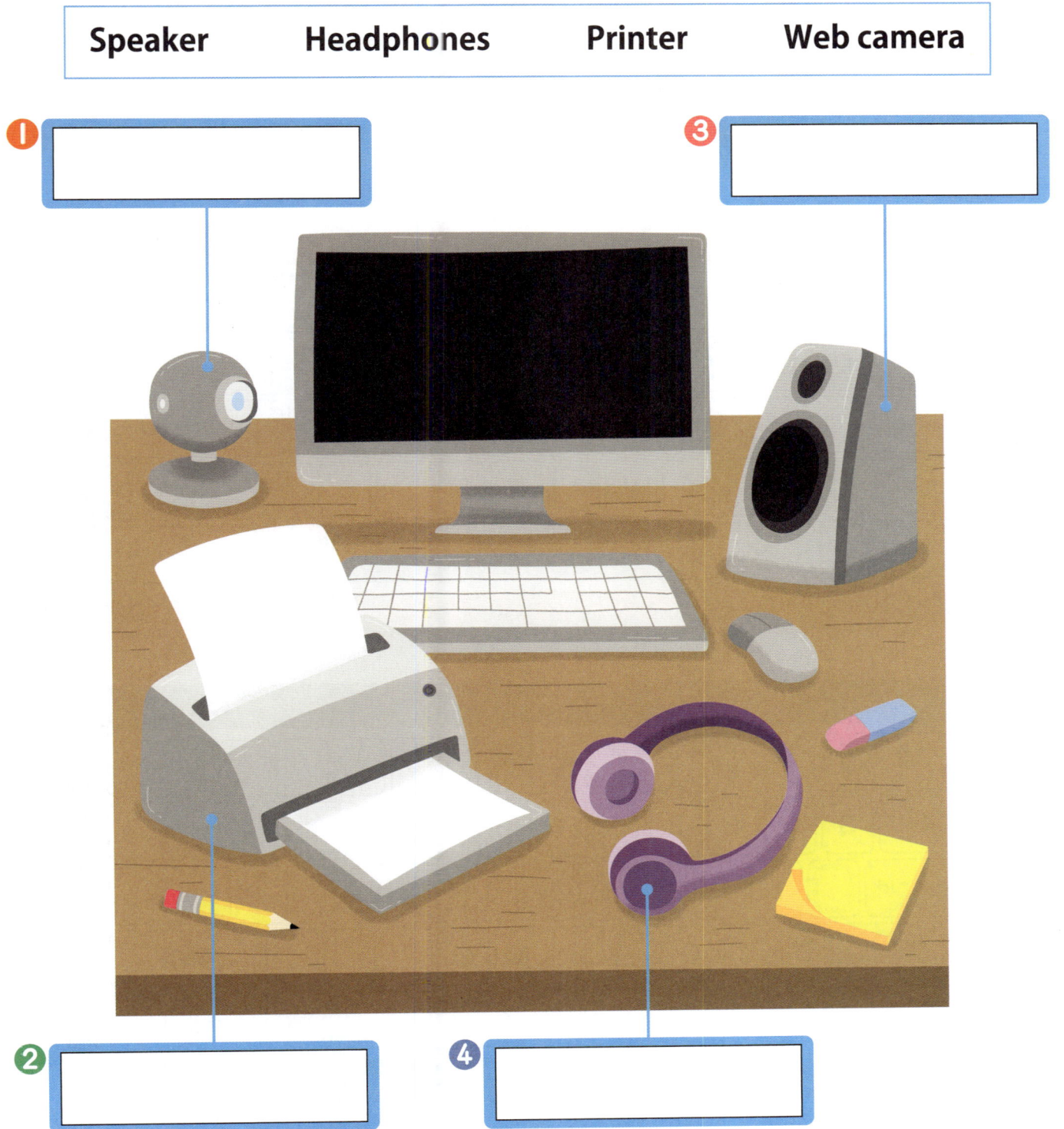

1 _____

2 _____

3 _____

4 _____

Keyboard Skills

KEY POINTS

The keyboard is the part of the computer used to enter information. It is made up of buttons called keys that stand for numbers and letters.

■ Fill in the missing keys on each keyboard.

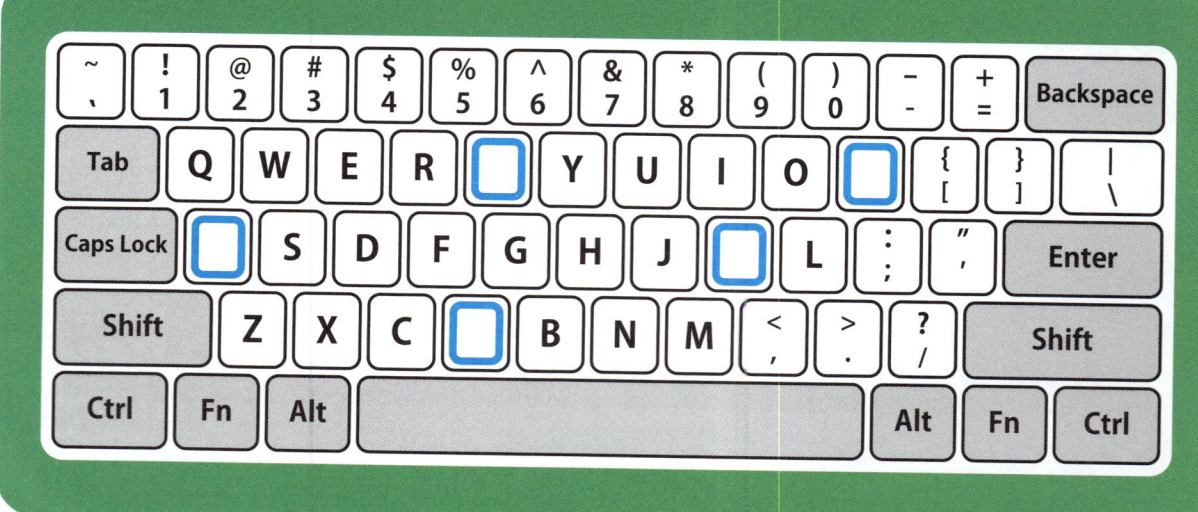

■ Name each key below. Use the Word Bank for help.

Enter	Shift	Backspace	Space	Period

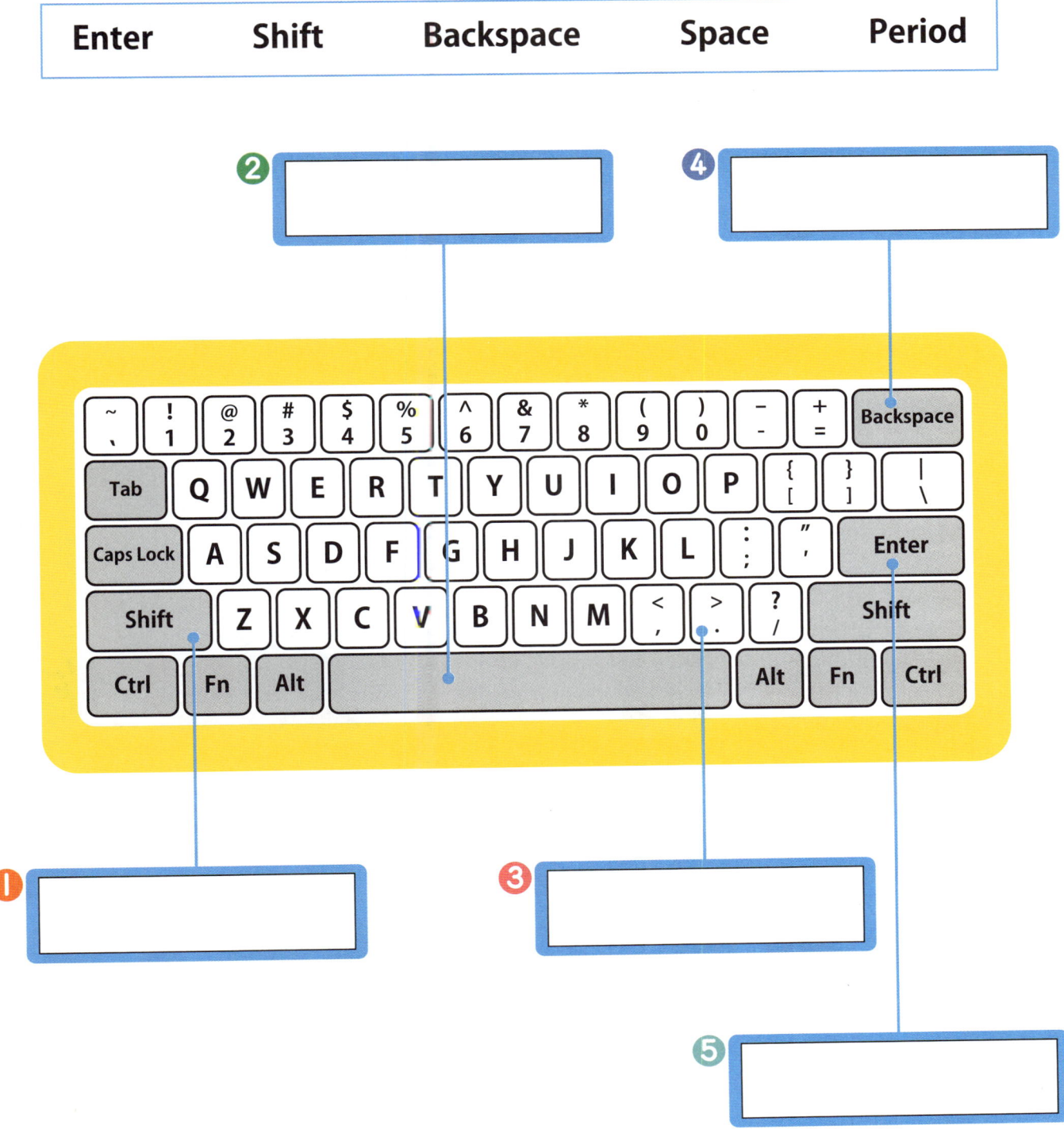

❷

❹

❶

❸

❺

Secret Code

■ Use the code in each box to find the secret word.

①

o	g	d

d o g

③

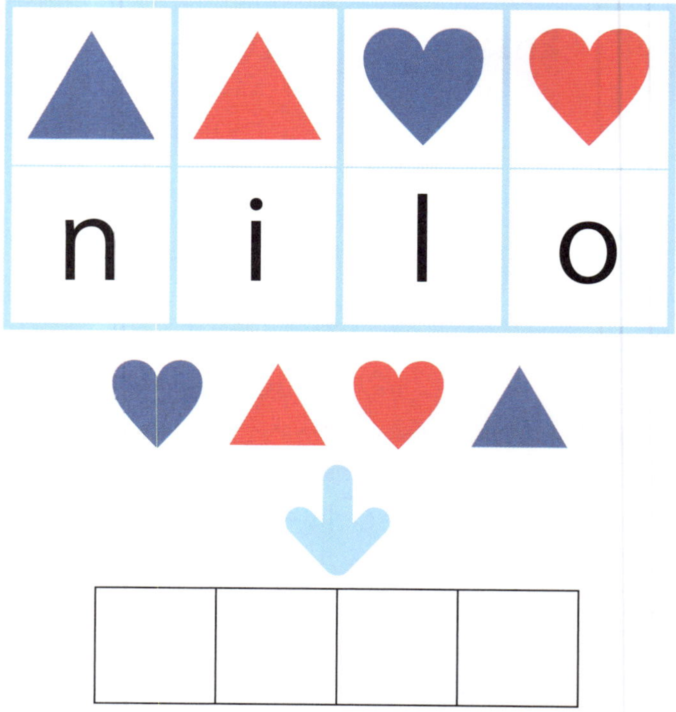

n	i	l	o

②

i	p	e

④

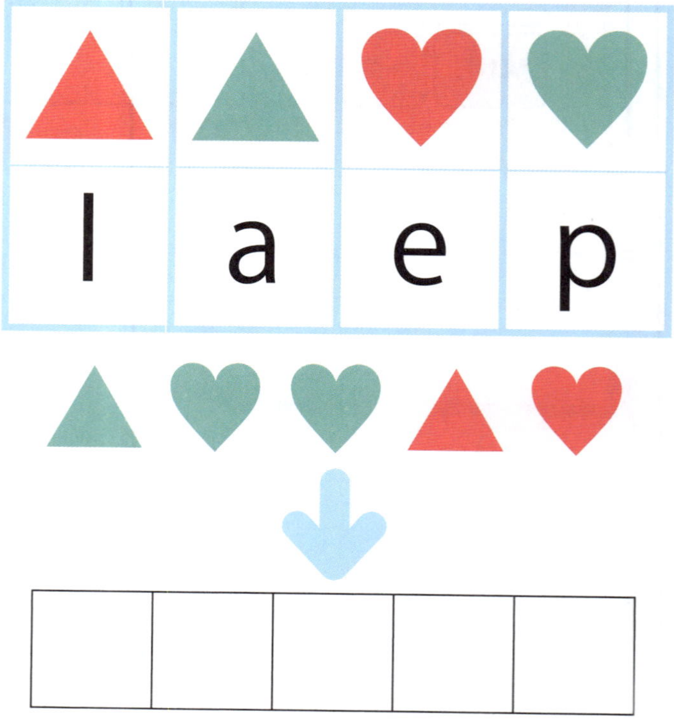

l	a	e	p

■ Draw a line to the word that matches each code.

Secret Code Spelling

| a | e | h | i | l | r | t | w |

• wheel

• white

• water

It's important to move your body and exercise!
Try this fun activity below for a study break!

■ Get a coin and flip it. If it lands on heads, do that activity.
If it lands on tails, do the activity from the tails column.

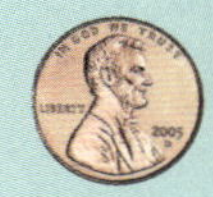 HEADS	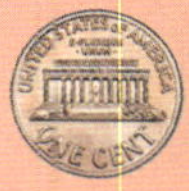 TAILS
1 5 jumping jacks	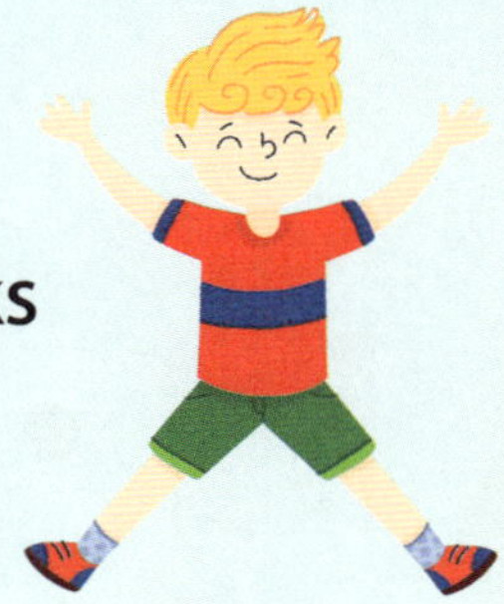 5 squats 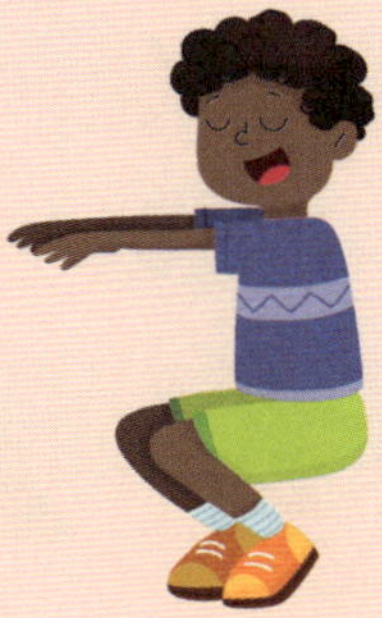
2 10 arm circles	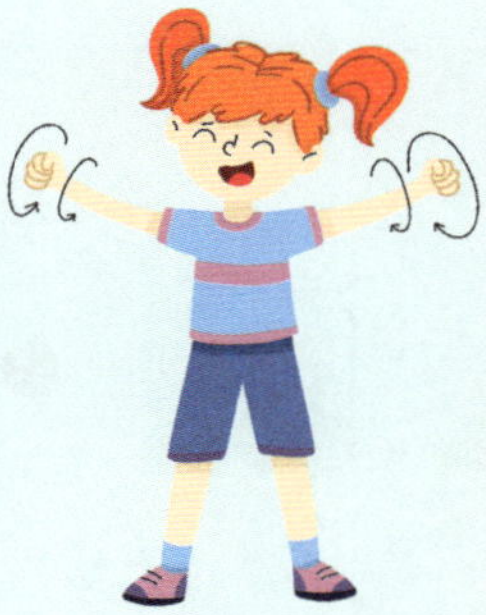 10 toe touches 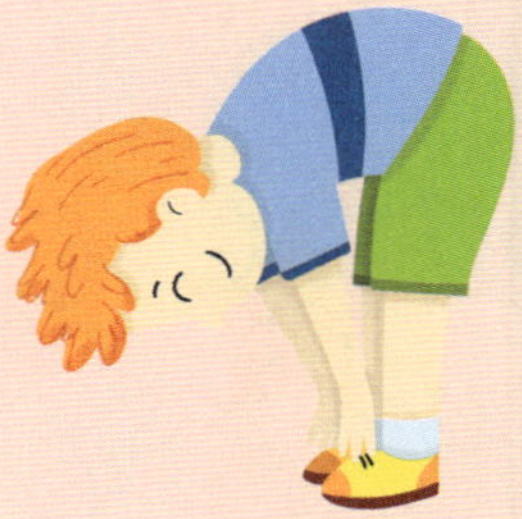
3 30 seconds run in place	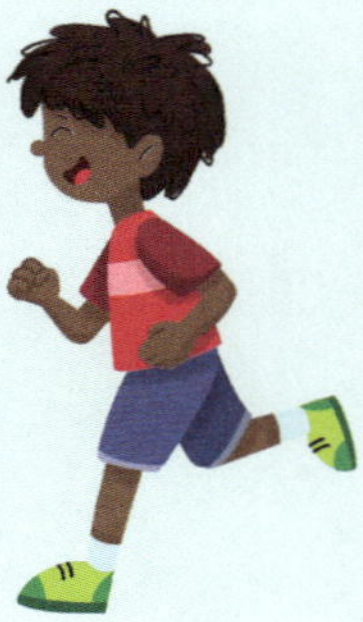 30 seconds march in place 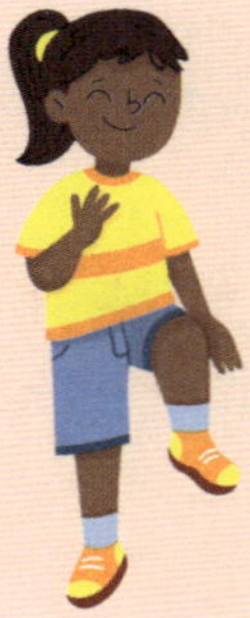

Unit **2** Table of Contents

Use this page to keep track of your progress throughout the book. Place a check mark in the box when you have completed a section.

Language Arts

- [ ] **Pronouns** — 066
- [ ] **Verb Tenses – Past/Present** — 068
- [ ] **Verb Tenses – Future/Mixed** — 070
- [ ] **Adjectives** — 072
- **Brain Break** — 074
- **Mindfulness Break!** — 075

Reading

- [ ] **Characters** — 076
- [ ] **Setting** — 078
- [ ] **Plot** — 080
- [ ] **Main Topic and Key Details** — 082
- **Brain Break** — 084
- **Mindfulness Break!** — 085

Math

- [ ] **Single Digit Addition 1** — 086
- [ ] **Single Digit Addition 2** — 088
- [ ] **2–Digit Addition** — 090
- [ ] **Single Digit Subtraction** — 092
- [ ] **2–Digit Subtraction** — 094
- **Brain Break** — 096
- **Maze Break!** — 097

Science

- [ ] **Animals** — 098
- [ ] **Animal Habitats** — 100
- [ ] **Animal Adaptations 1** — 102
- [ ] **Animal Adaptations 2** — 104
- **Brain Break** — 106
- **Art Break!** — 107

Social Studies

- [ ] **Communities and Citizens** — 108
- [ ] **Rules and Laws** — 110
- [ ] **Being a Good Citizen** — 112
- [ ] **Community** — 114
- **Brain Break** — 116
- **Mindfulness Break!** — 117

Technology

- [ ] **Coding 1** — 118
- [ ] **Coding 2** — 120
- [ ] **Coding 3** — 122
- [ ] **Coding 4** — 124
- **Physical Education Break!** — 126

Pronouns

KEY POINTS

A pronoun takes the place of a noun.
Some pronouns are: he, she, they, I, me, you.

We can rewrite this sentence using a pronoun:
Fred walked to the store → He walked to the store.

■ **Write the correct pronoun in the blank.**

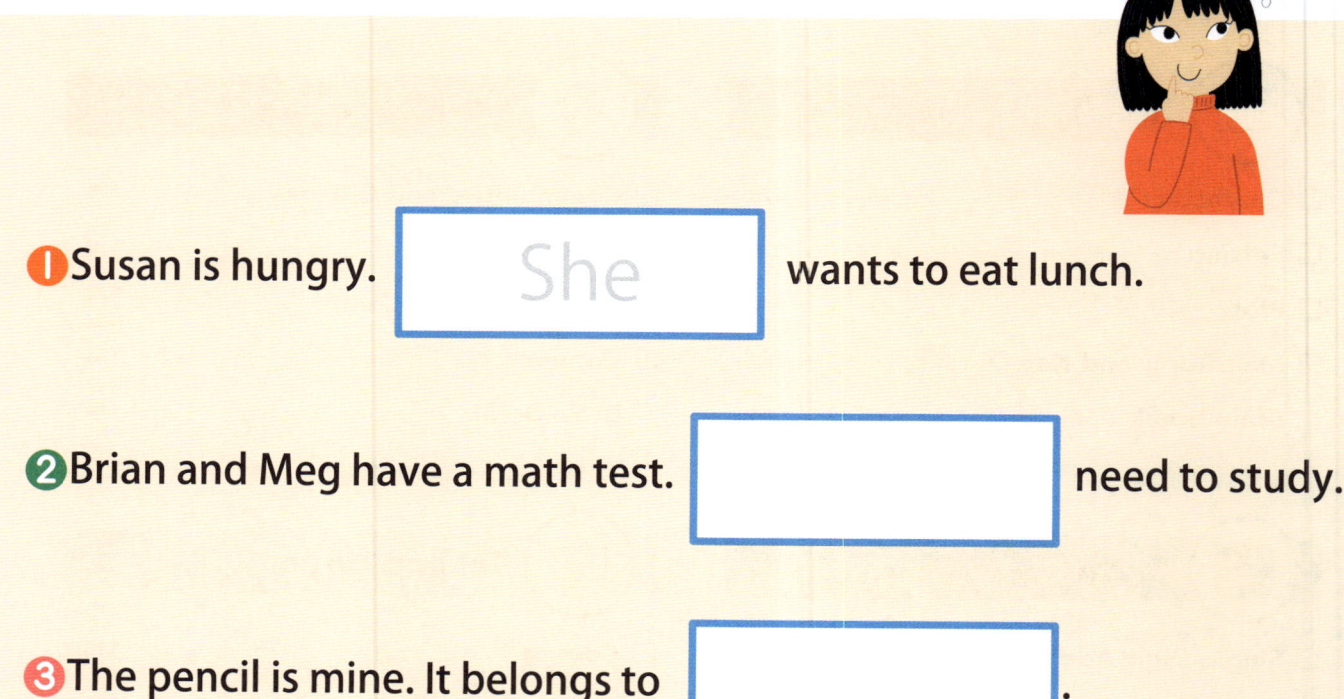

❶ Susan is hungry. [She] wants to eat lunch.

❷ Brian and Meg have a math test. [   ] need to study.

❸ The pencil is mine. It belongs to [   ].

KEY POINTS

Pronouns can also show who owns something. For example: his, hers, my, your, their.

We can rewrite this sentence using a pronoun:
Mary has a pet dog. Mary's dog is named Lucky.
→ Mary has a pet dog. Her dog is named Lucky.

■ Write the correct pronoun.

1 Shanae and Robin moved _____their_____ desks.

2 I watched _____ favorite movie.

3 You should do _____ homework.

67

Verb Tenses – Past/Present

KEY POINTS

Some verbs tell about an action that is happening now. These are present-tense verbs.

Today I walk home.

She plays piano.

You ride a bike.

■ Circle the present tense verb.

❶Lila (draws) a picture.

❷Theo builds a tower.

❸Kim reads a book.

Some verbs tell about an action that has already happened.
These are past tense verbs.

Yesterday I walked home.

She played piano.

You rode a bike.

■ Circle the past tense verb.

❶ I | **write** · **wrote** | **my name.**

❷ They | **eat** · **ate** | **pizza.**

❸ She | **kicked** · **kick** | **a soccer ball.**

Verb Tenses – Future/Mixed

KEY POINTS

Some verbs tell about an action that takes place in the future. These are future tense verbs.

Tomorrow I will walk home.

She will play piano.

You will ride a bike.

■ Write a check mark (✓) next to the sentences with a future tense verb.

☐ **She will eat fish for dinner.**

☐ **They drive to work.**

☐ **She will do her homework.**

☐ **He played the guitar.**

■ Circle the past tense verbs. Underline the present tense verbs.
Highlight the future tense verbs.

Miles watched his friends. They played

basketball. Miles liked basketball, but he

didn't know the rules. "I will show you!" said

Laura. "You stand here. I will pass the ball."

Laura taught Miles.

71

KEY POINTS

Adjectives describe nouns. Here are some adjectives that can describe an apple:

red   sweet

tasty   round

■ Circle the adjectives that describe each object.

1   yellow   small   sour

2   green   large   slimey

3   smelly   round   green

4   rough   sweet   noisy

■ Write an adjective that describes each noun.

1   a   black   **cat**

2   a   **eye**

3   a   **sock**

4   a   **dog**

5   a   **face**

Brain Break
Funny Fill–in!

■ Fill in the blanks with the correct part of speech to tell a story.

Jack and the [_____] went to the [_____]

animal noun   *place noun*

to find [_____] . They [_____]

thing noun   *past-tense verb*

past a lake and saw a duck swimming. They stopped to

ask if [_____] knew where they could find a

duck's name

[_____] . The duck said a [_____]

thing noun   *same thing noun*

was in [_____] . Jack and the [_____]

place noun   *animal noun*

started to [_____] to get to the object. When they

verb

found it they [_____] with [_____] !

past-tense verb   *noun*

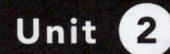

Mindfulness Break!

■ Write a positive affirmation for each situation.

A positive affirmation is a sentence that is thought or said out loud to help a person feel more positive or optimistic about a situation.

❶ First day of school:

I will make new friends!

❷ Meeting a new friend:

❸ Trying a new activity:

KEY POINTS

Characters are the people (or animals) in a story. A story might tell us about what a character is like or how they feel.

Will ran. He was late for the bus. He could hear it coming. He ran faster and faster. He was afraid to miss the bus.

■ Write a check mark (✓) next to the sentence that tells about how Will feels.

☐ **Will is running.**

☐ **Will is late for school.**

☐ **Will is afraid.**

■ Read the story below and circle the words that describe Taylor.

It was getting dark. Everyone was ready to leave the park. Taylor was hungry. But Ryan looked upset. "I can't find my soccer ball!" he said. Taylor wanted to go home, but he didn't want his friend to be sad. They looked for the ball . Then Taylor stood up. "I found it!" he yelled.

Sad   Hungry   (Helpful)

Angry   Upset

A setting is where a story happens.

Cindy walked on the sand. Then she stuck her toe in the water.

This setting is at the beach.

■ Circle things that could be a setting.

a library   a park

a book   a sweater

a dog   a school

■ Read the story below and write a check mark (✓) next to the sentences that are true.

> Stephanie and her mom walked to the park. The trees were changing. The leaves were red, orange, and yellow. The air was cool too. "Fall is finally here!" said Stephanie.

☐ Stephanie is in the park.

☐ It's warm out.

☐ The trees have colorful leaves.

Plot

KEY POINTS

The things that happen in the story make up the plot.
The plot is the events that happen.

Xavier woke up late. He rushed out of bed. His mom yelled,
"Don't forget to eat breakfast!" He ran to school.
He made it just on time!

■ Write a check mark (✓) next to the plot details. Remember that plot details are events that happen.

☐ Xavier is a boy.

☐ Xavier rushed out of bed.

☐ The school was big and full of people.

☐ Xavier made it to school on time.

■ Read the story below and number the events from 1 to 4 in the order they happened.

Sam really wanted a dog. His parents
said no. "I'll take care of it!" Sam said.
But they weren't sure. So Sam helped
his friend Emily with her dog Spot.
He took Spot for a walk every day.
He played with Spot. And he fed Spot
 dinner. Sam's parents saw him taking care of Spot.
"I can see you know a lot about dogs," said his
mom. "Maybe it's time we get one of our own."

☐ Sam's parents said no.

☐ Sam's parents agreed to get a dog.

☐ Sam wanted a dog.

☐ Sam took care of Spot.

Main Topic and Key Details

Stories have main topics and key details. Main topics are big ideas.

Main topics are what the story is all about. Details are small ideas that help tell about the topic.

■ Underline the main idea and circle the details.

I went to the beach. The water was scary! The waves were big. I saw a jellyfish in the water. I wondered if there were sharks.

■ Write a T next to the sentence that tells the topic. Write a D next to the details.

1 ☐ **There are many activities to do in gym class.**

2 ☐ **We play soccer.**

3 ☐ **Sometimes we play basketball.**

4 ☐ **Yesterday we ran a full mile!**

5 ☐ **Next week, we are going to practice throwing baseballs.**

Brain Break
Build Your Own Story!

■ Fill in each element box with your own ideas.

Main Character	**Narration**

Setting	**Main Points**

Mindfulness Break!

■ Write a response for each sentence.

> Be in the present moment. Write what you see, hear, feel, and smell right now.

❶ Right now I see...

❷ Right now I hear...

❸ Right now I feel...

❹ Right now I smell...

Single Digit Addition 1

■ Count the objects. Write the number in the box below. Then add the numbers.

1

| 2 | + | 3 | = | 5 |

2

| | + | | = |

3

| | + | | = |

4

| | + | | = |

■ **Add to get to the goal!**

$6 + 1 = \boxed{}$

$2 + 2 = \boxed{}$

$4 + 5 = \boxed{}$

$5 + 3 = \boxed{}$

$8 + 2 = \boxed{}$

Single Digit Addition 2

■ Draw more dots to make 10. Then write the missing numbers.

1

$4 + \boxed{6} = 10$

2
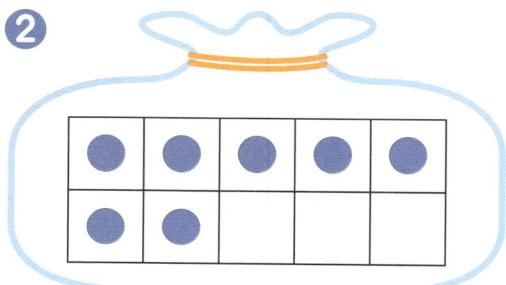

$7 + \boxed{} = 10$

3

$9 + \boxed{} = 10$

4

$2 + \boxed{} = 10$

5

$5 + \boxed{} = 10$

6
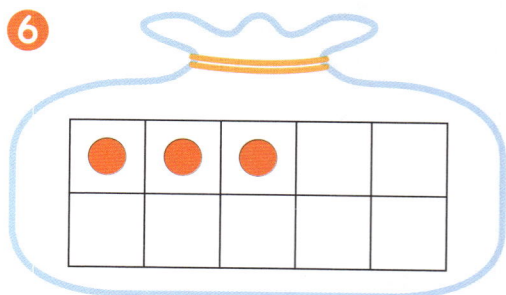

$3 + \boxed{} = 10$

■ Draw a line to the correct answer.

9 + 2 =   •   • 11
          •   • 12

7 + 6 =   •   • 12
          •   • 13

5 + 9 =   •   • 13
          •   • 14

8 + 8 =   •   • 16
          •   • 17

6 + 5 =   •   • 10
          •   • 11

3 + 9 =   •   • 12
          •   • 13

2–Digit Addition

■ Count the objects. Write the number in the box below. Then add the numbers.

①

$$\boxed{15} \; + \; \boxed{1} \; = \; 16$$

②

$$\boxed{} \; + \; \boxed{} \; =$$

③

$$\boxed{} \; + \; \boxed{} \; =$$

④

$$\boxed{} \; + \; \boxed{} \; =$$

■ Draw a line to the the same answer.

| 1 + 4 | • | • | 9 + 3 |

| 2 + 7 | • | • | 15 + 2 |

| 3 + 9 | • | • | 4 + 1 |

| 5 + 8 | • | • | 8 + 5 |

| 2 + 15 | • | • | 7 + 2 |

■ Subtract.

❶

3 − 1 = 2

❹

8 − 2 =

❷

7 − 3 =

❺

4 − 3 =

❸

9 − 4 =

❻

8 − 5 =

Subtract to get to the goal!

$$5 - 2 = \boxed{}$$

$$6 - 5 = \boxed{}$$

$$9 - 1 = \boxed{}$$

$$4 - 2 = \boxed{}$$

$$7 - 3 = \boxed{}$$

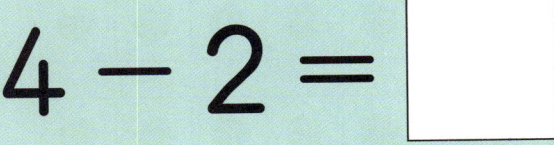

2–Digit Subtraction

■ **Cross out the dots so only ten are left. Then write the missing number.**

1

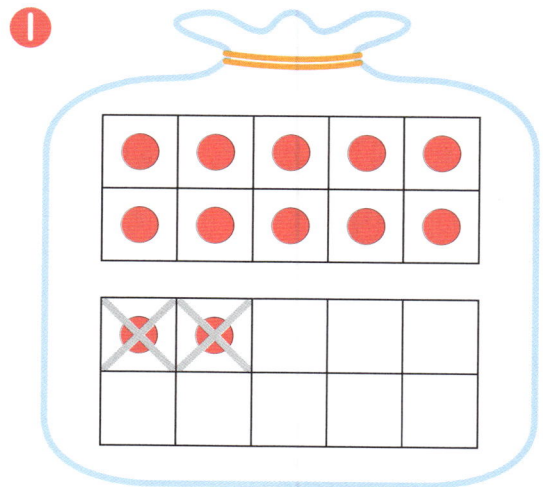

$$12 - \boxed{2} = 10$$

3

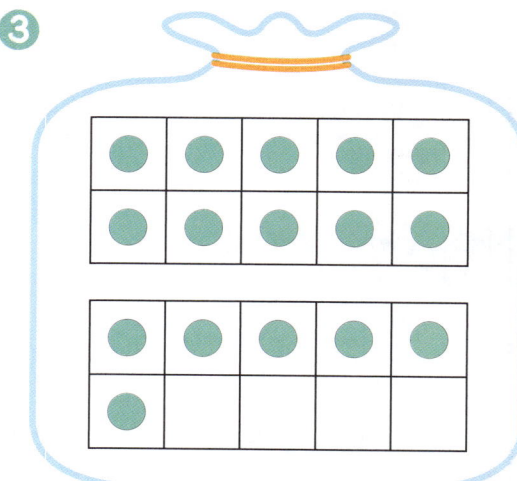

$$16 - \boxed{} = 10$$

2

$$15 - \boxed{} = 10$$

4

$$19 - \boxed{} = 10$$

■ **Draw a line to the correct answer.**

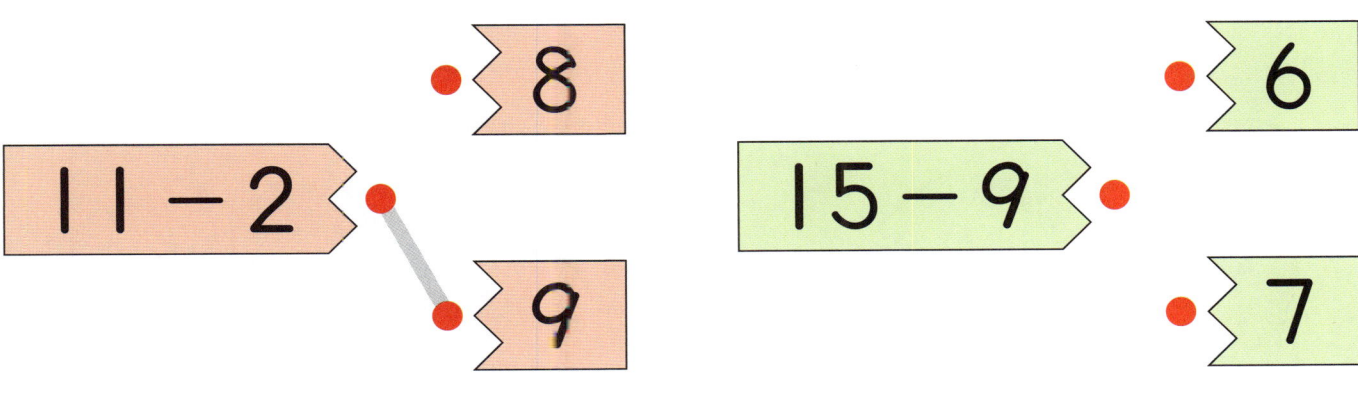

8

11 − 2

9

15 − 9

6

7

12 − 4

7

8

17 − 8

8

9

14 − 5

9

10

13 − 9

4

5

Brain Break
Coloring Game

■ Add or subtract. Then use the key below to color by answer.

4 = yellow	9 = green	15 = brown

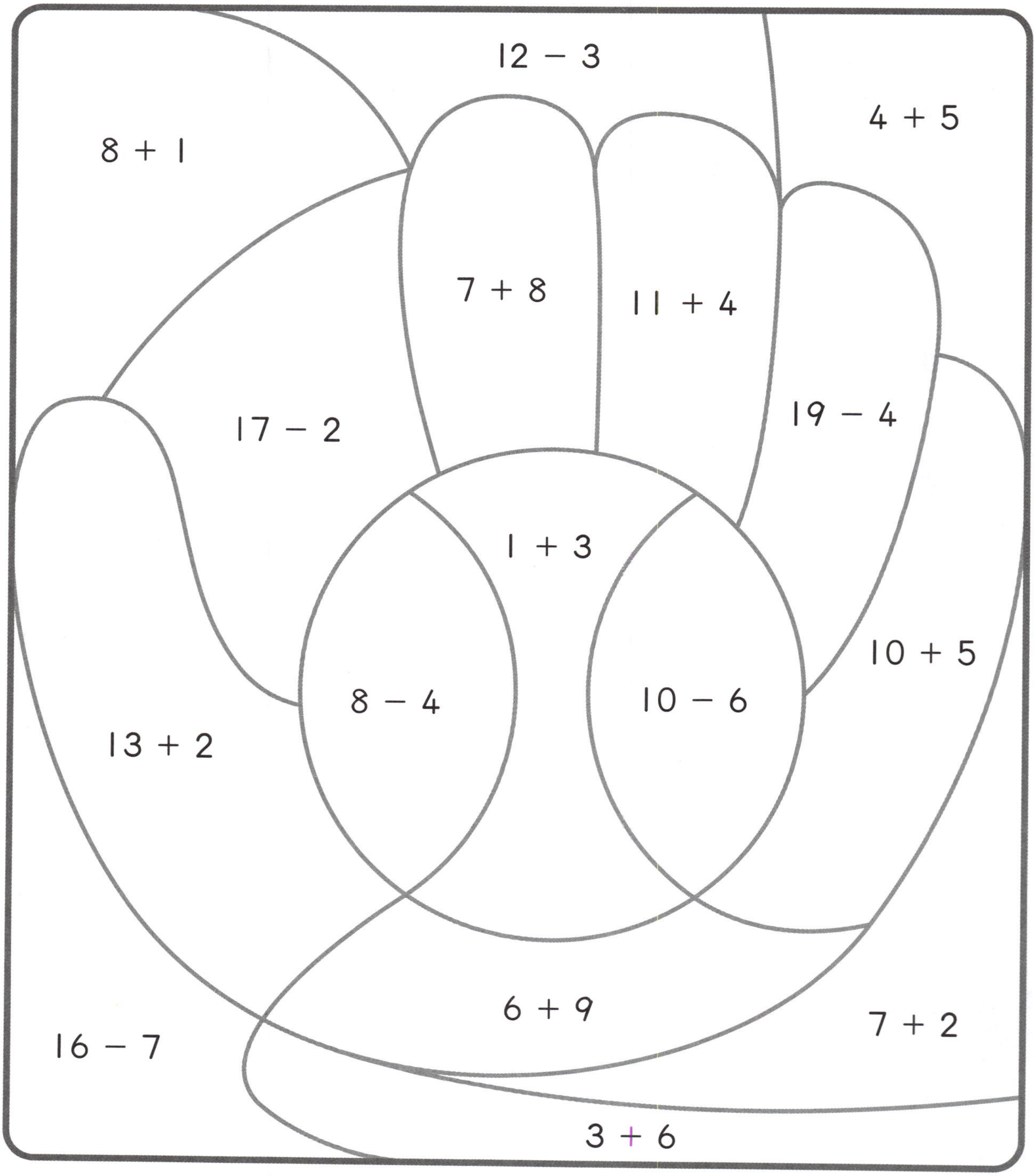

12 − 3

4 + 5

8 + 1

7 + 8

11 + 4

17 − 2

19 − 4

1 + 3

10 + 5

13 + 2

8 − 4

10 − 6

16 − 7

6 + 9

7 + 2

3 + 6

Unit 2

Maze Break!

■ Trace the path from start to finish!

Animals

In the last unit, we learned about plants as living things. Animals are also living things. Animals need food and water to live, they grow and reproduce, or make more animals. There are five main types of animals: mammals, birds, fish, reptiles, and amphibians.

■ **Answer the questions.**

❶ How many types of animals are there?

❷ What do animals need to live?

■ **Read the text and circle the correct animal.**

Mammals are warm-blooded and have bodies covered in fur or hair.

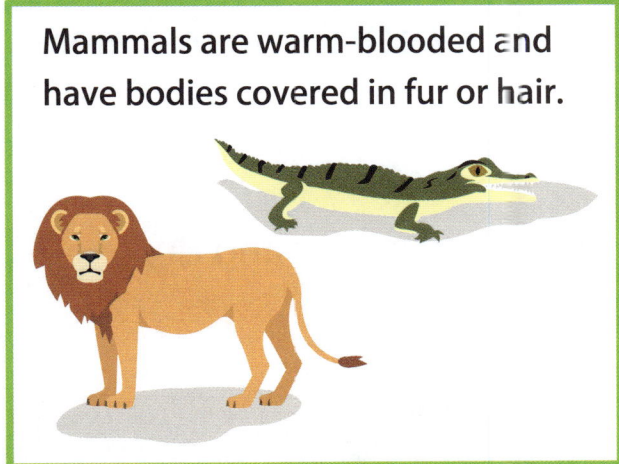

Fish are cold-blooded and live in the water.

Birds are warm-blooded and have bodies covered in feathers.

Amphibians are cold-blooded and live in the water and on land.

Reptiles are cold-blooded and covered in scales.

Did you know? Warm-blooded animals can keep their body temperature the same. They can adapt easily to different places and different types of weather. Cold-blooded animals rely on warmth from other sources.

Animal Habitats

Animals live in different places around the world. These places are called habitats. Just like plants, animals can live in cold areas, deserts, forests, and oceans.

1. Arctic: cold and snowy

2. Desert: hot and dry

3. Rainforest: warm and rainy

4. Northern Forest: changing temperature and weather

■ **Match the animals to their habitat.**

Desert

Arctic

Rainforest

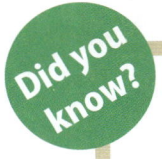 **Did you know?** Some animals can live in more than one habitat.

Animal Adaptations 1

Animals change to fit their habitats. These adaptations help them survive.

Giraffes have long necks to eat leaves from tall trees.

Polar bears have white fur to help them blend in to their habitat.

Hummingbirds have long beaks to drink nectar from flowers.

Sloths move very slowly to stop predators from seeing them.

Date

Great Job Sticker

Match the animal adaptation to the habitat.

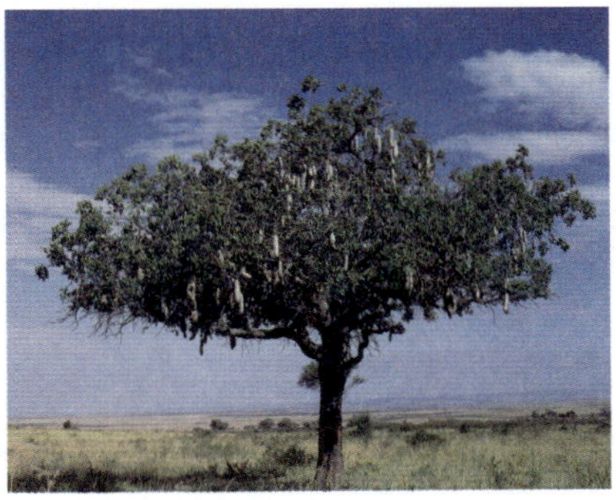

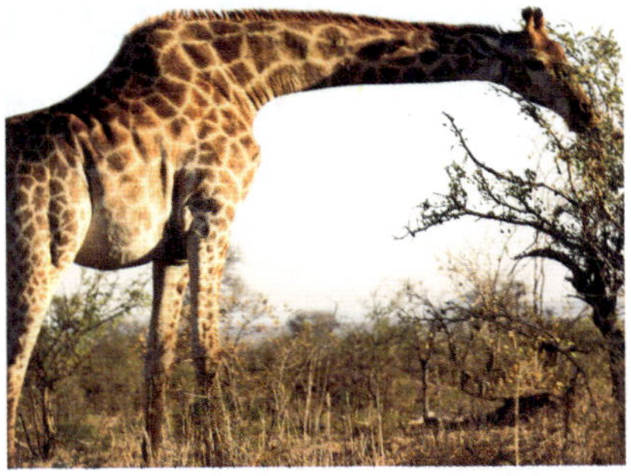

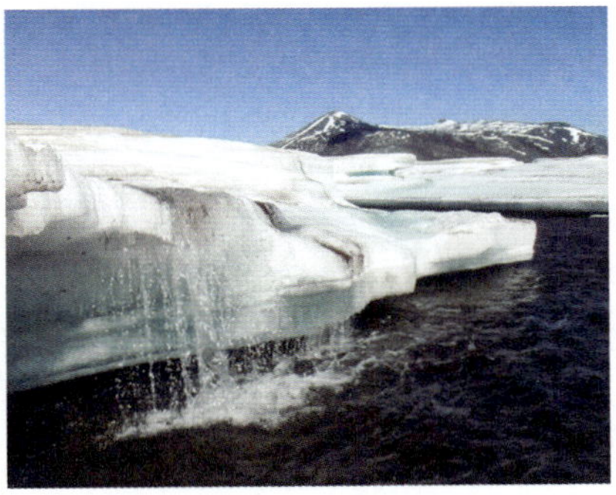

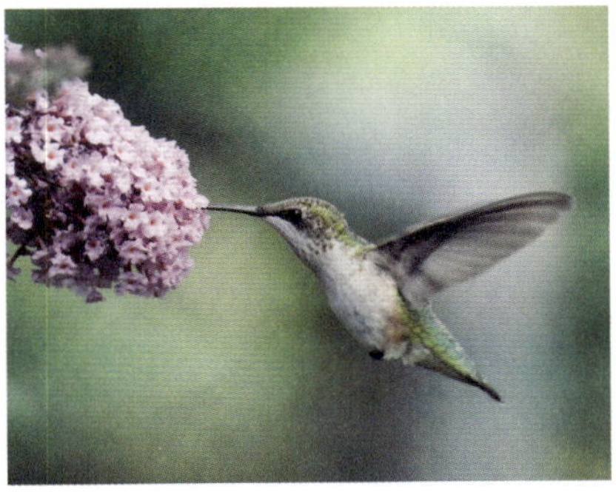

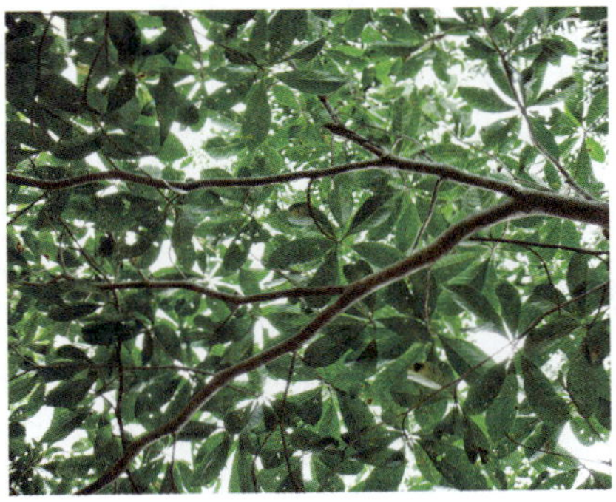

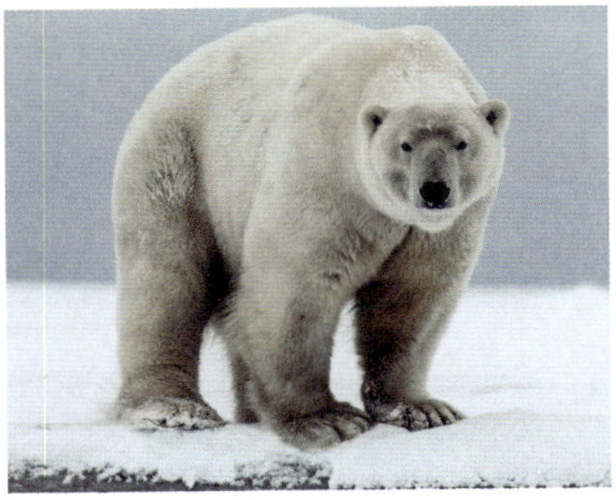

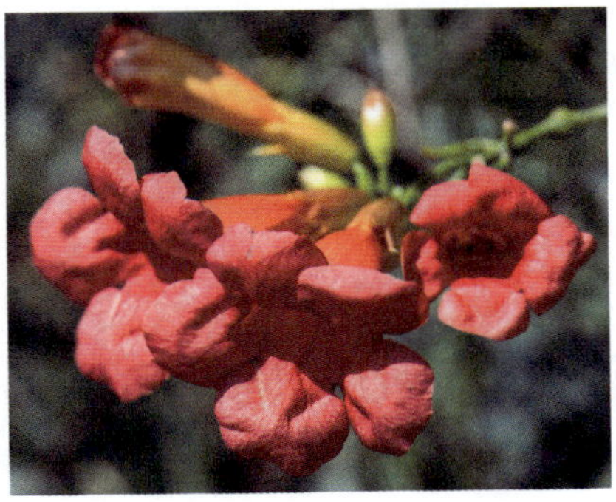

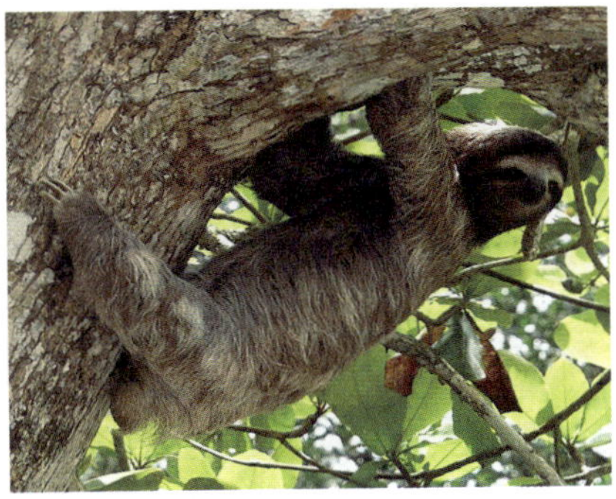

Animal Adaptations 2

KEY POINTS

Some adaptations help animals get food. For example, birds have different shapes and sizes of beaks. The shape and size of a bird's beak is made for the type of food it eats.

Hawks have sharp beaks to catch mice.

Sparrows have short beaks to help them eat seeds.

Ducks have flat beaks, called bills, that help them scoop up plants from the water.

■ **Draw a beak on each bird to help it eat the right food.**

A beak to eat seeds.

A beak to eat mice.

A beak to eat water plants.

A beak to eat flower nectar.

Brain Break
Science Journal 2

Camouflage is a trait that helps an animal blend in with its habitat. Color the animals below to match their habitat.

Art Break!

■ Create your own animal. What traits would it have? What would it eat? What habitat would it live in?

KEY POINTS

A community is a group of people who live and work together in the same area. Communities can be large like a country or small like a town. Communities have businesses, schools, parks, and other places where people work together and spend their time. A citizen is a member of a community. Citizens have civic responsibilities like following laws, being a good neighbor, and helping solve community problems.

■ Answer the questions.

❶ What is a community?

_____

❷ What is a citizen?

_____

❸ What type of responsibilities do citizens have?

_____

KEY POINTS

All people of the United States have rights. A right is freedom that is protected by law.

Examples of rights are:
The right to vote.
The right to education, like going to school.
The right say what you think.

■ **Answer the question.**

1 What other rights can you think of?

_____

_____

_____

_____

_____

Rules and Laws

KEY POINTS

All places have rules, but a law is a rule made by a country for all people to follow. Laws help keep people safe and make things fair.

An example of a rule is raising your hand before speaking.

An example of a law is don't steal or don't take things that don't belong to you.

CLASSROOM RULES

1. BE KIND
2. BE GENEROUS
3. BE READY TO LEARN
4. BE RESPECTFUL
5. BE HAPPY ☺

■ Answer the questions.

❶ What is a rule?

_____

❷ What is a law?

_____

■ Write "rule" or "law" next to each sentence.

❶ Raise your hand in a classroom.

_____

❷ Drive the speed limit.

_____

❸ Wear a seatbelt in the car.

_____

❹ Put your dish in the sink after dinner.

_____

❺ Throw trash in the trashcan.

_____

Being a Good Citizen

KEY POINTS

To be a good citizen, you need to follow your community's rules and respect others.

Respect means being kind and polite to others. Here are some examples:

Cross the street at a crosswalk.

Wait in line.

Throw out trash.

■ Place a check mark (✔) by the picture of the child following a rule.

Community

KEY POINTS

A community is an area where different people live. Communities can have schools, homes, businesses and other buildings in them. In order for a community to run smoothly and to grow, it is important that the people in the community follow rules and laws.

■ **Answer the questions.**

❶ What is a community?

❷ What does a community need to run smoothly?

■ Match the community building to its purpose.

Library

Town Hall

Fire Station

Police Station

to lend books
to people

to provide help in
case of a fire

to provide help and
protection

to create rules to
keep the town safe

Unit 2 Social Studies

Brain Break
Word Search

■ Circle the words in the Word Search.

respect	law	rule	citizen
town	good	litter	polite

R	E	T	T	I	L	X
E	R	Y	Q	I	E	C
S	T	L	A	W	V	Y
P	Y	Y	Z	A	C	H
E	U	G	R	U	L	E
C	J	R	C	L	A	V
T	K	N	P	T	G	A
W	L	P	O	W	O	L
S	M	O	L	R	O	W
D	H	L	E	E	D	Q
F	V	I	H	D	B	F
C	I	T	I	Z	E	N
A	B	E	B	T	C	T
Q	A	O	M	Y	N	P
T	O	W	N	K	E	O

Gratitude is feeling thankful for the people and things in your life.

■ Draw or write something you are grateful for on each piece of the wheel.

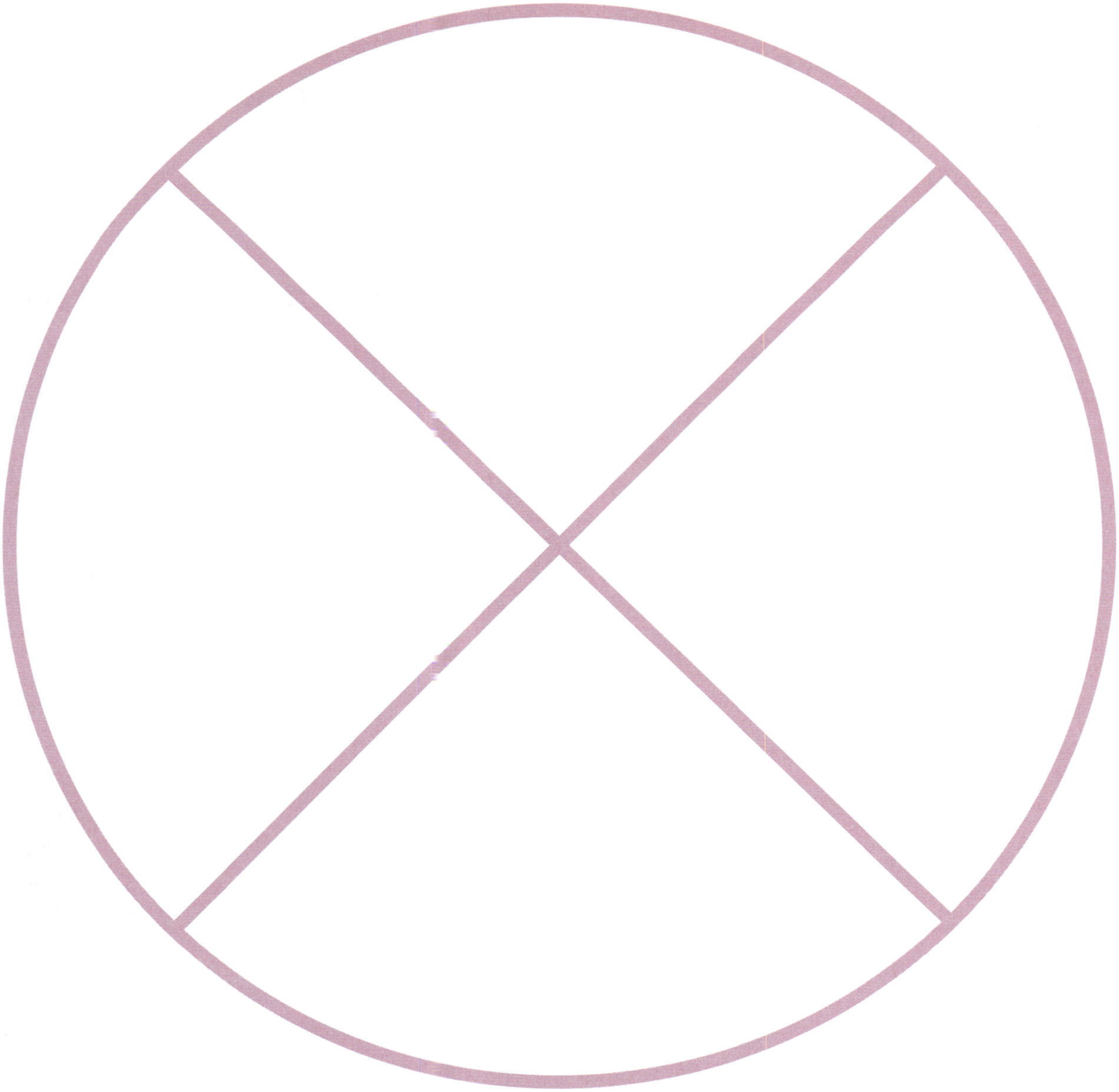

Coding 1

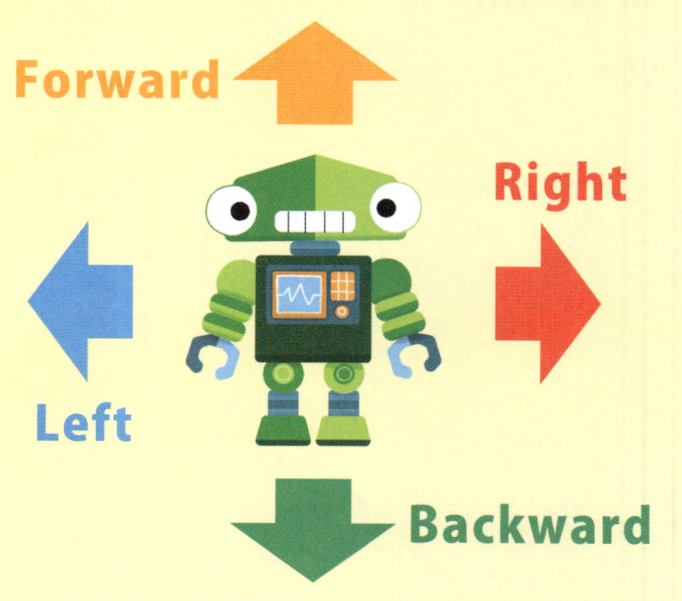

KEY POINTS

Coding is when we give a computer instructions to perform a task.

For example, you can use an arrow to show the direction you want an object to move. An arrow can make an object move right, left, forward, or backward.

Forward

Right

Left

Backward

■ Who will the robot meet if it follows the arrows from the start? Write a check mark (✔) next to the animal the robot will meet.

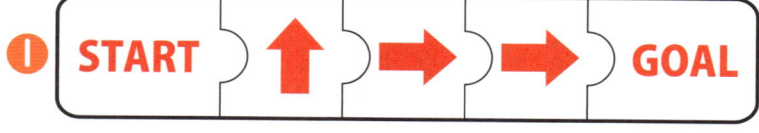

❶ START ⬆ ➡ ➡ GOAL

START

2 START ➡️ ⬇️ ➡️ ⬇️ GOAL

3 START ⬆️ ⬆️ ⬅️ ⬆️ GOAL

Coding 2

■ Which sequence below leads to the goal? Write a check mark (✓) for the correct answer.

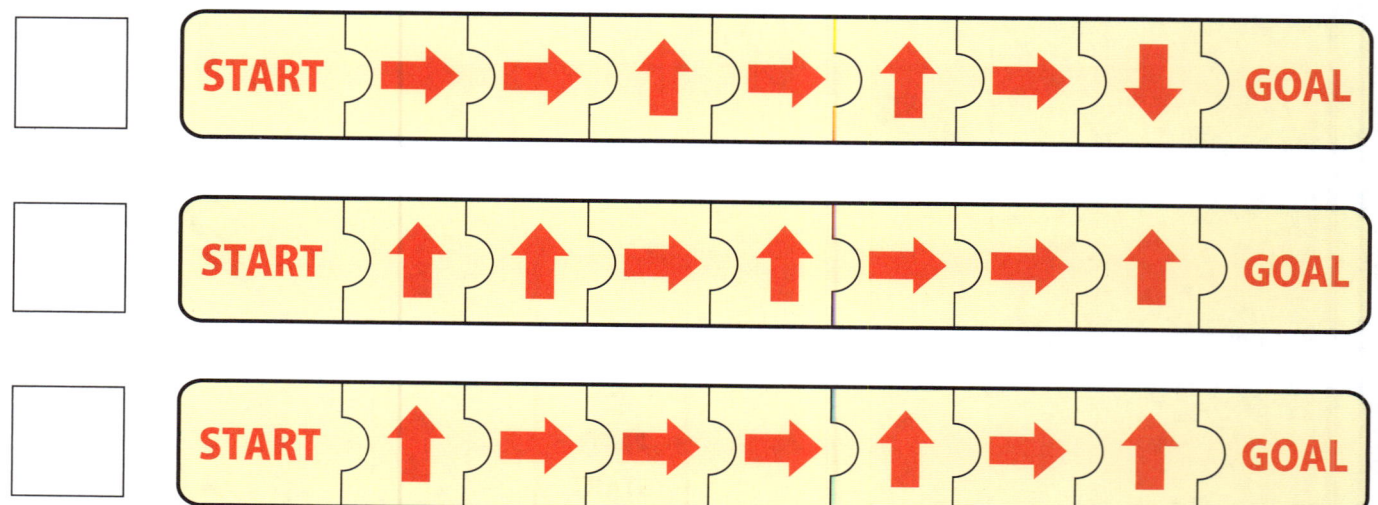

❷

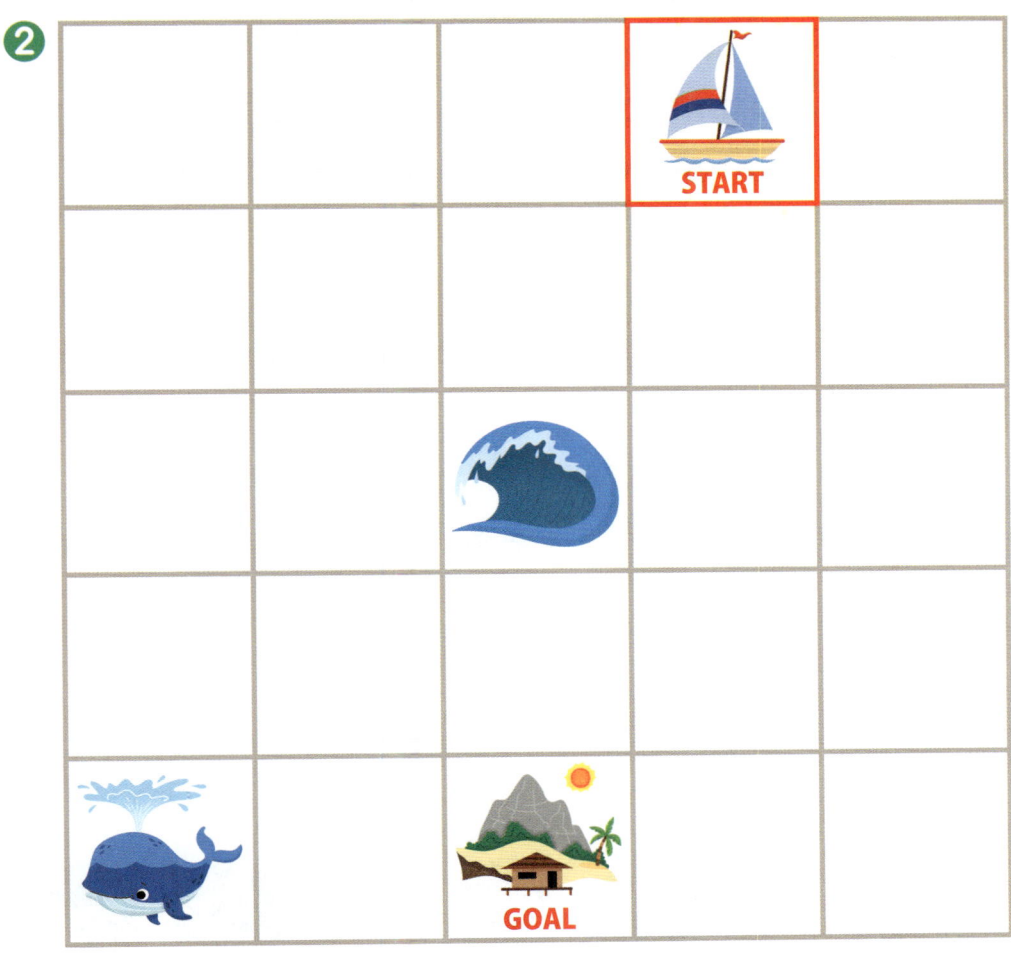

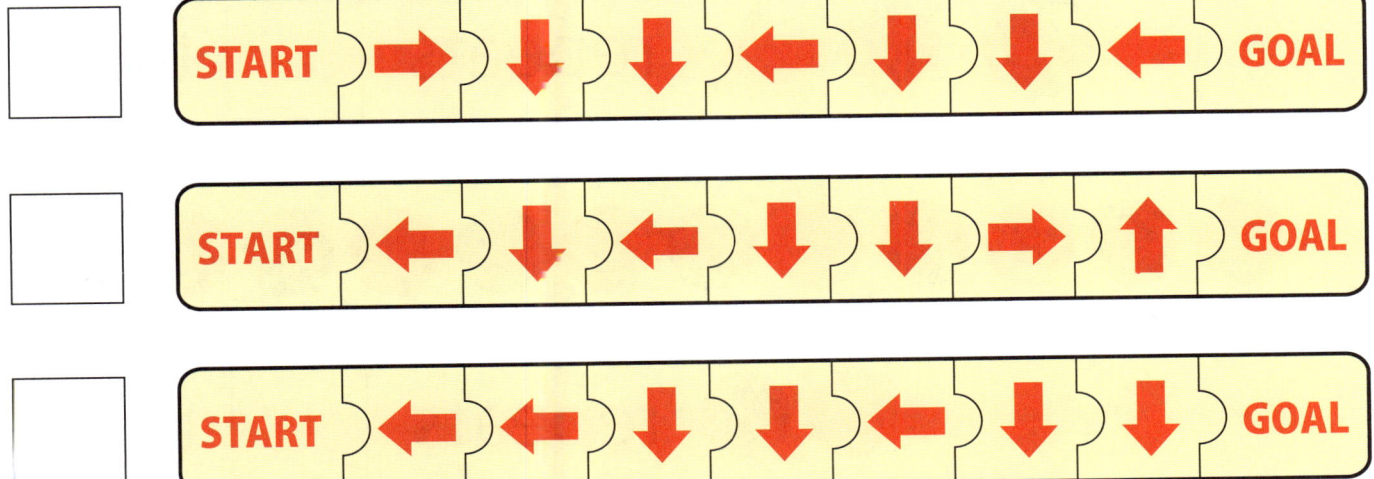

KEY POINTS

A command to repeat a piece of code until the desired process is completed is called a loop.

In coding, it is important to send the correct instructions to the computer about what pattern is to be repeated and how many times.

■ Each pattern below has a loop that repeats. Write how many times it repeats in the box.

1

★ ▲ repeats ☐ times

2

● ● ▲ repeats ☐ times

3

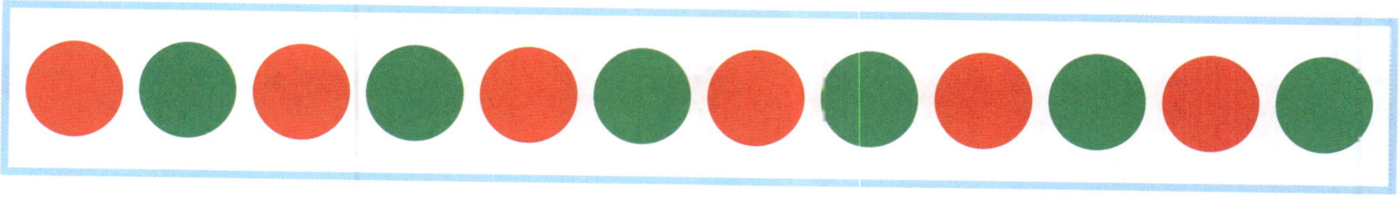

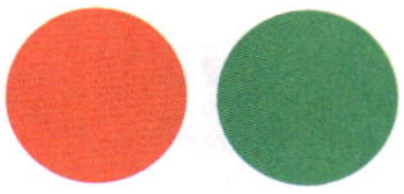

● ● repeats ☐ times

■ **Write a check mark (✓)next to the correct answer.**

1

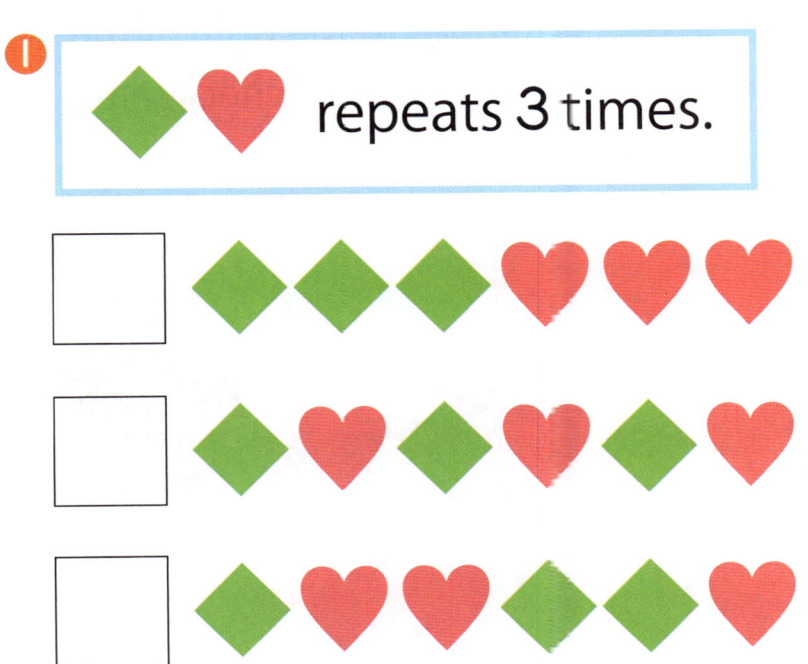

◆ ♥ repeats **3** times.

2

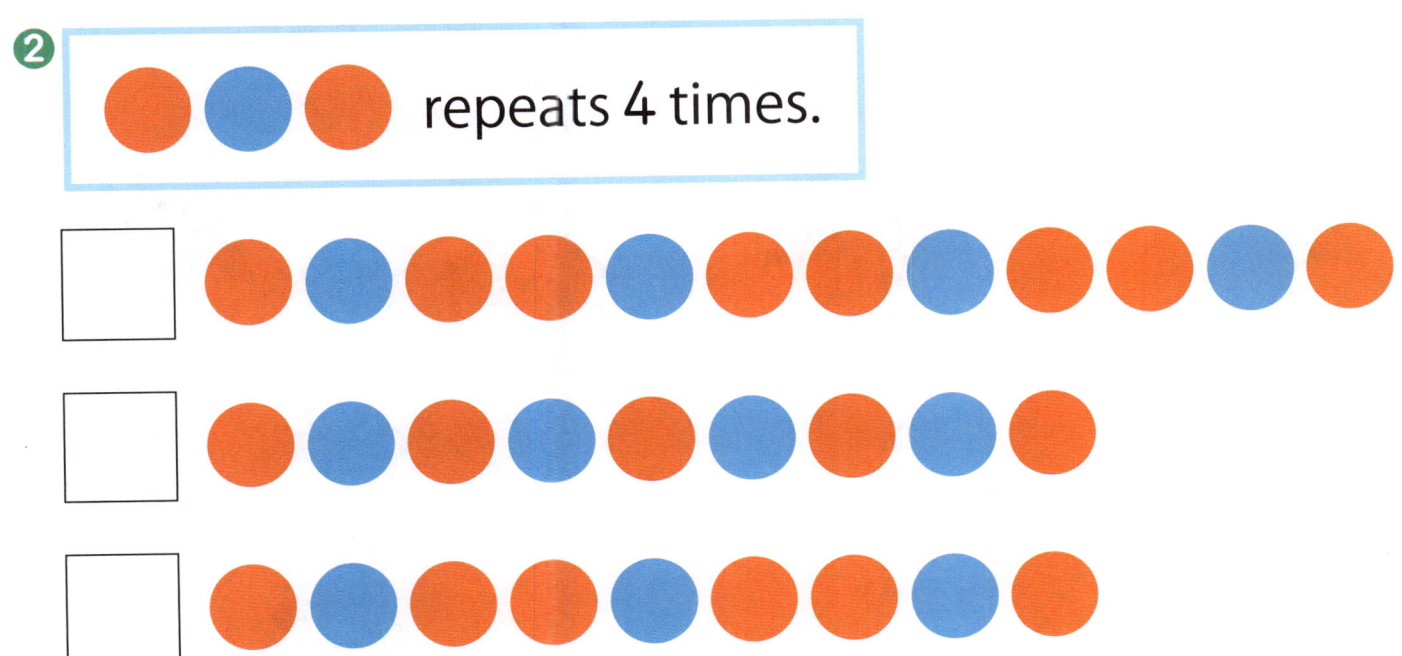

● ● ● repeats **4** times.

Coding 4

■ Usually, arrows point to where we go. But in this town, the color of the arrow shows which way the robot will go. If the arrow is red (← →), it goes to the left. If the arrow is blue (← →), it goes to the right. If the robot follows the path below, where does it go? Write a check mark (✓) in the box on the house.

> Careful! Remember that the color is the important part. It doesn't matter which way the arrow points.

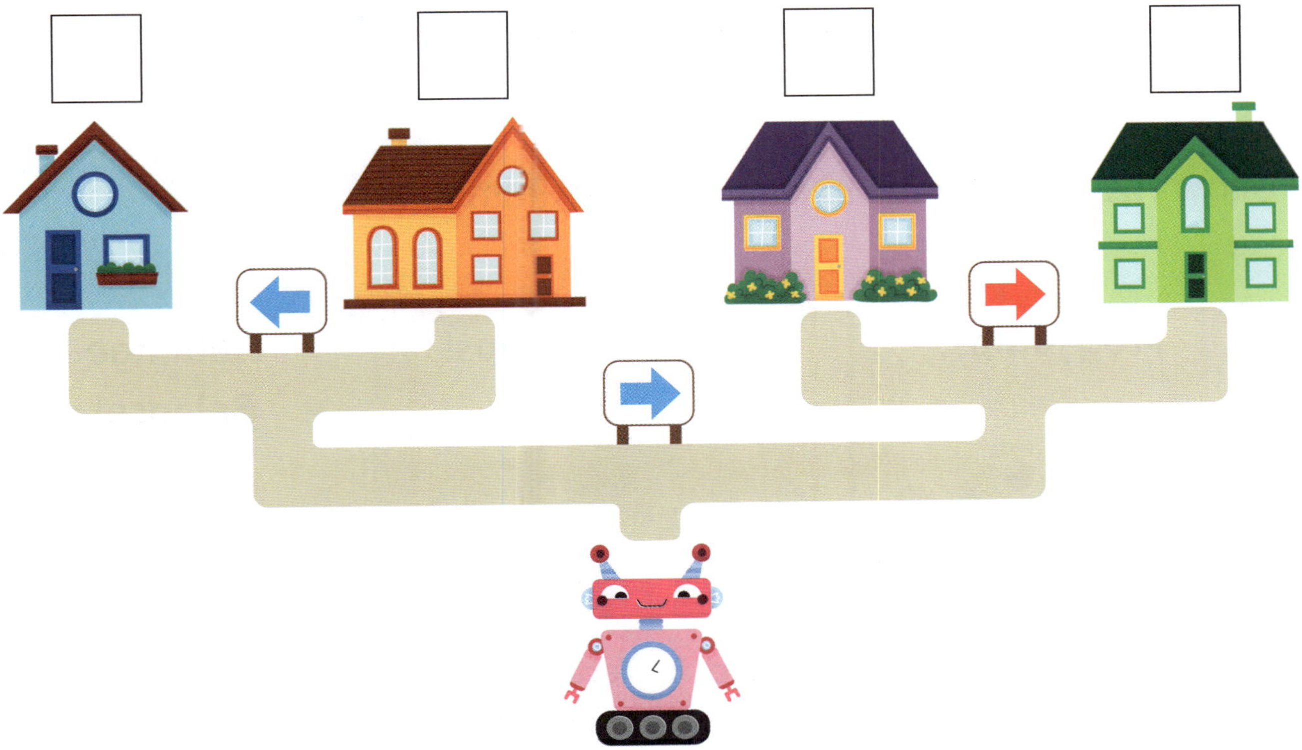

Physical Education Break!

It's important to move your body and exercise!
Try this fun activity below for a study break!

■ Follow the instructions to move like an animal!

Frog jumps!

Squat down and hop like a frog.

Elephant Stomps!

March in place, stomping your feet as hard as you can!

Flamingo Balance!

Try balancing as long as you can on one leg like a flamingo. Then try the other leg!

Crab Walk!

Sit down, place your palms on the ground behind you and lift your hips off the ground. Walk backwards like a crab!

Starfish Jumps

Jump up and down, spreading your arms wide like a starfish. Think of it like a jumping jack!

Did you try all five animal moves?

Unit **3** Table of Contents

Use this page to keep track of your progress throughout the book. Place a check mark in the box when you have completed a section.

Language Arts

- ☐ Prepositions 128
- ☐ Capitalization 130
- ☐ End Punctuation 132
- ☐ Commas 134
- Brain Break 136
- **Mindfulness Break!** 137

Reading

- ☐ Reading Comprehension Literature 1 ---- 138
- ☐ Reading Comprehension Literature 2 ---- 140
- ☐ Reading Comprehension Literature 3 ---- 142
- ☐ Reading Comprehension Literature 4 --- 144
- Brain Break 146
- **Mindfulness Break!** 147

Math

- ☐ Length 1 148
- ☐ Length 2 150
- ☐ Telling Time ☐:00 152
- ☐ Telling Time ☐:30 154
- ☐ Telling Time 156
- Brain Break 158
- **Maze Break!** 159

Science

- ☐ Earth and Space 160
- ☐ Earth, Sun, and Moon 162
- ☐ Seasons 164
- ☐ Weather 166
- Brain Break 168
- **Art Break!** 169

Social Studies

- ☐ Geography and the Environment ------ 170
- ☐ Maps / Cardinal Directions ---------- 172
- ☐ Physical vs Human Features --------- 174
- ☐ Maps Symbols 176
- Brain Break 178
- **Mindfulness Break!** 179

Personal Finance

- ☐ Identifying Coins 180
- ☐ Counting Coins 1 182
- ☐ Counting Coins 2 184
- ☐ Financial Literacy 186
- **Physical Education Break!** 188

Prepositions

A preposition is a word that can show time, where something is, and how two things are related.

For example: in   outside

on   inside

up   before

down   after

■ Circle the prepositions below.

❶He sat (on) the bench.

❷We walked outside.

❸I washed my hands before dinner.

❹The rain came down.

■ Write the correct preposition in the blank.

1

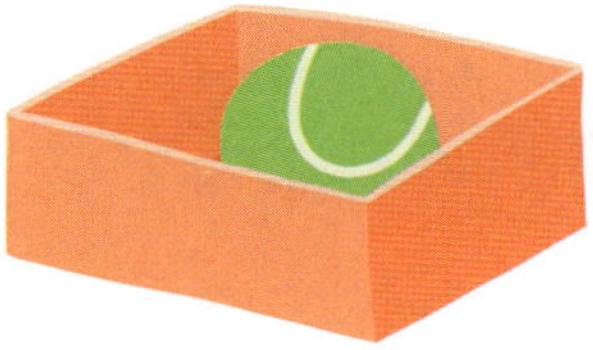

The ball is [in] the box.

2

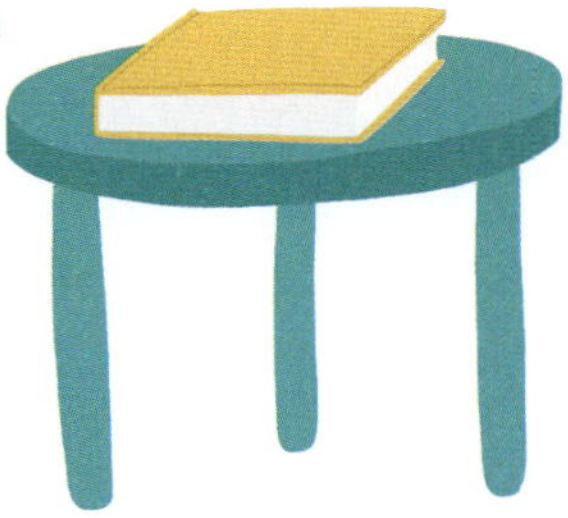

The book is [ ] the table.

3

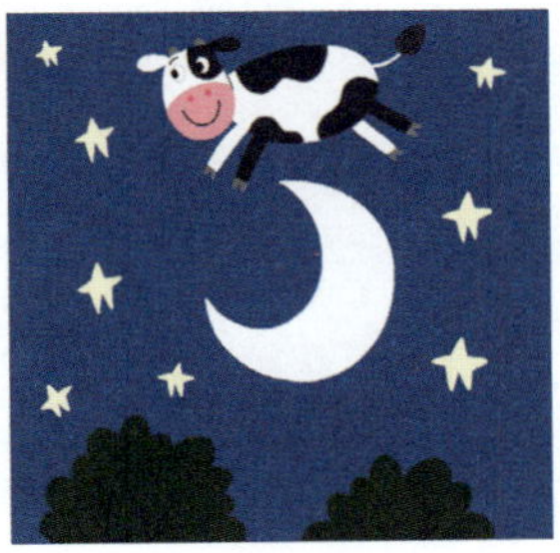

The cow is [ ] the moon.

4

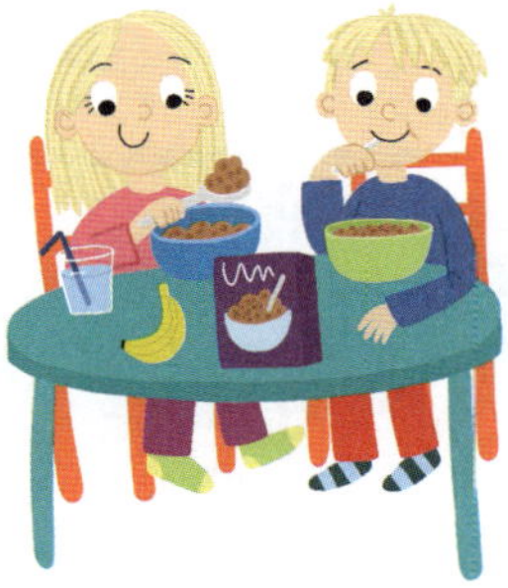

We eat breakfast [ ] home.

5

The dog is [ ] the rug.

Capitalization

KEY POINTS

We use capital letters for the first letters of a name.

Lucy

Steve

Ms. Fisher

Aunt Amy

Grandpa Bob

■ Rewrite each name using capital letters.

1 bill   Bill

2 mr. gordon

3 ms. eden

4 uncle joe

5 mia thomas

6 grandma nina

KEY POINTS

We also use capital letters when writing dates. Capitalize the first letter of a month or day.

January	Monday
June	Wednesday
December	Saturday

■ Rewrite each date using capital letters.

❶ tuesday, may 7 → Tuesday, May 7

❷ friday, october 19

❸ sunday, february 26

❹ thursday, july 1

End Punctuation

KEY POINTS

Sentences can end with a period, question mark, or an exclamation point.

. Most sentences end with a **period**.
This type of sentence tells information.
The average cat weighs ten pounds.

? Sentences that ask a question end with a **question mark**.
Do you have a pet cat?

! Sentences that share something exciting end with an **exclamation mark**.
The oldest cat lived to be 38 years old!

■ Circle the correct punctuation for each sentence.

1 I have three brothers   **.**   **?**   **!**

2 Do you have a brother   **.**   **?**   **!**

3 Sam has 13 brothers and sisters   **.**   **?**   **!**

4 Does your brother have a dog   **.**   **?**   **!**

■ Add punctation for each sentence in the story below.

Max wanted a job ☐ He asked his mom, "How do

I get a job ☐ " His mom said, "you are very good

at taking care of Luna ☐ " Max made signs

☐ The signs said, "Dog Walker Max—only ten

dollars a walk ☐ " He got a call just 20 minutes

later ☐ "You're hired ☐ Can you start

tomorrow ☐ "

Commas

KEY POINTS

A comma is written like this: **,**

A comma shows a pause in a sentence.
Commas are used in lists.
red, blue, and orange

Commas are also used in dates.
January 12, 2025

■ Circle the places where a comma is missing.

We started school on August 28 2023.

My favorite animals are monkeys cows, and snakes.

I was born on June 11 2018.

I like to sing dance and play piano.

- If the sentence is correct, put a check (✓) If it is wrong, put an ✕ . Then write it correctly.

❶ I have a green yellow, and blue backpack.

✕

I have a green, yellow, and blue backpack.

❷ We moved to Texas on October 5, 2021.

❸ I have three cats, two dogs and a frog.

❹ For lunch I ate a sandwich, an apple, and nuts.

❺ Our last day of school is May, 29 2024.

❻ At the park we saw a squirrel a deer and a raccoon.

■ Correct the punctuation errors in the story!

Samson and the Garden

Samson was a bunny who loved to eat carrots?

One day he found a garden that had carrots

tomatoes and corn. He ate so many carrots.

He got a tummy ache! He lay down in a flower

bed to sleep. Samson woke up and felt much

better, The end.

Mindfulness Break!

■ Match the emotions.

surprised

mad

happy

sad

KEY POINTS

Key details are small but important parts of a story.

■ Read the story. Then put a check mark (✓) next to the details that are true and an ✗ next to the details that are not true.

> Where was her sock? Sasha couldn't find it anywhere. She looked under the bed. No luck. She checked behind the door. Nope! Finally she found it under her desk.

☐ Sasha looked in the closet.

☐ Sasha searched under the bed.

☐ Sasha sat down at her desk.

■ **Read the story and answer the questions below.**

Spencer was sad. His friend Jessica was going on vacation for a whole week! He didn't know what he would do while she was gone. Who would he play baseball with? Who would he watch movies with? He decided to write her a letter to tell her all about what was happening at home.

❶ How did Spencer feel?

_____

❷ Why was Spencer sad?

_____

❸ What did he decide to do?

_____

Reading Comprehension Literature 2

KEY POINTS

To retell a story, use your own words to describe the key details. Also think about what lesson the story may have.

■ Read the story. Circle the lesson.

> Jack studied all weekend for the test. He did very well on the test. Tim didn't do as well. Tim told Jack he hadn't studied at all. He played basketball all weekend.

Playing basketball helps your grades.

Studying can help you do well on tests.

Jack is a good friend.

■ Read the story. Then draw a picture of what happens and write about it in your own words.

Mindy told her mom that she was old enough to walk home from school by herself. Her mom gave her keys and told her to be careful. The next day, Mindy started walking home. She stopped and looked around. She was lost! Then she looked again. She knew where she was. She was just nervous. Mindy walked the rest of the way home.

KEY POINTS

Key details can describe characters, settings, and events.

■ Read the story and then write a check mark (✓) next to the statements that are true.

> Mateo looked outside. He could see the full moon. Then he heard a noise right outside his bedroom door. He jumped! But it was just his dog Lola.

☐ It is daytime.

☐ Lola made a noise outside his door.

☐ Mateo is being noisy.

■ Read the story. Then write a detail that describes the characters and setting.

> Sophie's grandmother mixed the batter. "I'm glad I can show you how to bake this. My mother showed me and now I'm teaching you." "I'm glad too," said Sophie. "I love to eat your chocolate cake." Sophie spilled some batter on the kitchen counter. She wiped it up quickly. "Don't worry about it," Sophie's grandmother said.

Sophie: loves her grandma's chocolate cake

Sophie's grandmother:

The setting:

Reading Comprehension Literature 4

KEY POINTS

Sensory word appeal to the five senses: sight, touch, smell, taste, and hearing. We use sensory word to make a story feel more real.

■ Match the word with the correct category.

sour •	• smell
soft •	• taste
stinky •	• touch
bright •	• hearing
loud •	• sight

■ Circle the sensory words in the story.

It was a hot summer day. Daisy felt sticky. She went to the beach with her family and could smell the salty sea. The waves crashed loudly on the shore. She walked into the cool water. She felt a pinch. It was a tiny crab!

Brain Break
Riddle and Maze

■ Follow the path through the maze. Write each letter as you pass it below to solve the riddle.

Riddle: What can you break, even if you never pick it up or touch it?

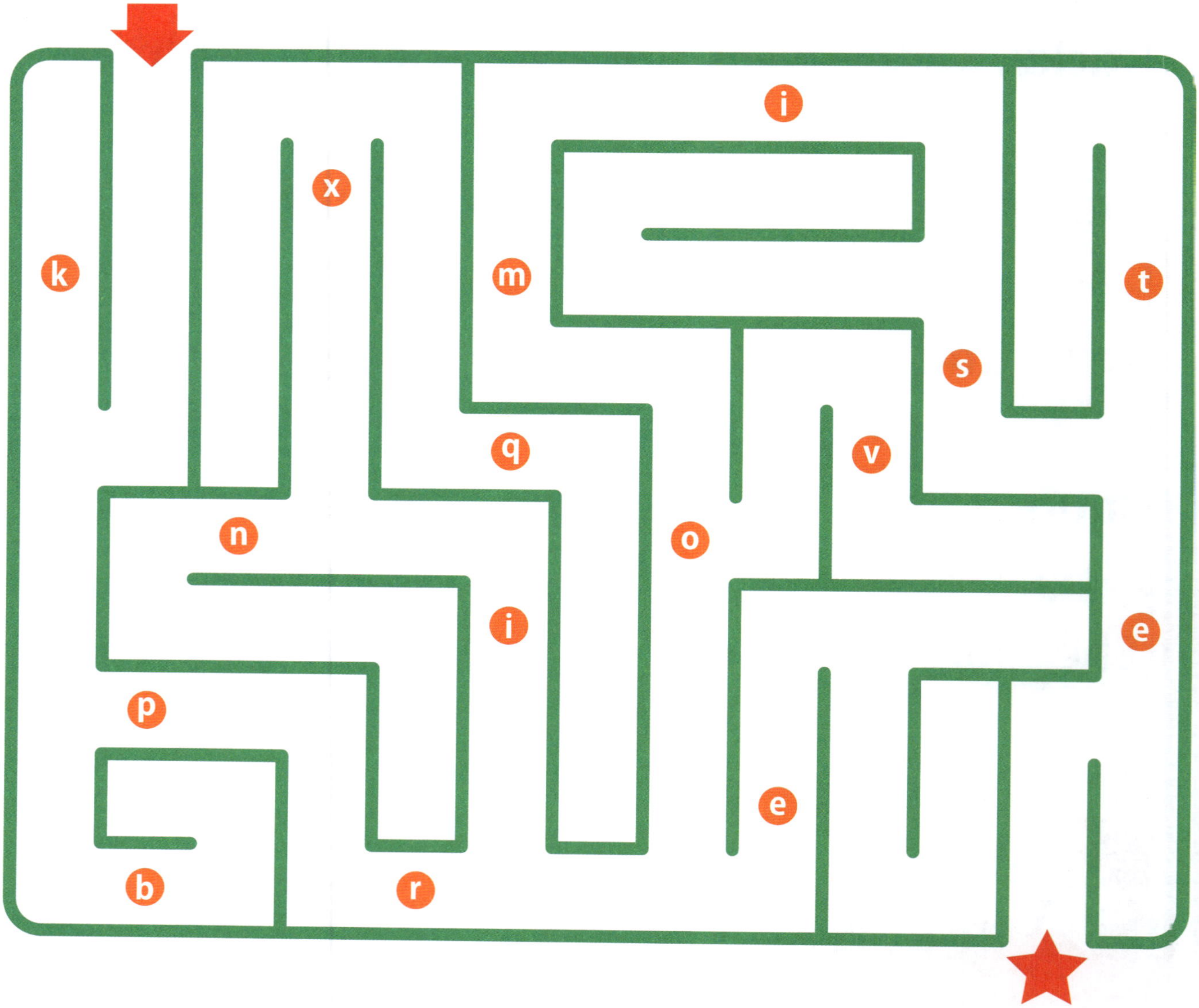

i

x

k   m   t

s

q   v

n   o

i   e

p

e

b   r

Answer: A ☐ ☐ ☐ ☐ ☐ ☐ ☐

Mindfulness Break!

■ Fill in the boxes using the prompts.

When something happens that we do not like or that is upsetting, we can try and change our mindset with positive thinking.

Situation: You did not make the team or club you tried out for...

1 What happened?

2 Why did it happen?

3 Can I change the outcome?

4 If yes...how?

5 If no...then what's next?

6 How does it make me feel?

Unit 3 Math

Length 1

KEY POINTS

Objects can have different lengths. We can compare how long they are and measure their length in inches.

■ Which is the longest? Write a check mark (✓) next to the longest bar.

(   )

(   )

(   )

(   )

(   )

(   )

(   )

(   )

(   )

(   )

(   )

(   )

(   )

(   )

(   )

Length 2

■ How long is each bar? Answer in inches.

❶

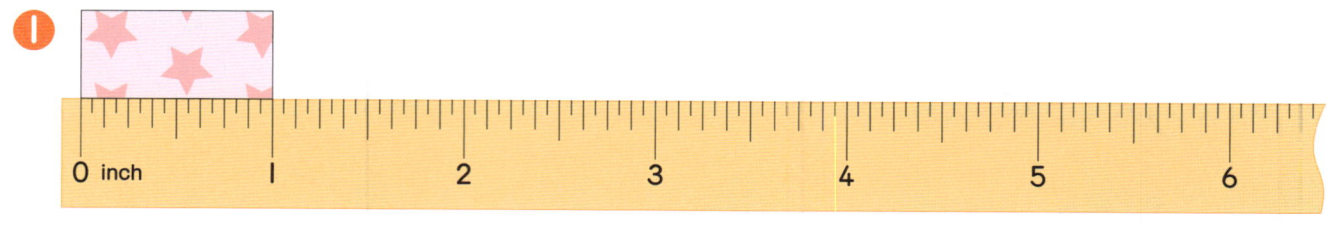

| | in. |

❷

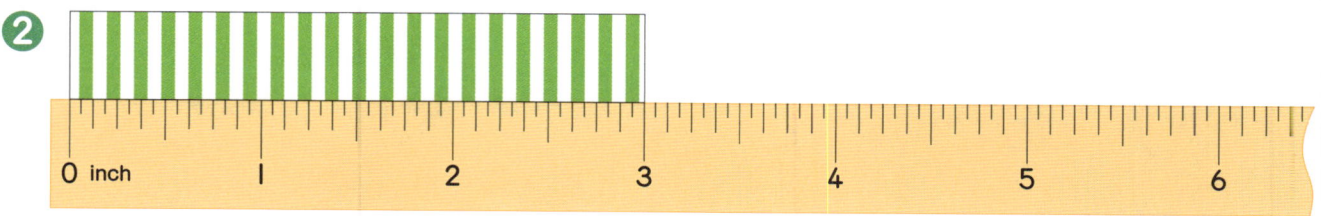

| | in. |

❸

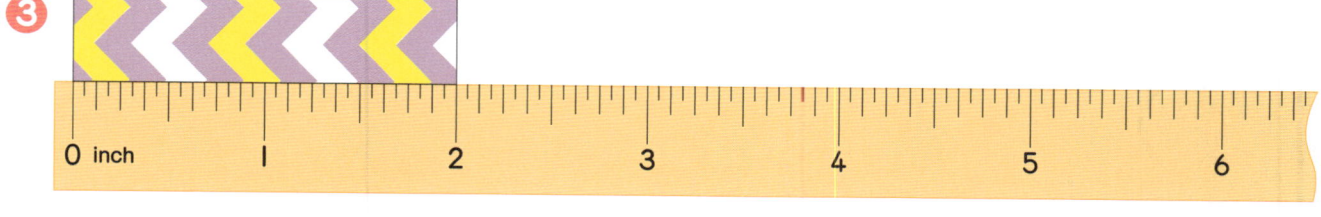

| | in. |

❹

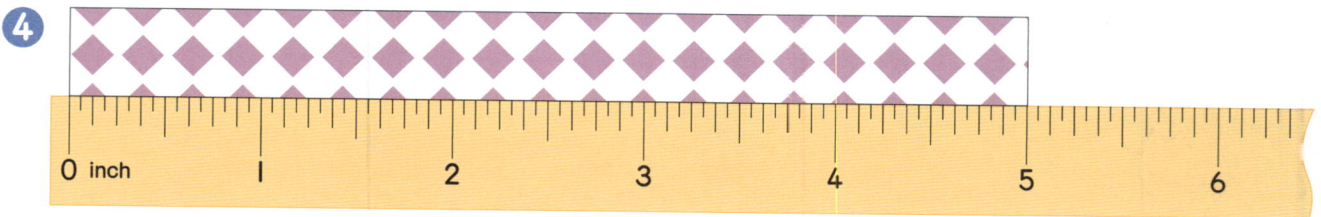

| | in. |

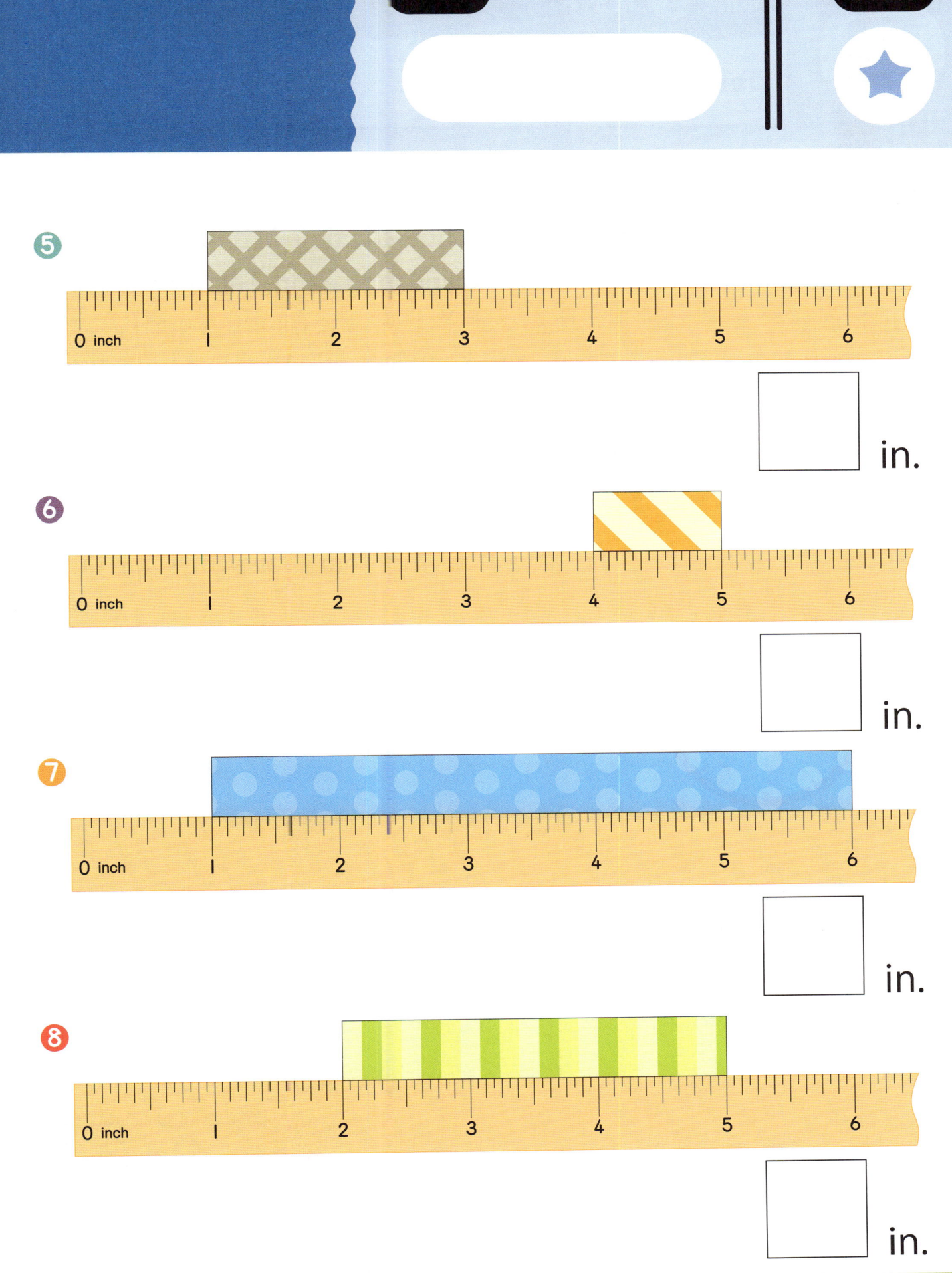

5

[ ] in.

6

[ ] in.

7

[ ] in.

8

[ ] in.

Telling Time ☐:00

Analog clocks and digital clocks show the time in different ways.
Analog clocks have a short hand and long hand. The short hand points to the hour. The long hand shows the minutes, and it starts at the 12 at the top. When it is zero minutes past the hour, it points to the 12.

Digital clocks show the time in this format: Hour: Minutes. So one o'clock is written as 1:00.

■ Match the analog clock to the digital clock that shows the same time.

10:00

8:00

3:00

■ **What time is it? Write the time under the clock.**

1

```
7:00
```

4

7

2

5

8

3

6

9

Telling Time □:30

An hour has sixty minutes. So when it is thirty minutes past the hour, the long hand moves halfway around the clock and points at six.

■ Match the analog clock to the digital clock that shows the same time.

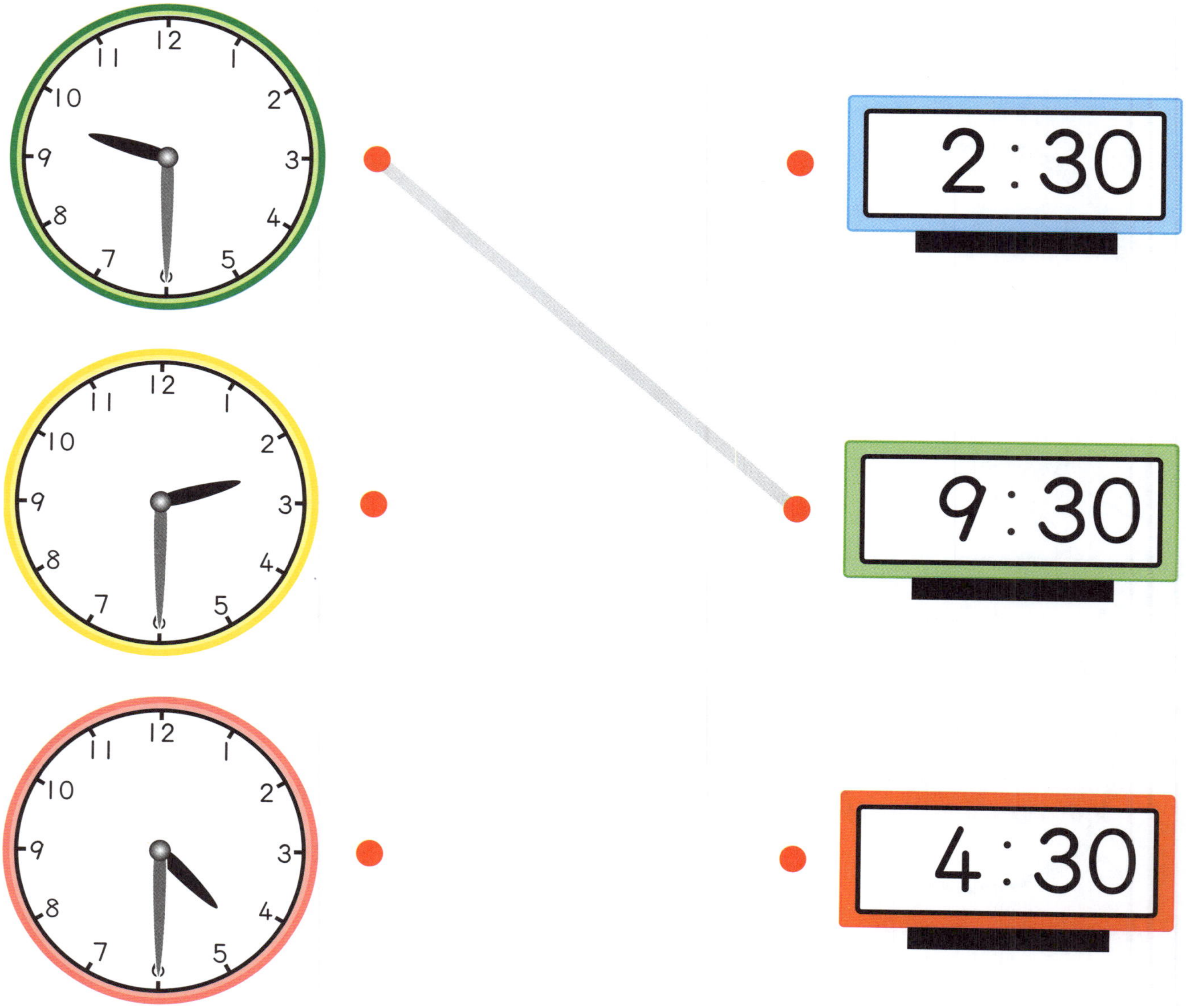

| 2 : 30 |

| 9 : 30 |

| 4 : 30 |

■ **What time is it? Write the time under the clock.**

$8:30$

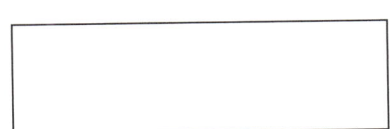

Telling Time

■ **Draw the hands on each clock to show the time.**

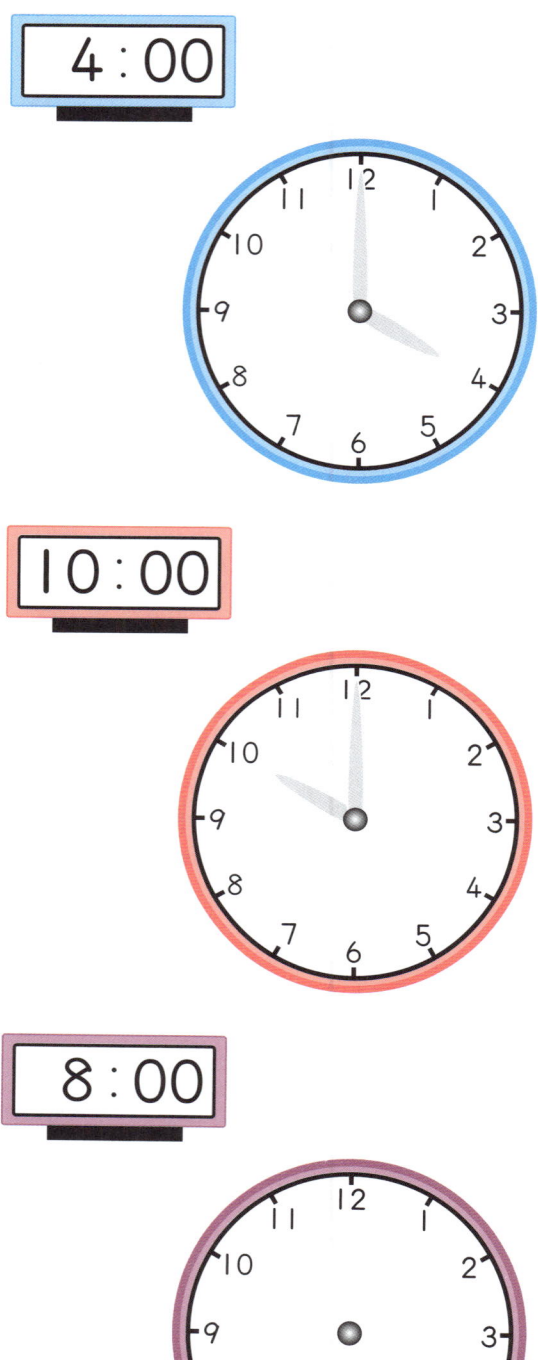

4 : 00

10 : 00

8 : 00

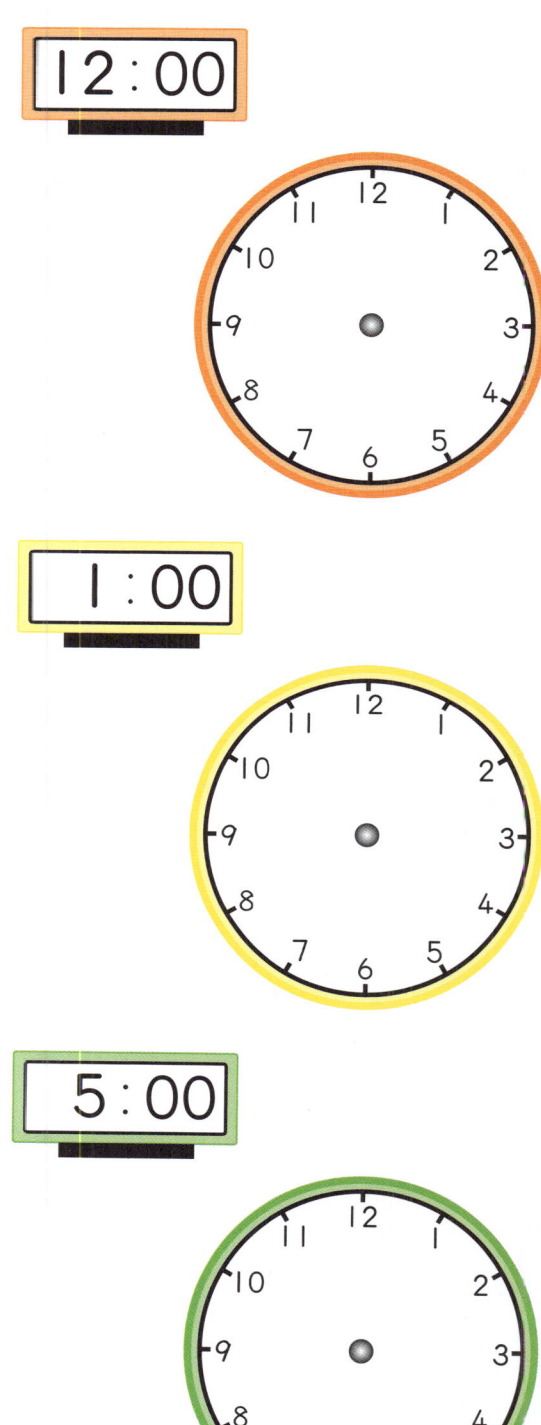

12 : 00

1 : 00

5 : 00

9 : 30

3 : 30

2 : 30

7 : 30

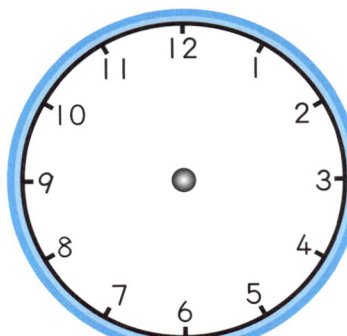

11 : 30

6 : 30

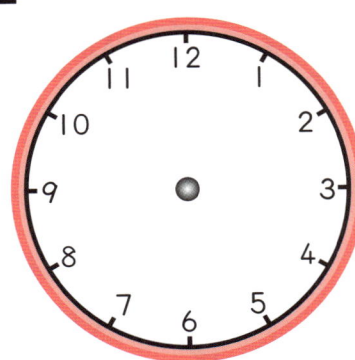

Brain Break
Find the Clock!

■ Find the clock below that shows the same time as the one on the right and circle it. How many seconds did it take you to find it?

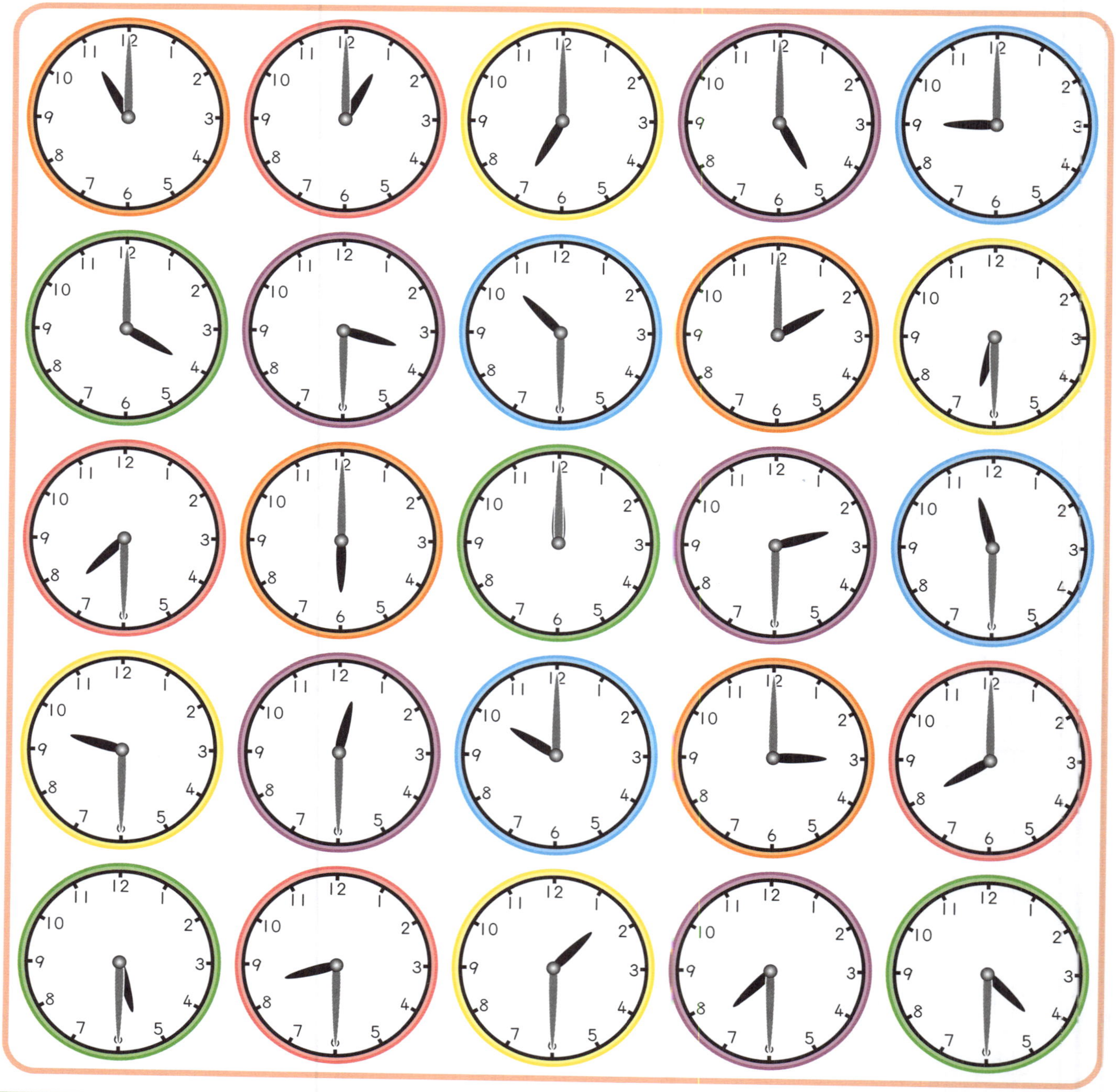

Unit 3

Maze Break!

■ Trace the path from start to finish!

Earth and Space

There are eight planets in our solar system. One of them is Earth! All of the planets orbit the sun. This means that they move around the sun. The closest planet to the sun is Mercury, and then Venus, Earth, Mars, Jupiter, Saturn, Uranus, and Neptune.

■ Answer the questions.

❶ How many planets are there?

_____

❷ What does *orbit* mean?

_____

■ Label each planet.

Sun   Earth   Mercury   Venus   Mars
Uranus   Neptune   Saturn   Jupiter

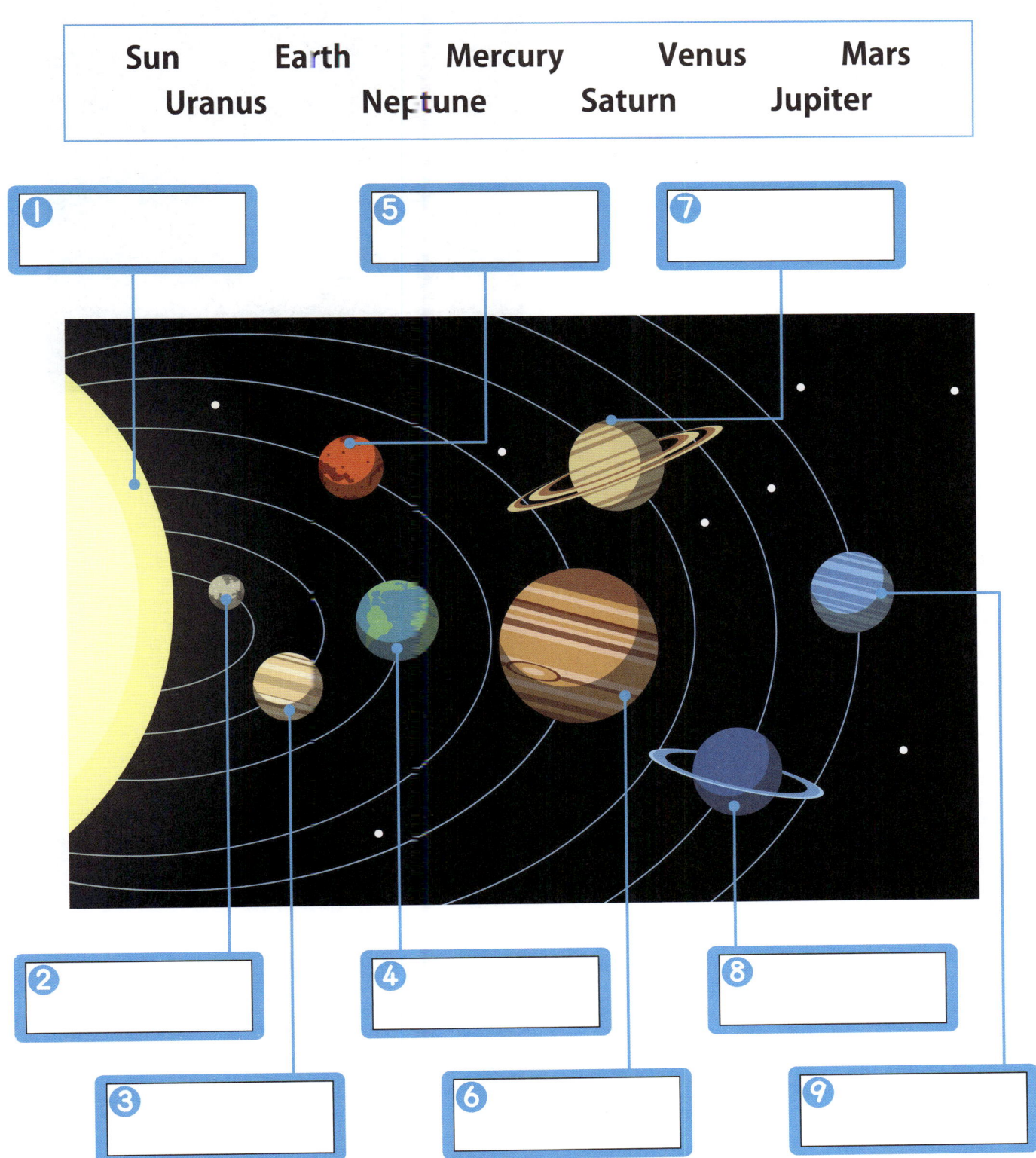

1. _____

2. _____

3. _____

4. _____

5. _____

6. _____

7. _____

8. _____

9. _____

Earth, Sun, and Moon

KEY POINTS

When Earth orbits the sun, it also spins. The side that faces the sun has sunlight. This causes daytime. When it spins away, it becomes night on that side, and day on the other side of Earth. Just like Earth orbits the sun, the moon orbits Earth.

■ **Answer the questions.**

❶ What does the moon orbit?

_____

❷ What causes daytime?

_____

Date

Great Job Sticker

■ Write day or night beneath the picture.

1
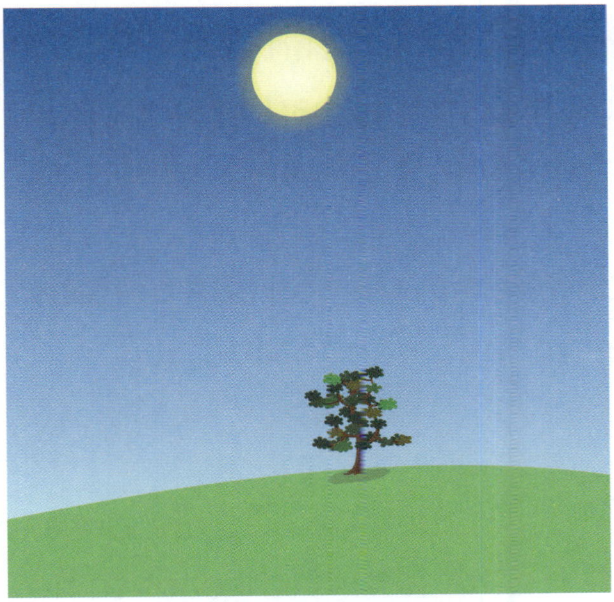

3
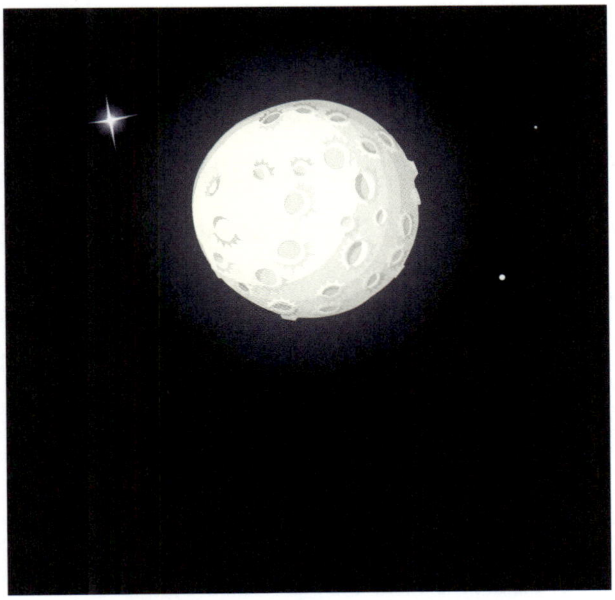

2
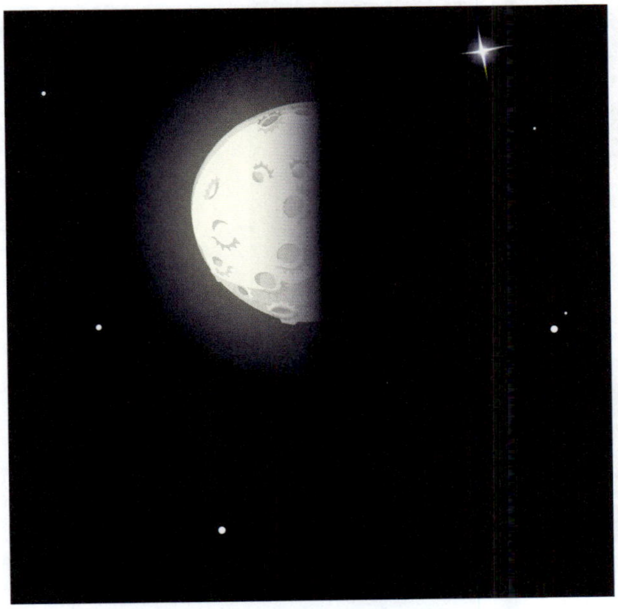

4

Seasons

KEY POINTS

The earth moves in many ways. It orbits the sun. It spins. And it also tilts in back and forth. Sometimes, the top part of the world tilts closer to the sun. Then it is summer in that part of the world. When the top part tilts away from the sun, it becomes winter in that part of the world.

Because of this, the seasons are different in the top and bottom half of the world. When it is winter in the United States, it is summer in Australia!

In winter, you are far from the sun and very cold.

In summer, you are close to the sun which leads to hot weather.

In spring, you get closer to the sun and plants start to bloom from the warmer weather.

In fall, you start to move further from the sun and the weather cools down.

■ Match the seasons.

   ●  ● **Fall**

   ● ● **Winter**

   ●  ● **Summer**

   ● ● **Spring**

Weather

KEY POINTS

Every season has different weather. In summer it is often very hot. In the fall, it begins to cool down. In the winter, it can be cold. Spring is warmer than winter, but not as hot as summer.

■ Answer the questions.

❶ What season is the hottest?

_____

❷ In what season might it snow?

_____

■ Circle the objects that you would need in each season.

①

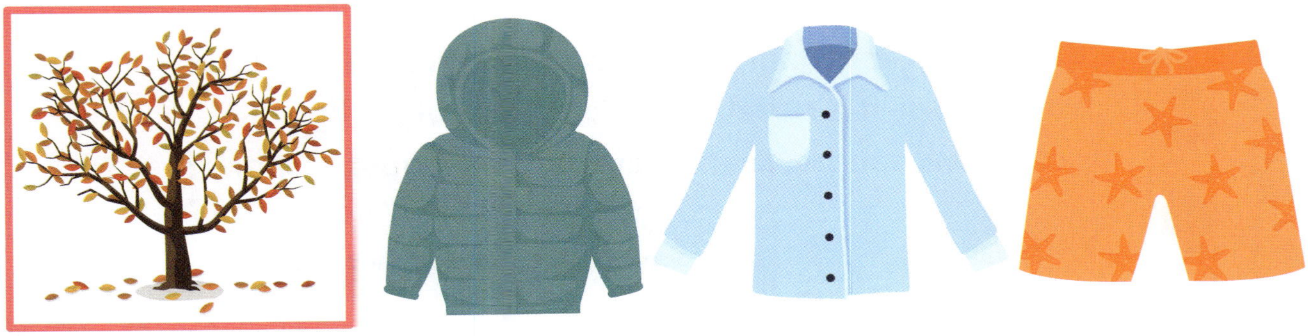

②

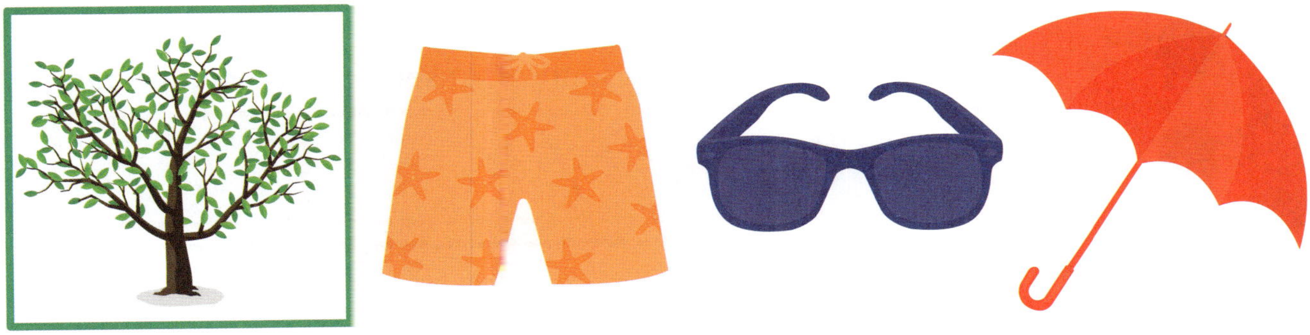

③

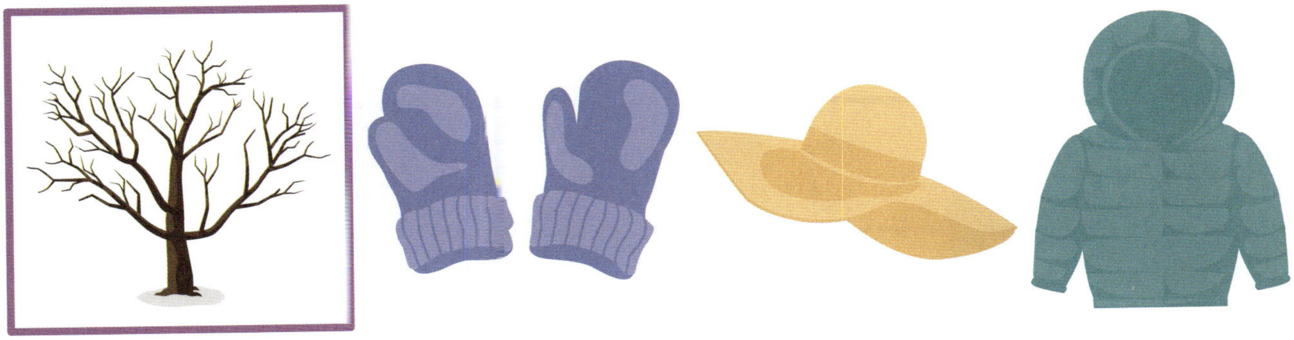

④

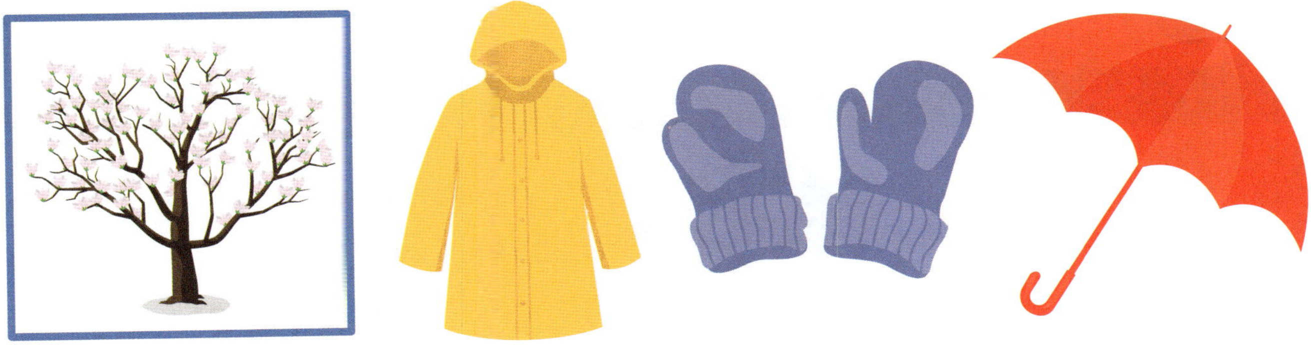

Brain Break
Science Journal 3

Fill in the science journal and record information based on what season it is currently. Record hours of daylight and sunset and sunrise. Are the days getting longer or shorter?

What season is it?

	Date	When is sunrise/sunset?	Daylight Hours
❶		/	
❷		/	
❸		/	

Did you know? The days are longer in the summer and shorter in the winter.

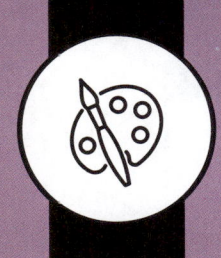

Art Break!

■ Draw what you do, wear, or eat in your favorite season.

What is your favorite activity in this season?

Geography and the Environment

KEY POINTS

A map is a drawing that represents a place. A map can show countries, landforms, oceans, places and buildings. The purpose of a map is to show where places are. Maps help people find the location of places or things.

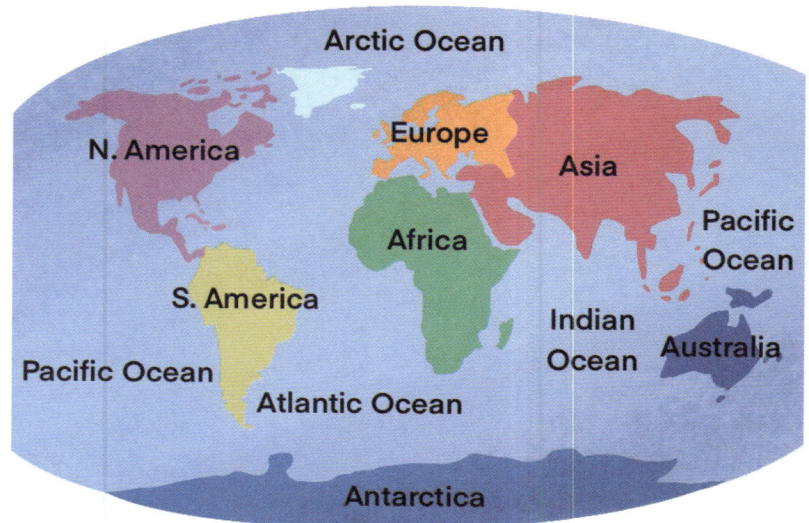

■ **Answer the questions.**

❶ What is a map used for?

_____

❷ What do maps show?

_____

■ Use the pictures to help answer the questions.

A Country map　　**B Town map**　　**C Store map**

❶ Which map would you use to find the post office in your town?

❷ Which map would you use to find the capital of a country?

❸ Which map would you use to find milk in a store?

Maps / Cardinal Directions

KEY POINTS

Maps use a compass rose to show the four directions: north, east, south, and west. When describing where places are on a map you can use these direction words.

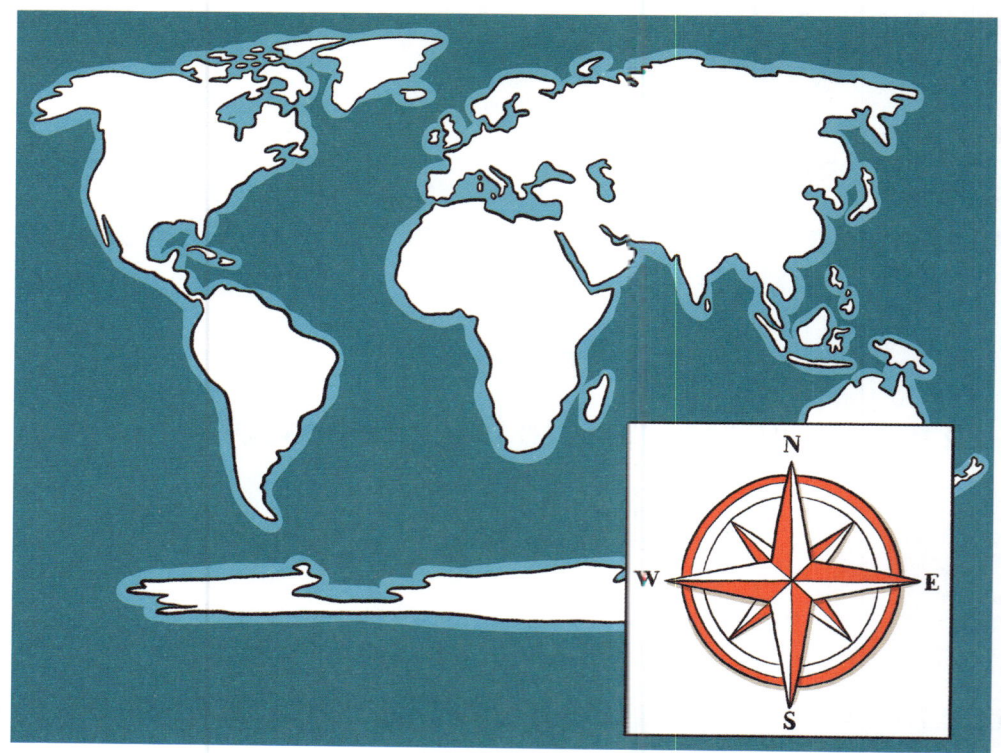

■ Answer the questions.

❶ What is a compass rose used for?

_____

❷ What are the four main directions?

_____

■ Use the compass rose to write the directions.

❶ What direction is the library from the river?

_____

❷ What direction is the Town Hall from the park?

_____

❸ What direction is the post office from the library?

_____

❹ What direction is the park from the library?

_____

Physical vs Human Features

KEY POINTS

Maps have both physical and man-made features. Physical features are natural, like mountains, rivers, or plains. Man-made features are created by humans, such as houses, stores, and roads.

■ Answer the questions.

❶ What is a physical feature on a map?

<hr>

❷ Is a house man-made or a physical feature?

■ Circle the correct picture.

Man-made

Natural

Man-made

Map Symbols

KEY POINTS

Some maps use symbols to show features. This makes the map easier to read. A map can have different symbols for cities, rivers, lakes, roads, and railroad tracks. A legend is a list on a map that shows what the symbols stand for.

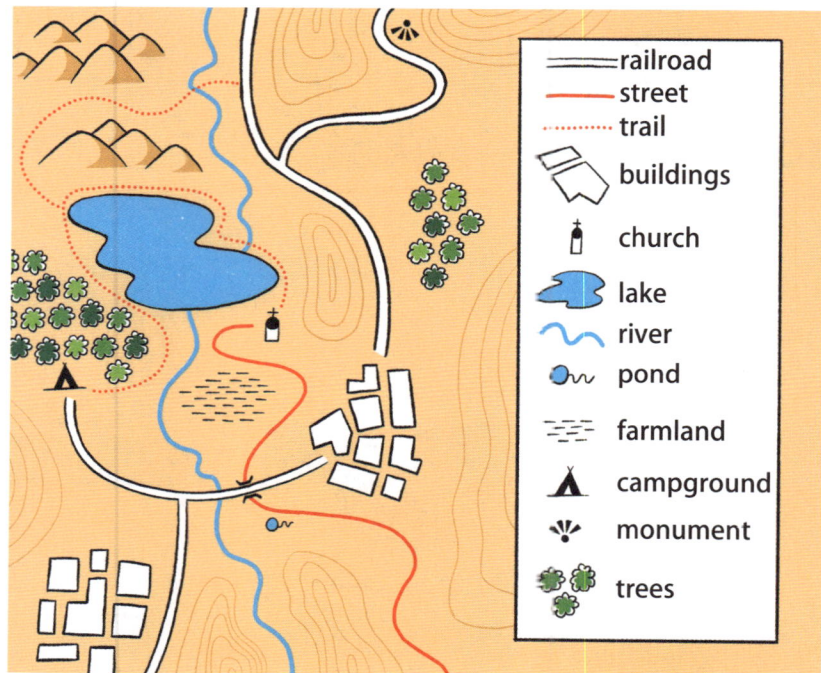

■ **Answer the questions.**

❶ What are map symbols used to show?

❷ What is a legend?

■ Match the symbols to what they stand for on the map.

cave

tree

mountain

river

Brain Break
Map Maze

■ Complete the activity.

START

SCHOOL

LIBRARY

GOAL

■ **Choose an emotion to illustrate and answer the questions.**

❶Choose an emotion and draw what it means to you.

❷How can you be mindful of the emotion you picked?

Identifying Coins

Coins

	Coin Front (heads)	Coin Back (tails)	Name	Value

Coin Front (heads)				
Coin Back (tails)				
Name	**Penny**	**Nickel**	**Dime**	**Quarter**
Value	1¢ (cent)	5¢ (cents)	10¢ (cents)	25¢ (cents)

■ Draw a line to the same coin.

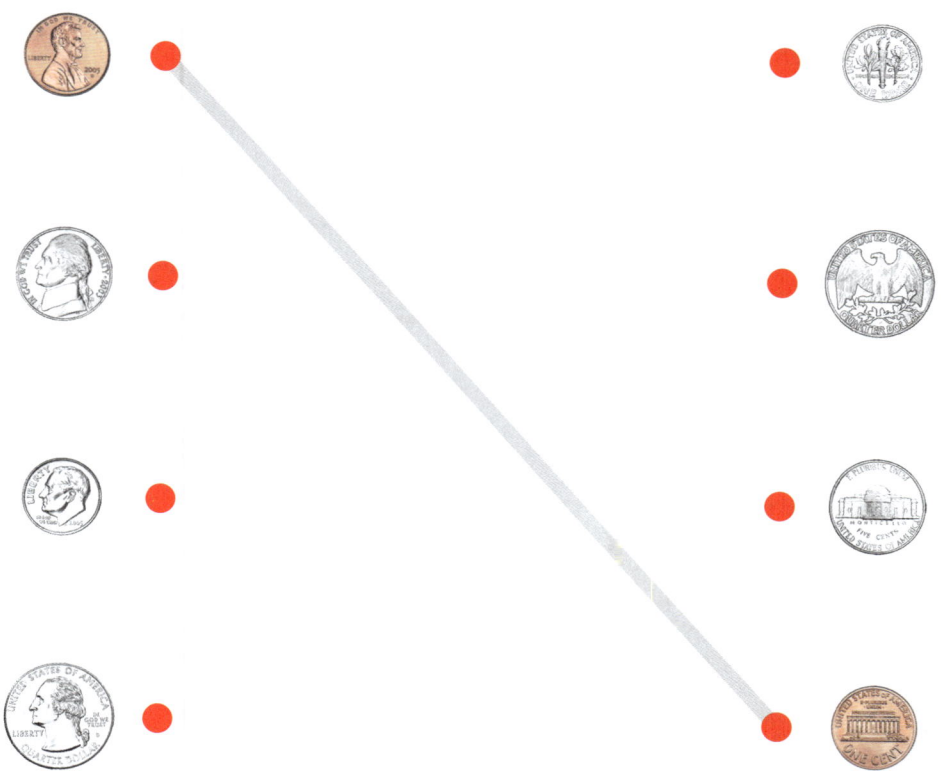

■ Circle both sides of the coin.

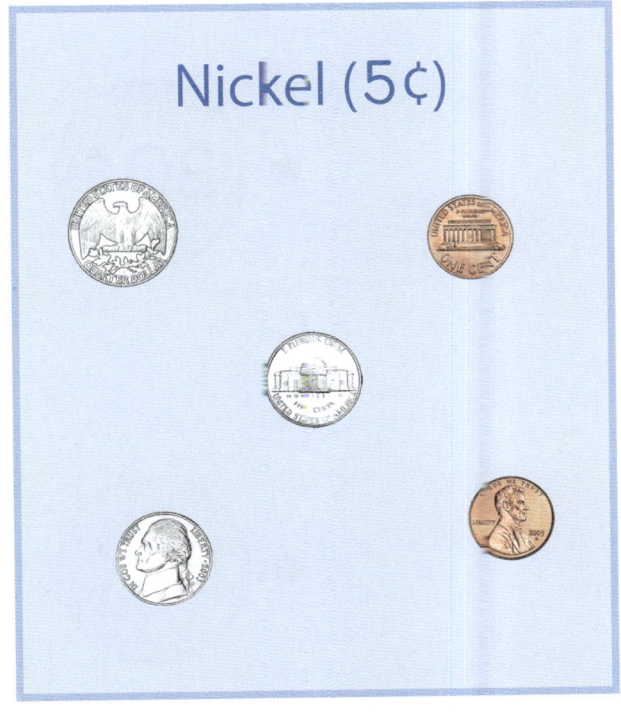

Counting Coins 1

■ Draw a line to match each set of coins with the correct coin with correct amount of money.

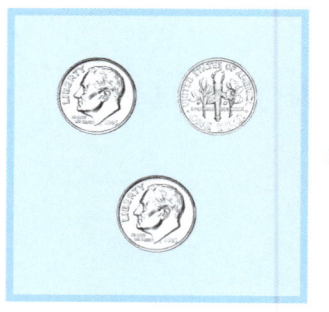   •   •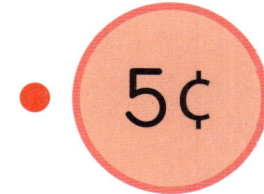

   •   •

   •   •

   •   •

Date

Great Job Sticker

Add the value of the coins and write the amount in the box.

1

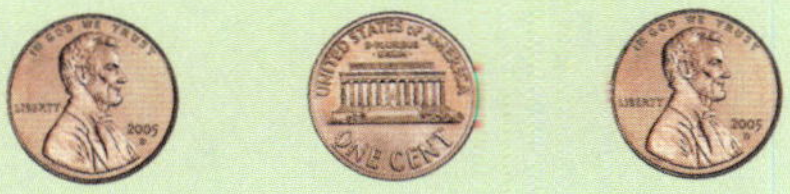

☐ ¢

2

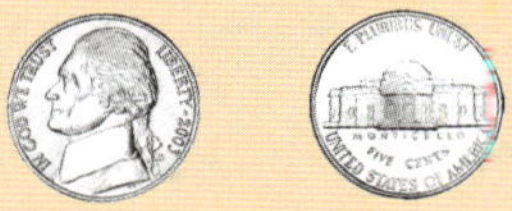

☐ ¢

3

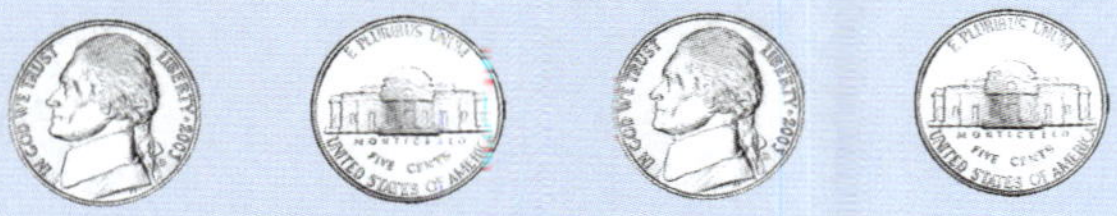

☐ ¢

4

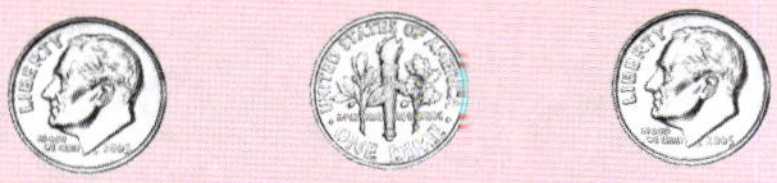

☐ ¢

5

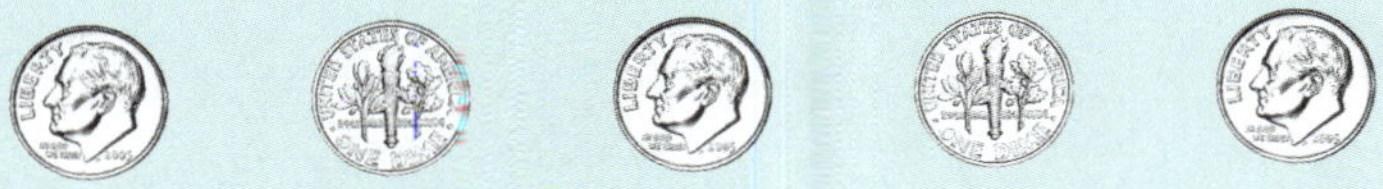

☐ ¢

6

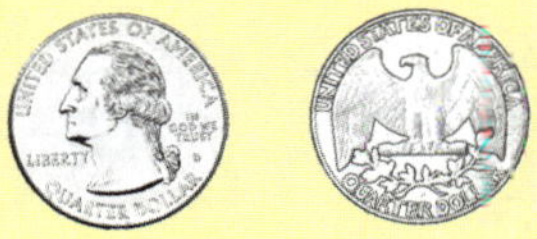

☐ ¢

Counting Coins 2

■ Add the value of the coins and circle the correct answer.

1

3¢ • ⓐ7¢

2

17¢ • 32¢

3

14¢ • 29¢

4

13¢ • 23¢

5

15¢ • 25¢

6

40¢ • 45¢

■ Draw a line to the purse with the money you need to buy each item.

9¢

20¢

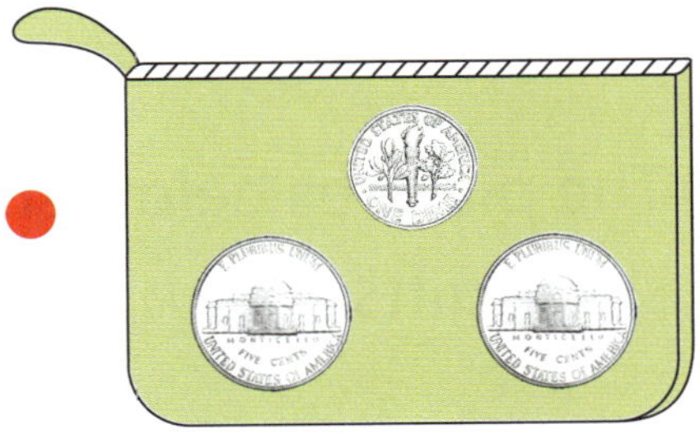

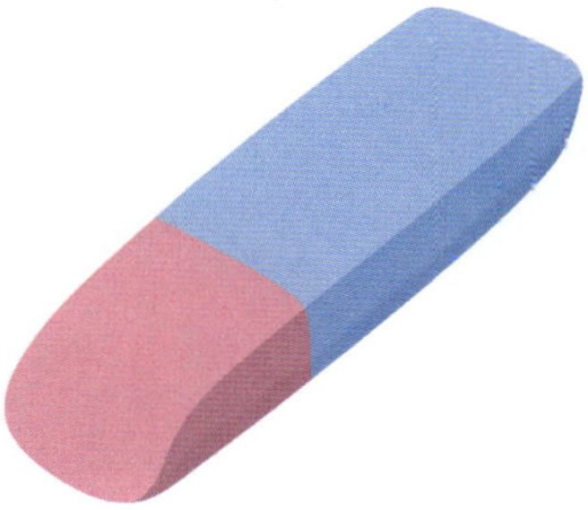

70¢

90¢

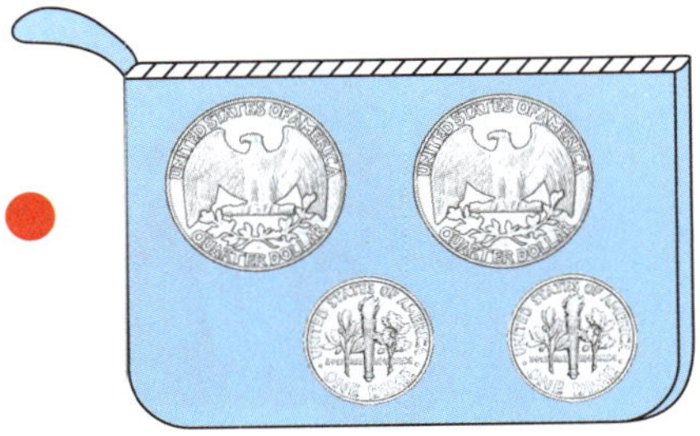

Financial Literacy

KEY POINTS

Income is money that you earn from a job.

A **gift** is money you are given as a present.

■ The pictures below show income or gifts. Circle the pictures that show gifts.

KEY POINTS

Needs are things that you must have to live and survive.

Wants are things that you would like to have, but don't need.

■ Circle the picture that shows *needs*.

187

It's important to move your body and exercise!
Try this fun activity below for a study break!

■ Look at the images and read the text below. Try the yoga poses!

Mountain Pose

Stand up straight with your feet apart and your arms out to the side with palms facing foward. Imagine being strong and unmovable like a mountain.

Butterfly Pose

Sit on your behind with your back straight. Bend your legs and place the bottom of your feet together.

Tree Pose

Stand on one leg. Bend the knee of the leg you are not standing on, place the bottom of your foot on the inside of your leg, and then balance.

Frog Pose

Squat down with your knees apart and your arms resting between your knees. Touch your hands to the ground. Hold.

Unit **4** Table of Contents

Use this page to keep track of your progress throughout the book. Place a check mark in the box when you have completed a section.

Writing

☐ Writing Sentences 1 — 190
☐ Writing Sentences 2 — 192
☐ Word Families — 194
☐ Spelling Irregular Words — 196
Brain Break — 198
Mindfulness Break! — 199

Reading

☐ Reading Comprehension Informational 1 — 200
☐ Reading Comprehension Informational 2 — 202
☐ Reading Comprehension Informational 3 — 204
☐ Reading Comprehension Informational 4 — 206
Brain Break — 208
Mindfulness Break! — 209

Math

☐ 3D Shapes 1 — 210
☐ 3D Shapes 2 — 212
☐ 2D Shapes 1 — 214
☐ 2D Shapes 2 — 216
☐ Partitioning Shapes — 218
Brain Break — 220
Maze Break! — 221

Science

☐ States of Matter 1 — 222
☐ States of Matter 2 — 224
☐ Changes in Matter — 226
☐ Describing Matter — 228
Brain Break — 230
Art Break! — 231

Social Studies

☐ Culture — 232
☐ Culture Celebrations — 234
☐ Culture and Languages — 236
☐ My Culture — 238
Brain Break — 240
Mindfulness Break! — 241

Thinking Skills

☐ Jigsaw Puzzles — 242
☐ Copying Shapes — 244
☐ Direction Words — 246
☐ Matching — 248
Physical Education Break! — 250

Writing Sentences 1

KEY POINTS

Some sentences share information. They end with a period.

I like cheese.

Some sentences ask a question. They end with a question mark.

Do you like cheese?

■ Write an I next to the sentence if it shares information. Write a Q if it is a question.

Q | Do you like the beach?

She collects shells.

Some beaches are sandy.

Do you live near a beach?

KEY POINTS

Commands tell someone to do something. They might end with a period or an exclamation mark.

Give me the book.
Don't do that!

Some sentences show surprise.

Wow! I never knew that!

■ Write a C next to the sentence if it is a command. Write a S if it shows surprise.

| S | Oh, I really like your shoes! |

| | Go away! |

| | Tie your laces. |

| | Ouch, my feet hurt! |

Writing Sentences 2

■ Look at the picture. Write two of each sentence type based on what you see in the picture.

Share information: ❶ The boy is wearing a green shirt.

❷

Ask question: ❶ Is he making lunch?

❷

Commands: ❶ Add mustard, please!

❷

Show surprise: ❶ That is a lot of cheese!

❷

■ Look at the picture. Write two of each sentence type based on what you see in the picture.

Share information:

Ask question:

Commands:

Show surprise:

Word Families

KEY POINTS

Some words follow spelling patterns. These words can be called word families. Here are some examples.

ig	ap	ack	ake
pig	nap	snack	snake
big	map	track	rake
wig	trap	lack	take
dig	cap	pack	bake

■ Circle the words that belong to the word family.

all	ink	eat
tall	thank	neat
tell	pink	feet
mall	win	meat

■ Write a word that fits into each word family.

aw	eel	ish	ell
paw	feel	dish	smell

ight	ife	ock	orn
night	knife	sock	born

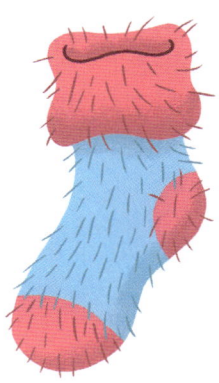

Spelling Irregular Words

KEY POINTS

Some words don't follow normal spelling patterns. Some common irregular words include:

the, of, there, is, you, they, said, were, do, one

■ Circle the correctly spelled word.

❶ "Hand me the phone," she   (**said**) • **sed**

❷ I put the box over   **there** • **thare**   .

❸ I'm not sure what to   **due** • **do**   .

❹ **You** • **Yoo**   have a new book.

■ Circle the words that are spelled incorrectly. Then write them correctly above the word.

was

I (wus) excited. Today we would find

out about thee school play. I wanted

to be in the play. But I wasn't sure I

would get a part. Thare wore a lot of

students who wanted to act. Our teacher

siad she would tell us before lunch.

Finally it was time. I got thu part!

■ Use the picture to write sentences.

1
2
3

Mindfulness Break!

■ Write a letter to someone to make them feel better.

KEY POINTS

KEY POINTS

Informational texts have key details. These are small pieces of information in a text.

■ Read the text and circle the key details in the text.

> Trees are important to have in cities. Their leaves make shade. Squirrels and other animals live in their branches. And trees help to clean our air.

Trees clean air.

Trees are used to make paper.

Squirrels live in trees.

■ Read the text and write a check mark (✓) next to the correct answer.

Have you ever wondered how carrots grow? The part of the carrot that we eat grows underground. The greens grow above ground. After the carrot has grown, the farmer pulls it out of the ground.

❶ Where do carrots grow?

   ☐ underground

   ☐ in water

❷ How are carrots picked?

   ☐ they are pulled out of the ground

   ☐ they are picked from a tree

KEY POINTS

The main topic is what the text is all about. The key details give information about the main topic.

Main topic: Bees live in hives.

Key details: A hive has one queen bee.
A hive has many worker bees.
Hives are full of honey.

■ Read the topic. Then pick details to support it.

Main topic: **Ants work together**

Ants carry large objects together.

Bees work together in a hive.

Ants dig huge nests together.

■ Read the text. Circle the main topic. Underline the key details.

Spiders should be man's best friend!

Some people think spiders look scary.

But they help us. Spiders trap and

eat other bugs. They weave webs. The

webs catch the bugs. So spiders help

keep your home bug-free.

KEY POINTS

Retell an informational text by focusing on the main topic and key details. Be sure to use your own words.

■ Underline the parts of the informational text that are most important to retell.

Have you ever looked up at the sky and wondered about clouds? Clouds look fluffy and soft. But clouds are actually made of tiny drops of water and ice. There are different types of clouds. Some clouds are high in the sky. Some are lower. Rain clouds usually are lower in the sky.

Date

Great Job Sticker

■ Retell the text in your own words. Use the pictures to help.

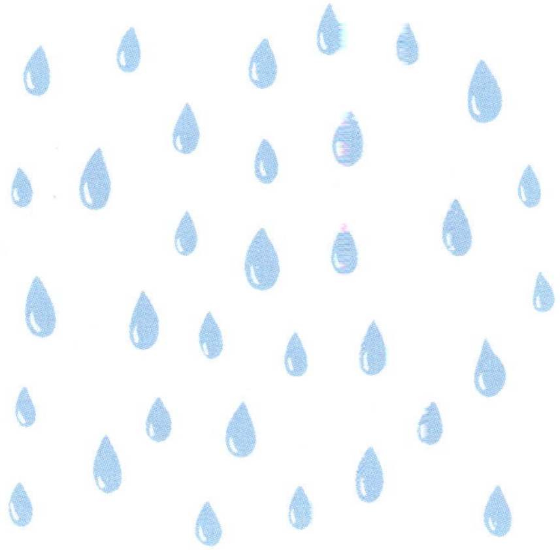

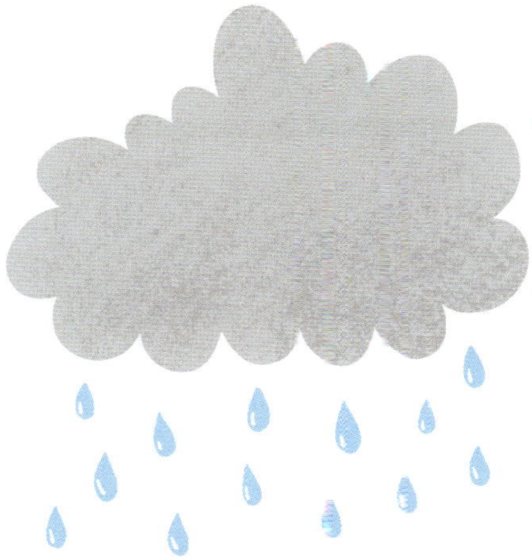

Reading Comprehension Informational 4

KEY POINTS

If you see a word you don't know, you can look for clues. For example, if you read "He sat at his typewriter and wrote a letter." you might wonder what a typewriter is. But you know it is something used for writing! This is a clue.

■ Read the sentence. Circle the word that is most similar to the underlined word.

My cat only likes wet food. He is very **particular** about what he eats.

kind   picky   angry

■ **Read the text. Then answer the questions.**

> Did you know dogs are **related** to wolves? That's right! Some wolves learned to live with humans a long time ago. Many many years later, their **offspring** are still living with humans. And now they are friendly and cute!

❶ What does *related* mean in the first sentence?

☐ family

☐ different

☐ better

❷ What does *offspring* mean in this text?

☐ children's children

☐ parents

☐ enemy

Brain Break
Creative Writing!

■ Write a story.

Once upon a time there was a monster named...

■ Circle how the action makes you feel.

Helping others can make us feel: happy, thankful, and loved.

❶ You help clean up your toys.

You feel:

> **happy** • **thankful** • **loved**

❷ You help your teacher hand out papers to the class.

You feel:

> **happy** • **thankful** • **loved**

❸ You help your parent or guardian make your favorite dinner.

You feel:

> **happy** • **thankful** • **loved**

3D Shapes 1

■ Draw a line from the pictures to shapes that are similar.

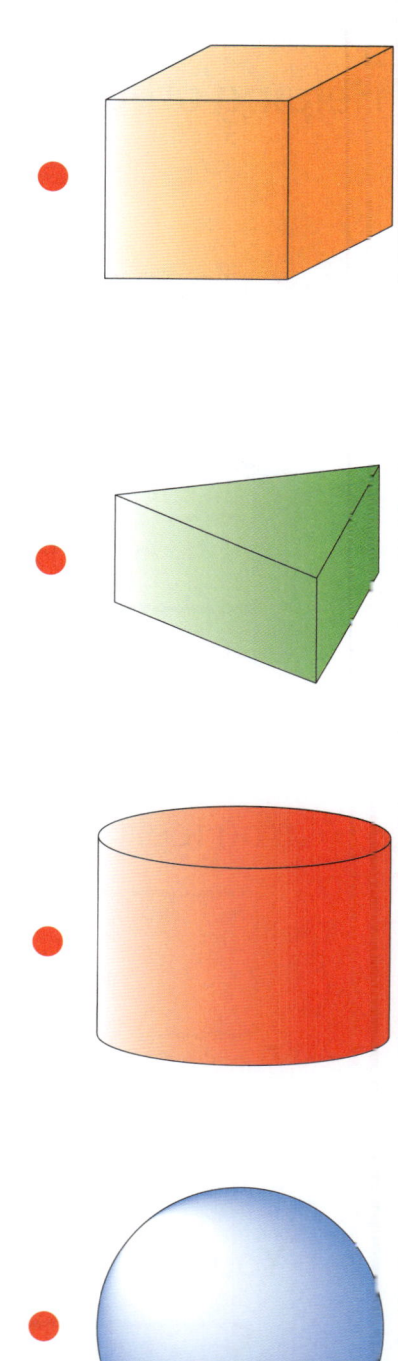

■ Find the shapes shown in the sample below. Then color them the same color as the sample.

Sample

 = Blue   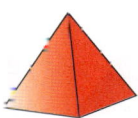 = Red    = Yellow

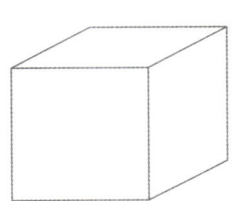
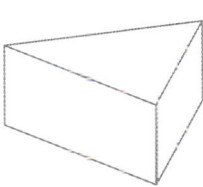
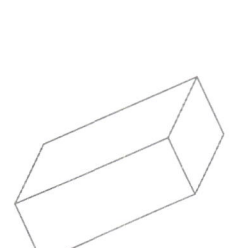
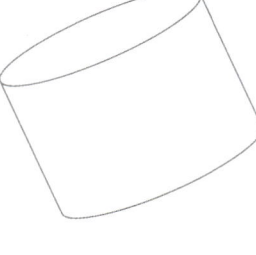

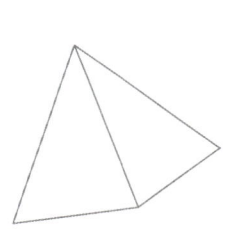
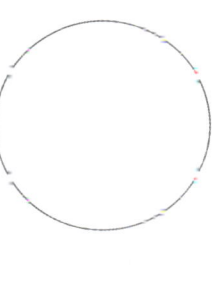
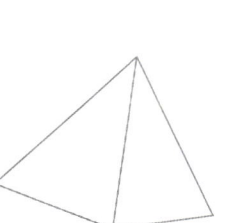
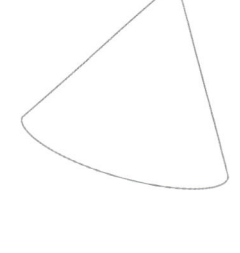

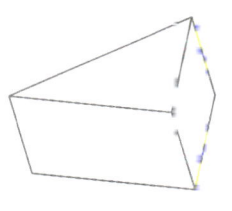
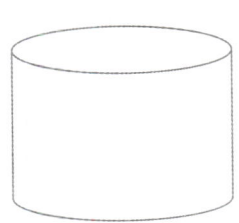
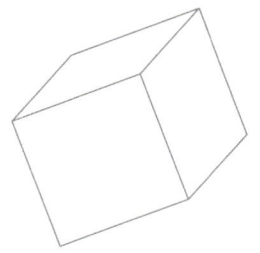

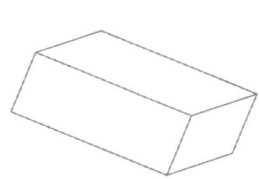
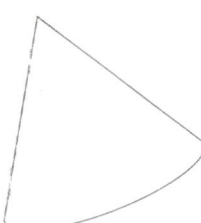
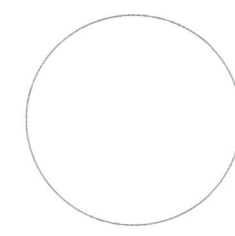

3D Shapes 2

■ Draw a line from the arrow (↓) to the star (★) by connecting the 🛢 , ▲ , and ⬤ .

■ How many 3D shapes are there? Write the answer in the box.

①

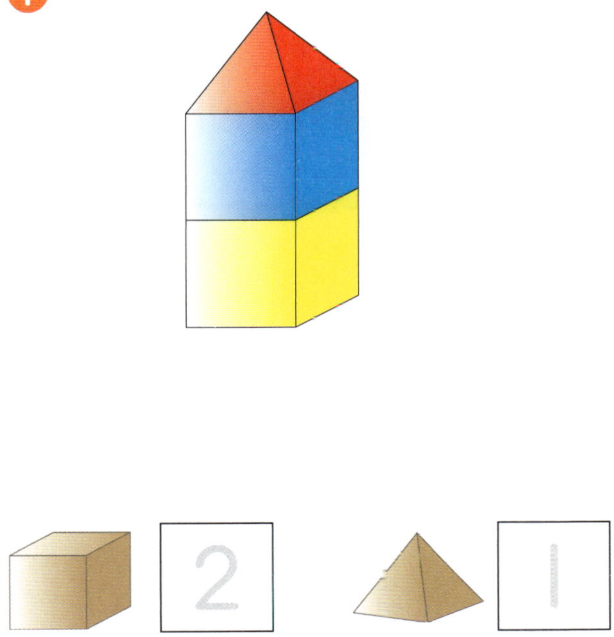

	2		1

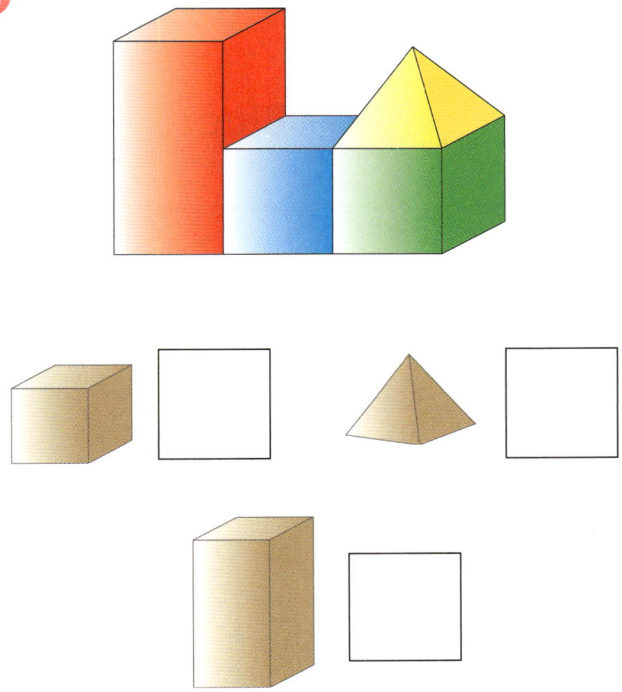

②

③

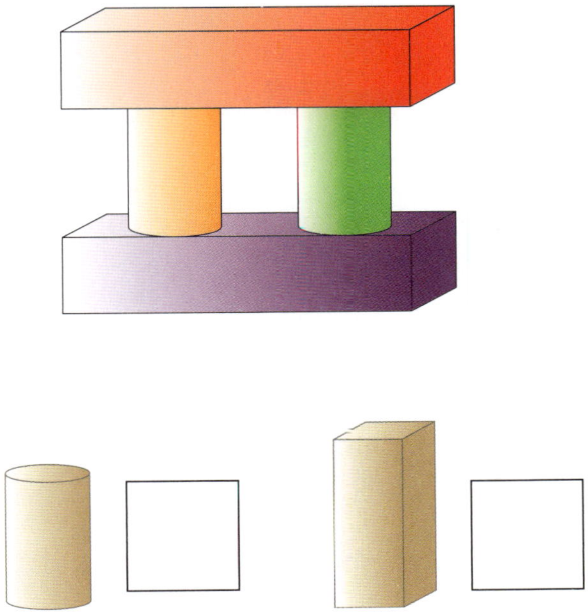

④

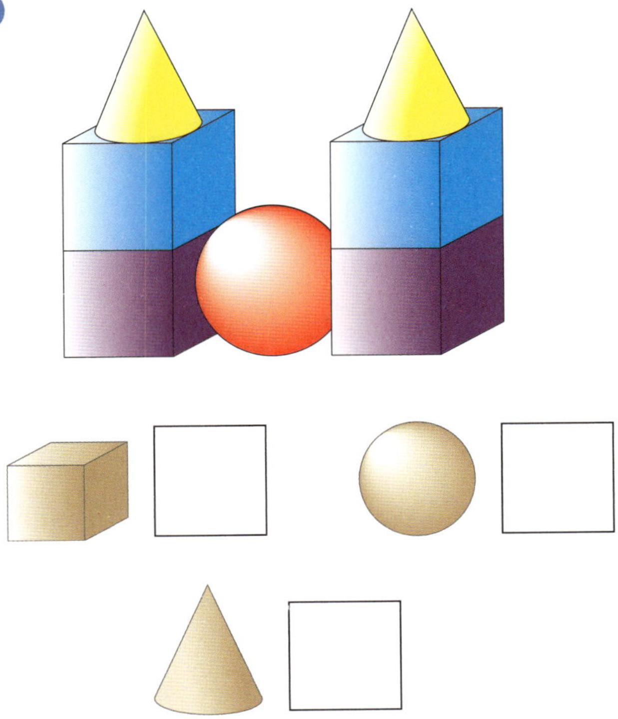

2D Shapes 1

■ Find the shapes shown in the sample below. Then color them the same color as the sample.

Sample

 = Blue   ⬛ = Red   ⬤ = Yellow

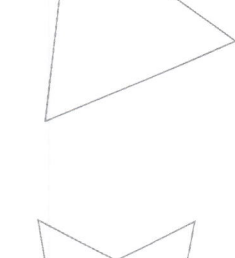

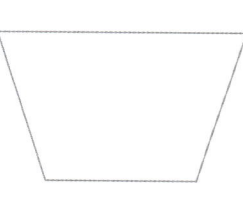

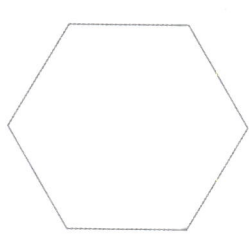

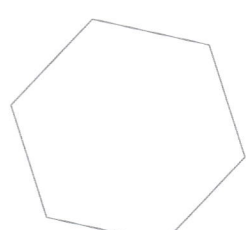
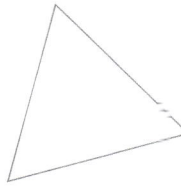

■ Draw a line from the arrow (↓) to the star (★) by connecting the ▬ , ◆ , and ⬭ .

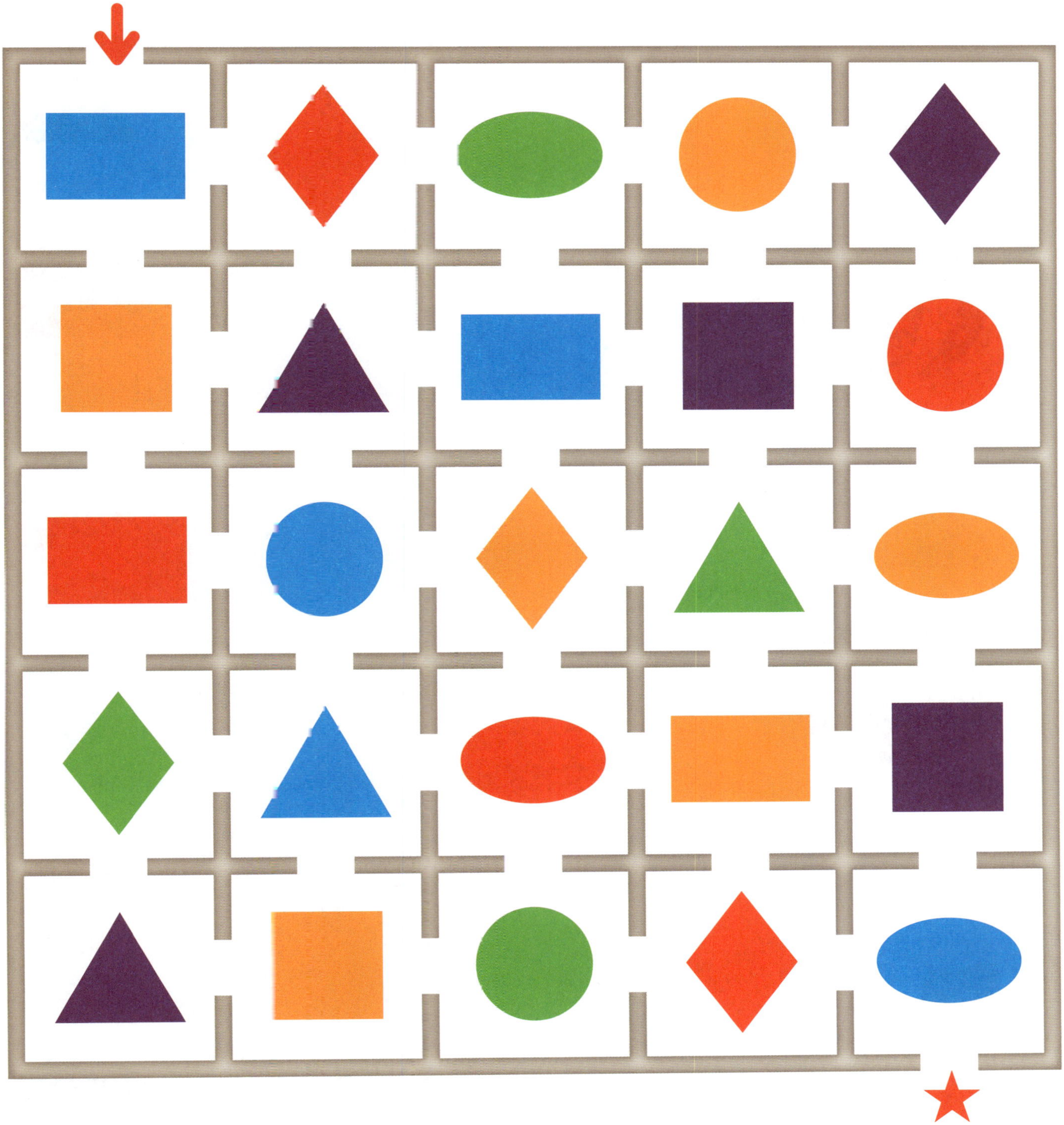

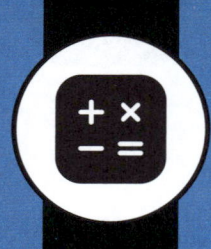
2D Shapes 2

■ Draw a line from the pictures to the shapes that are similar.

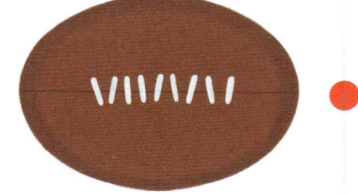

● Triangle

● Rectangle

● Square

● Diamond

● Circle

● Oval

Date

Great Job Sticker

■ How many 2D shapes are there? Write numbers in the box.

1
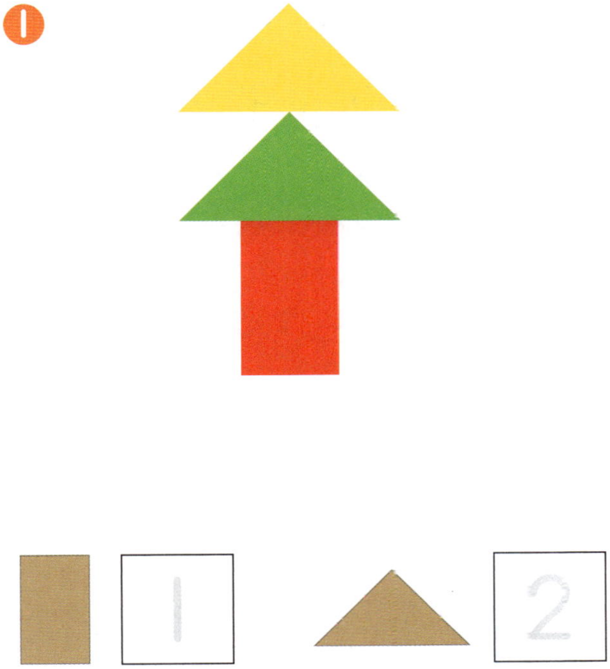

3
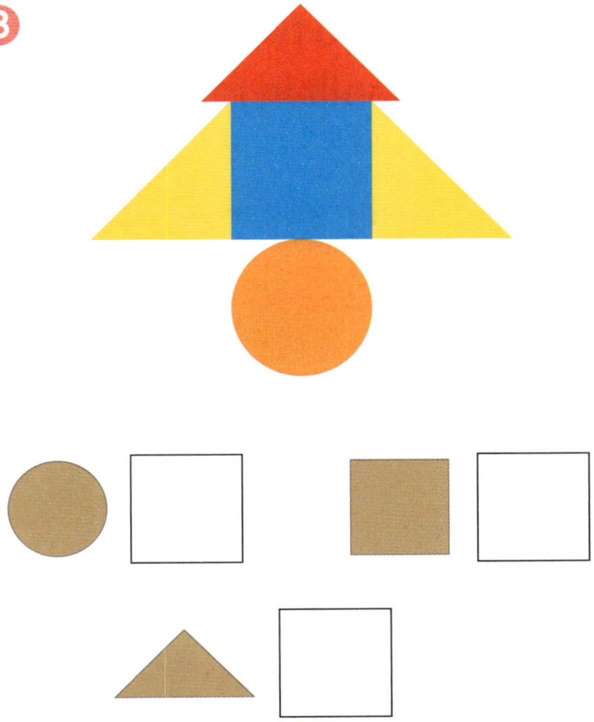

2
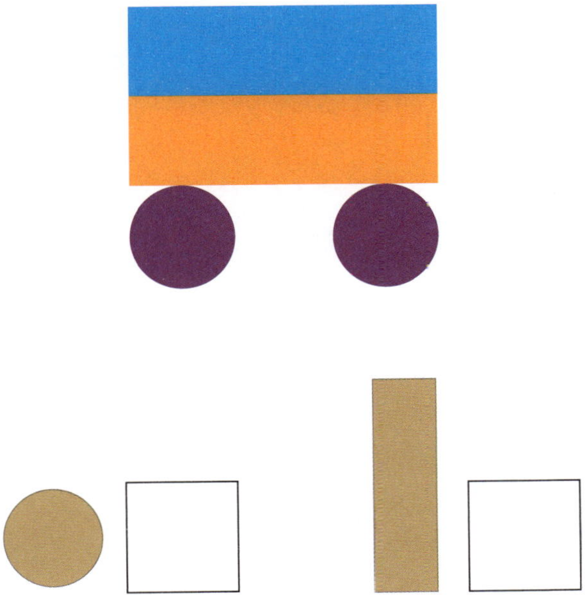

4
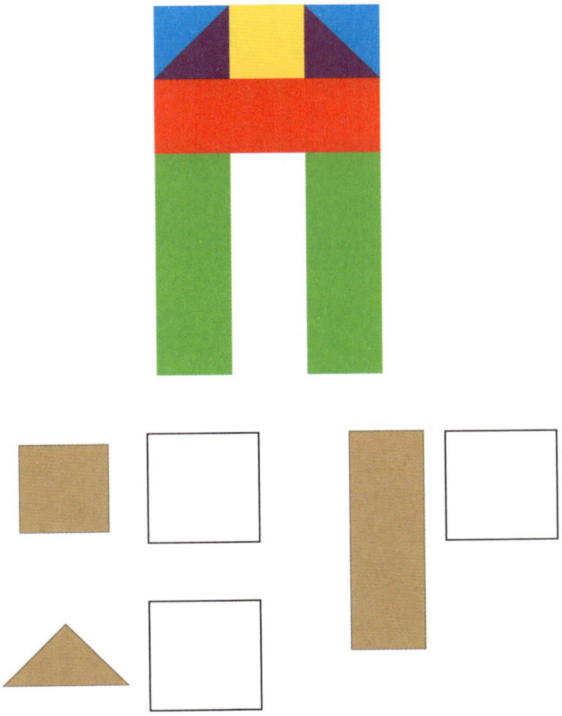

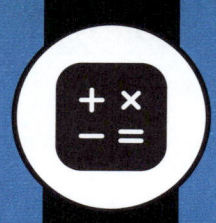

Partitioning Shapes

KEY POINTS

Shapes can be split, or partitioned, into equal pieces. If you split a shape into two pieces, then the pieces are called halves. If the shape is split in four, the pieces are called fourths or quarters.

■ Partition each shape into halves.

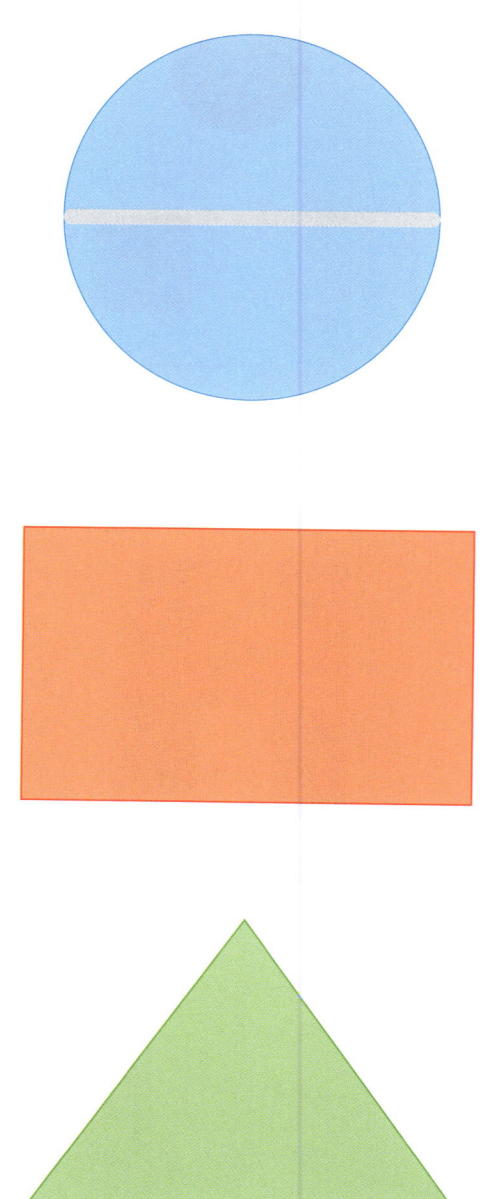

■ Circle the shapes that are partitioned into fourths.

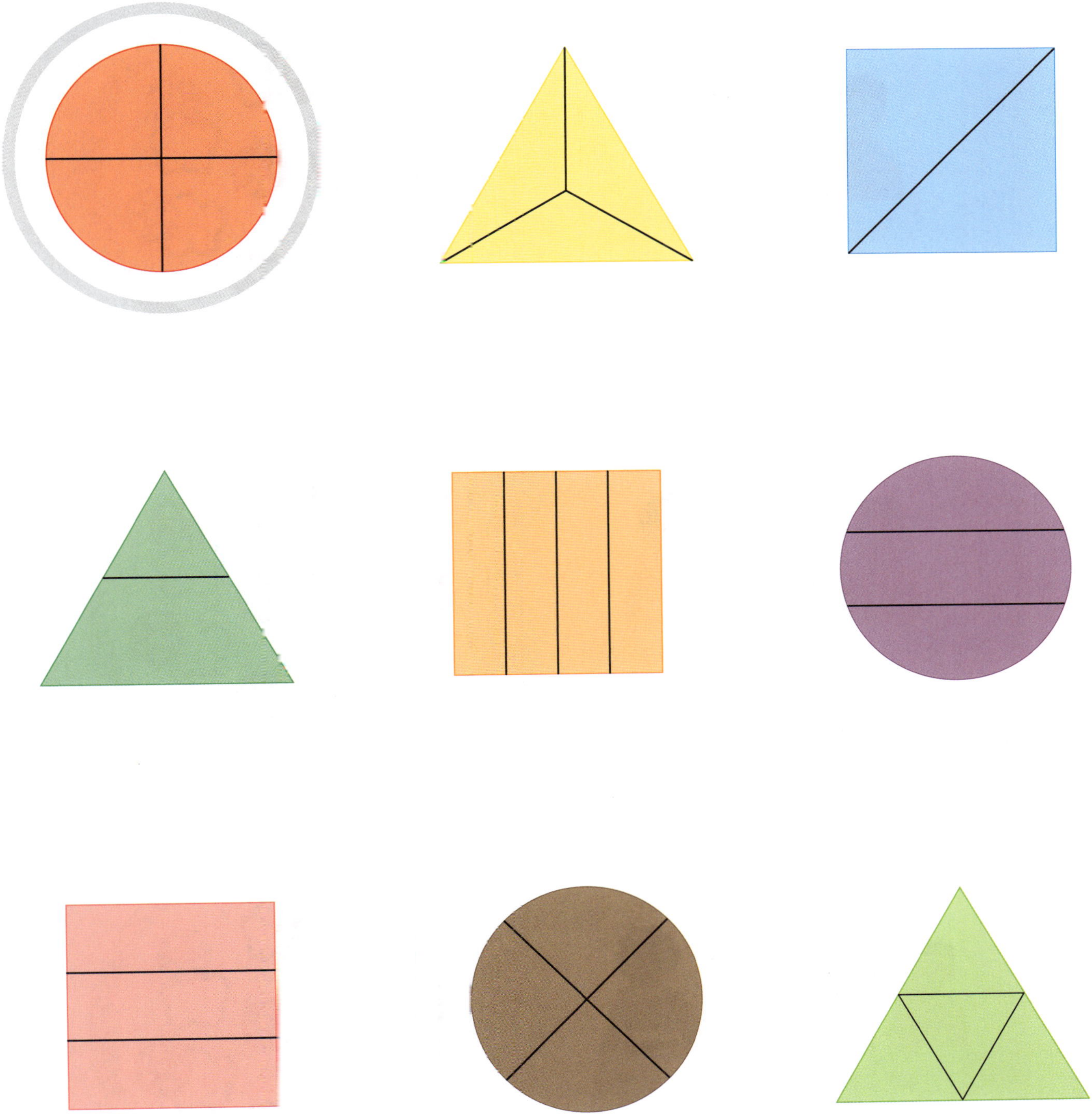

Brain Break
Cutting Foods

■ Listen to what the children say, and partition the pizza equally.

1

LET'S DIVIDE IT INTO TWO!

2

LET'S DIVIDE IT INTO THREE!

3

LET'S DIVIDE IT INTO FOUR!

Maze Break!

■ Trace the path from start to finish!

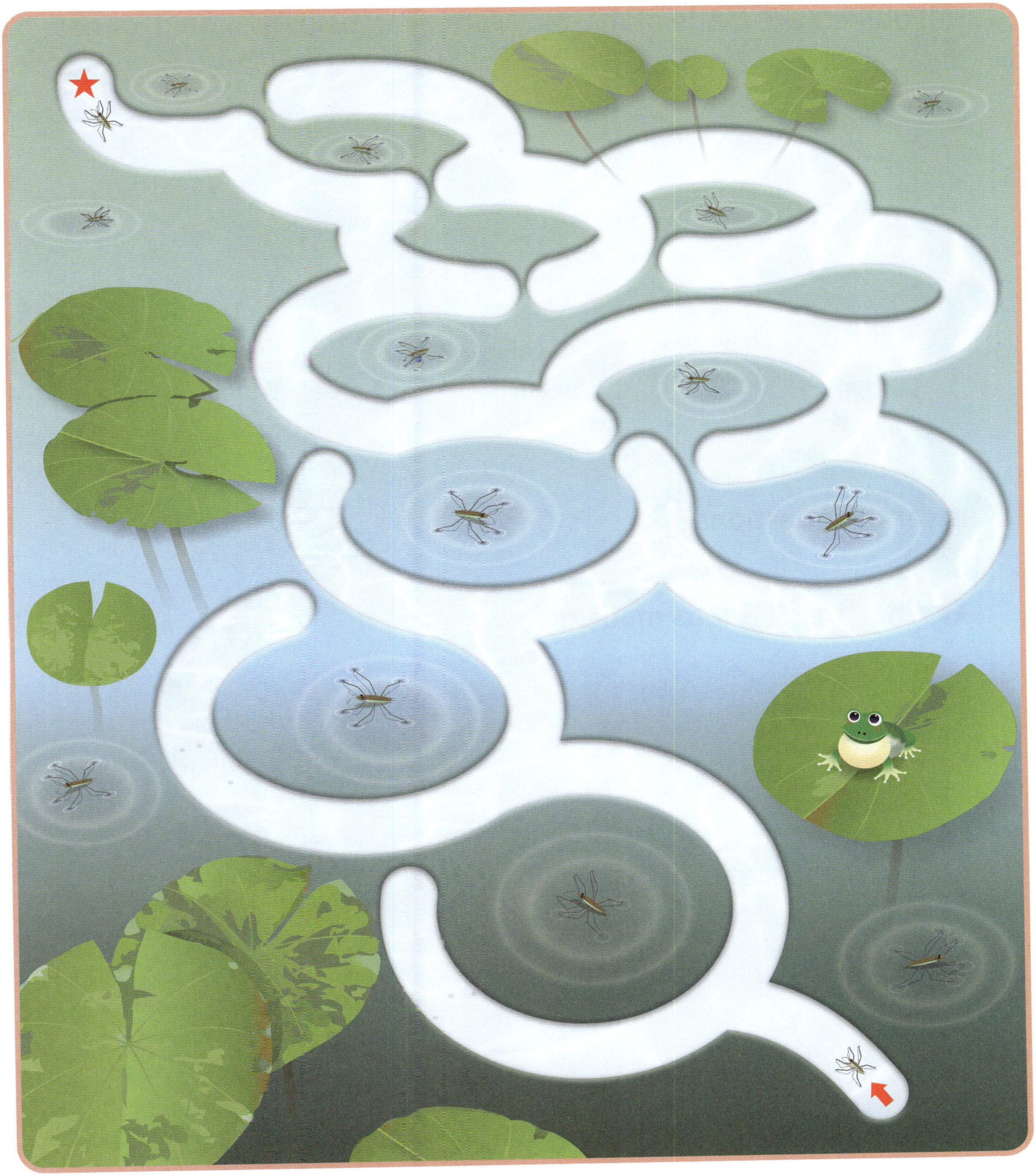

States of Matter 1

KEY POINTS

All objects are made of matter. Matter can be solid, liquid, or gas.

Ice is a solid.

Steam is a gas.

Water is a liquid.

■ Answer the questions.

❶ What are all things made of?

_____

❷ How many states of matter are there?

_____

■ Match the object to the correct state of matter.

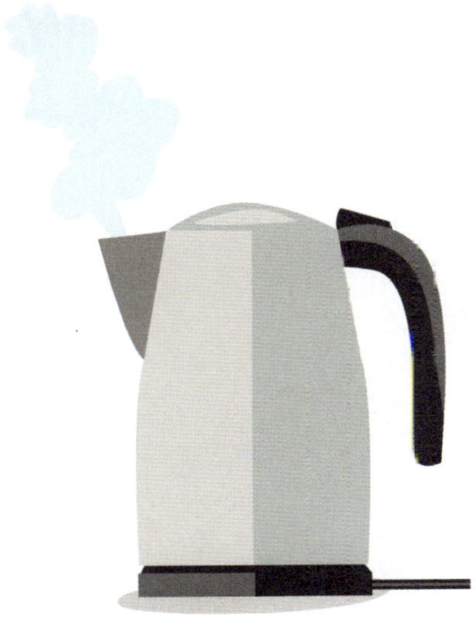

Solid

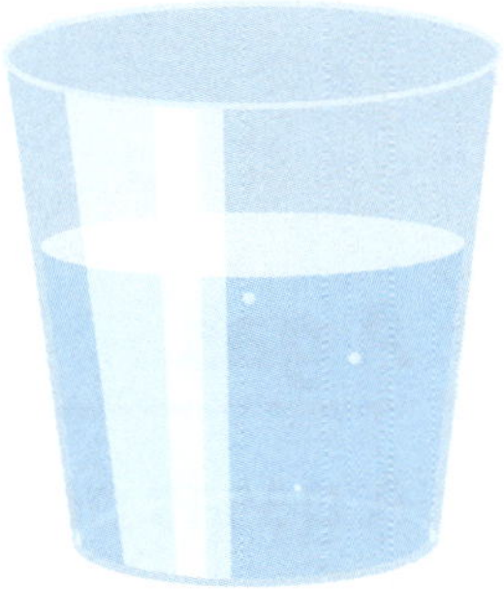

Gas

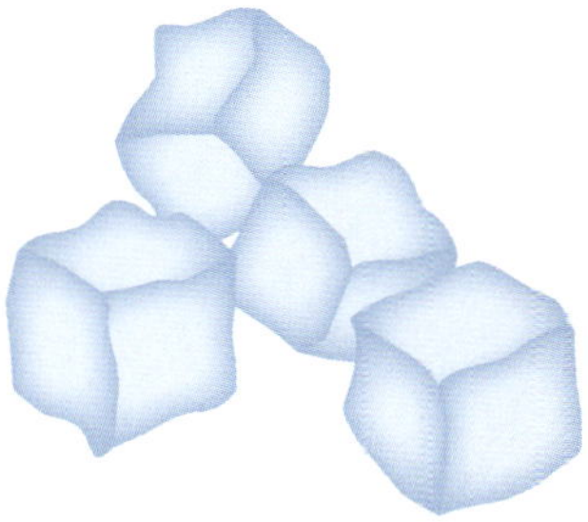

Liquid

States of Matter 2

Solids, liquids, and gases are different from each other in many ways.

A solid

A solid takes one shape and is firm.

A liquid

A liquid is not firm and takes the shape of the container it is put in.

A gas

A gas is not firm and fills all the space around it. Gases cannot be seen.

Date

Great Job Sticker

What is each object filled with?
Fill in the blank with solid, liquid or gas.

1
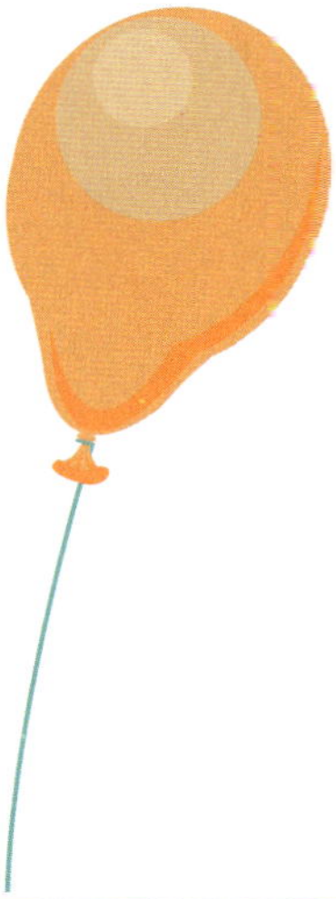

gas

3
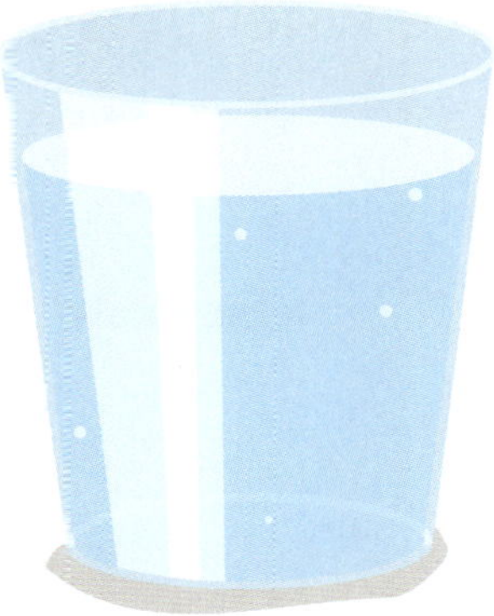

5
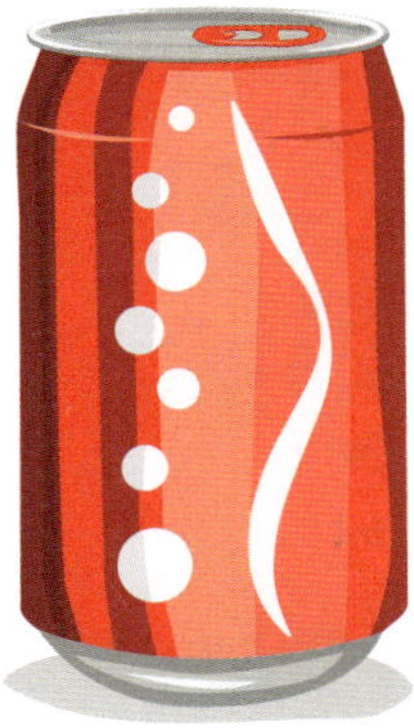

2
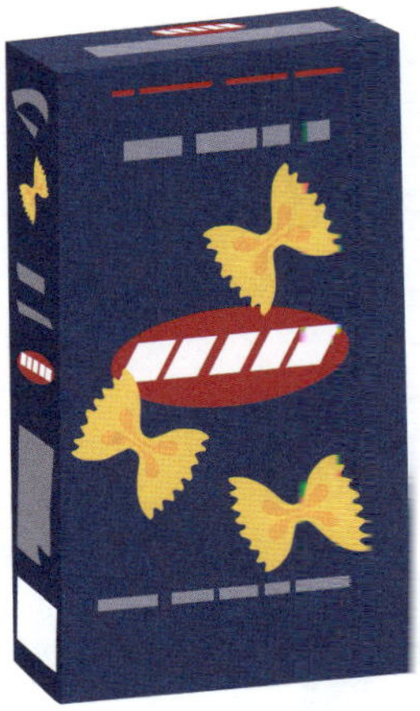

4
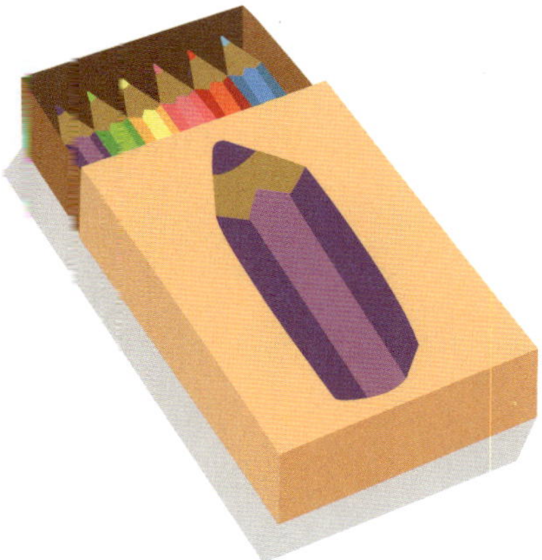

6
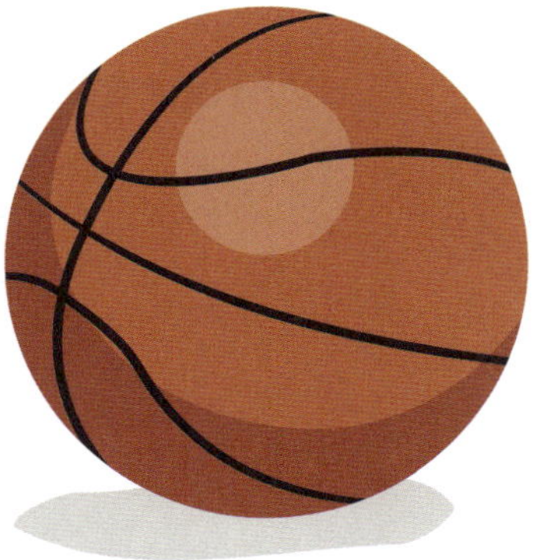

Changes in Matter

Matter can changes states when it is heated or cooled.

Water changes to ice when it is cooled.

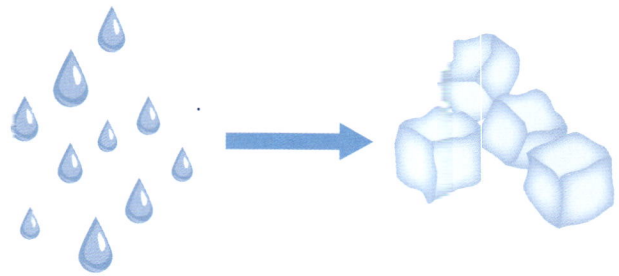

Ice changes to water when it is heated.

Water changes to water vapor when it is heated.

■ Write a check mark (✓) for the correct answer, whether the matter is heated or cooled.

❶

heated

cooled

❷

heated

cooled

❸

heated

cooled

Describing Matter

KEY POINTS

All matter can be described by its physical traits. A physical trait is something that can be seen, felt, or tasted. There are many words that can be used to describe the physical traits of objects.

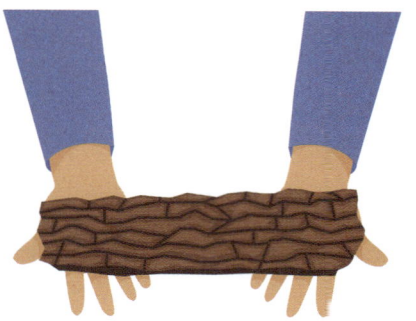

Texture

can be soft, rough, bumpy, or smooth.

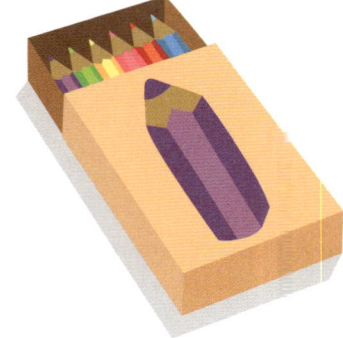

Color

can be red, green, yellow, blue, pink, etc.

Smell

can be good, bad, or strong.

Taste

can be sweet, sour, bitter, etc.

Size

can be big, small, or in between.

Date

Great Job Sticker

Describe the objects below using their traits.

1
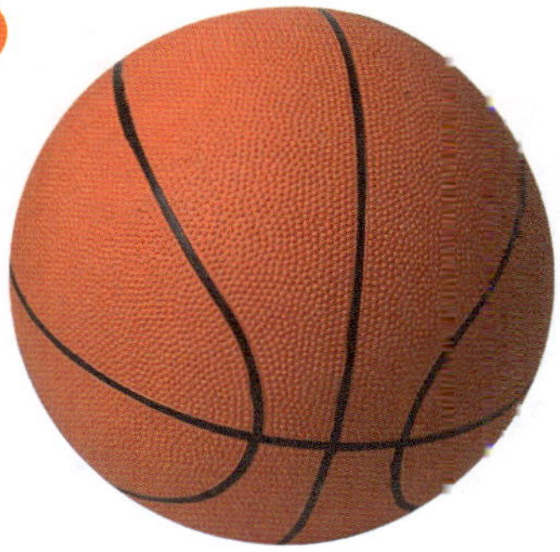

2
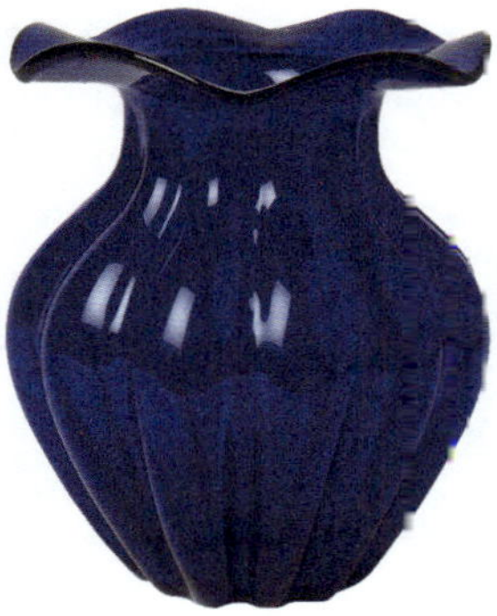

3
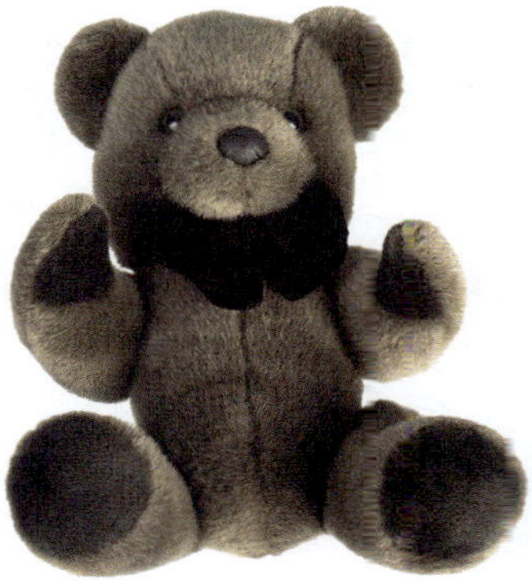

4
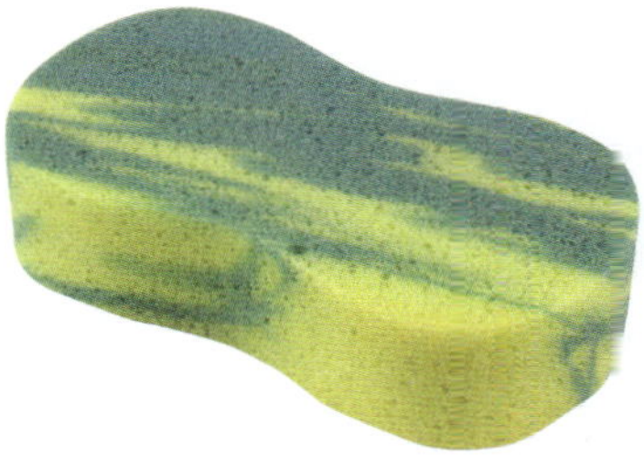

Brain Break
Science Journal 4

Choose three objects from around your home.
Draw and describe them below.

■ Find small objects with different textures to create a rubbing on the page below. Place the object under the paper in line with the box below and use a crayon to "rub" a copy of the object in to the box.

Culture

KEY POINTS

People in a community can have many different cultures. Culture comes from a community's shared celebrations, foods, languages, art, and clothes. The United States is a society made up of people from many different cultures!

■ Answer the questions.

1 What is culture?

_____

2 What are some things a community might share as part of its culture?

_____

3 Can you think of some other examples of culture in the United States?

_____

Cultures have their own celebrations, languages, and foods.
Look at the examples below.

■ Look at the examples, then fill in the blanks using your own culture.

Name:	Jon
Country:	Sweden
Culture:	Swedish
Language:	Swedish
Food:	Pickled herring

Name:	Kumi
Country:	Japan
Culture:	Japanese
Language:	Japanese
Food:	Udon noodles

Name:	
Country:	
Culture:	
Language:	
Food:	

Cultural Celebrations

KEY POINTS

Cultures have their own languages and rules. They celebrate their own holidays throughout the year....

The Culture: The United States
Celebration: The 4th of July

The United States celebrates its Independence Day on the 4th of July. People celebrate with fireworks, parades, and BBQs.

The Culture: Asian Countries
Celebration: Lunar New Year

Many Asian cultures celebrate the Lunar New Year. They mark the new year by sharing gifts in red envelopes for good fortune in the coming year.

The Culture: Mexico
Celebration: Dia de Los Muertos

In Mexico, people celebrate Dia de Los Muertos, or the Day of the Dead, to remember lost family members and celebrate them. People lay ofrendas with photos of family members and food to honor them.

Cultures celebrate different holidays with special activities and foods.

■ Circle the images that match each celebration.

1 American Culture
4th of July

2 Many Asian Cultures
Lunar New Year

3 Mexican Culture
Dia de Los Muertos

Culture and Languages

KEY POINTS

Language is a way people communicate. We use language when we speak and when we write. Some languages, like American Sign Language, communicate through moving your body. Language is an important part of culture because it is how we share ideas. Most people in the United States speak English, but many people speak other languages, too.

■ Answer the questions.

❶ What is language?

❷ Why is language an important part of culture?

■ Ask a family member or frienc to help you write the English phrases in another language.

❶ Hello, how are you?

❷ Happy Birthday!

❸ Goodnight!

❹ Let's play together!

My Culture

KEY POINTS

All people participate in some kind of culture. Some people have one culture and other people are part of many cultures. Think about your own culture.

■ Write or draw examples below using your own culture.

My Culture

My Celebrations

My Food

My Language

■ The people around us might not have the same culture as we do. Ask a friend about their culture and fill in the boxes below.

Culture

Celebrations

Food

Language

Brain Break
Crossword Puzzle

■ Use the clues to complete the crossword puzzle.

community
culture
holiday
language
food
tradition
people

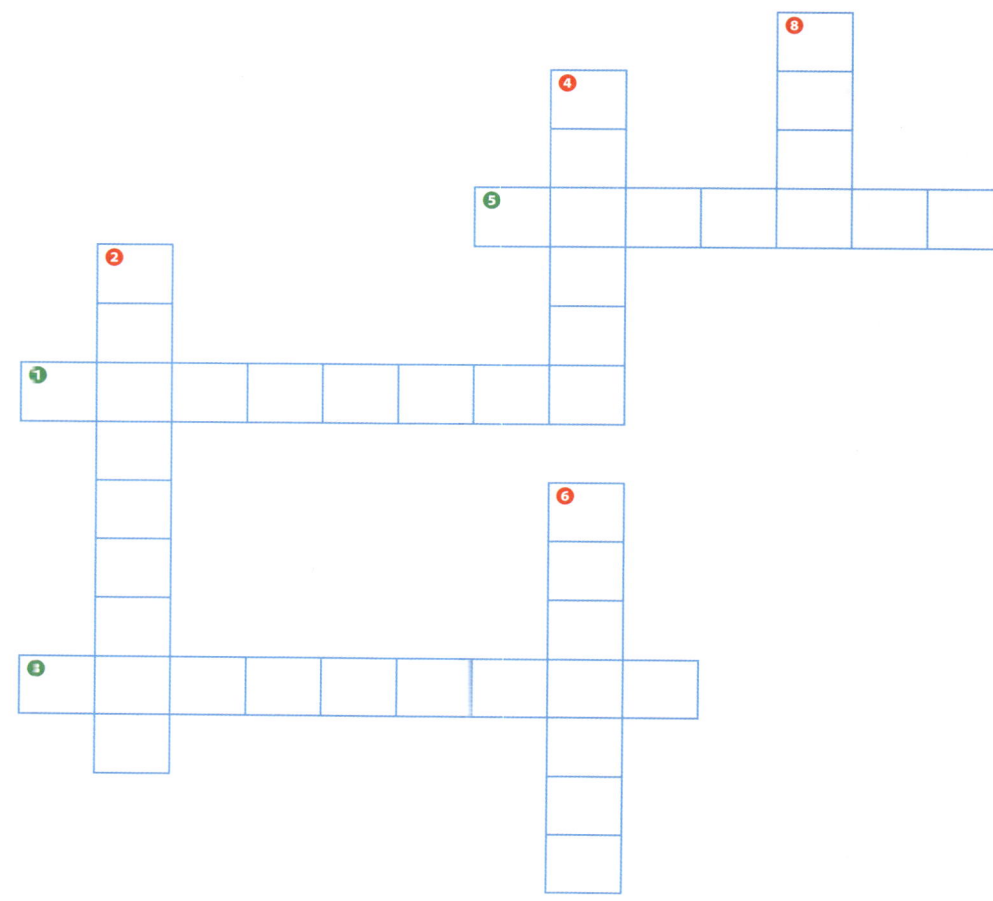

Across
1 How a culture communicates, usually by speaking or writing.
3 A group of people who live and work in an area.
5 A day that celebrates something.

Down
2 Sharing a cultures ideas from parent to child.
4 Members of a culture.
6 The shared way of life of a society or group of people.
8 What we eat. Also an important part of our cultures.

Mindfulness Break!

■ Color the picture. Focus only on coloring and your breathing.

Jigsaw Puzzles

■ Circle the piece that fits.

1

2

3

4

Copying Shapes

■ Draw the same shape.

1

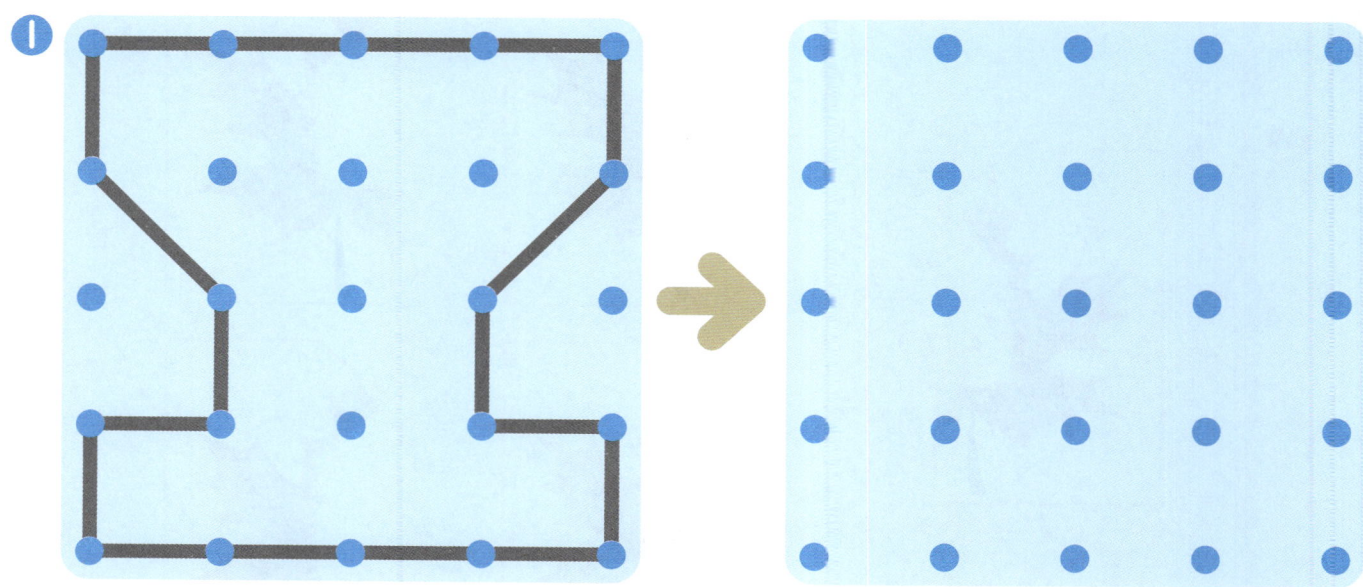

2

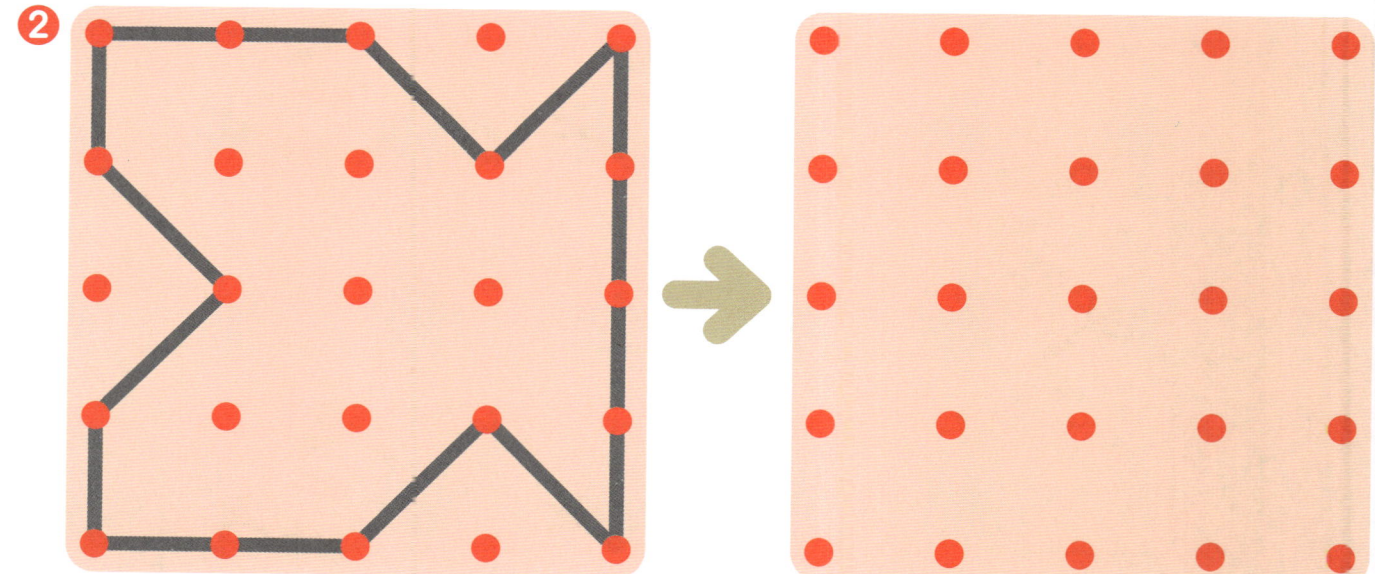

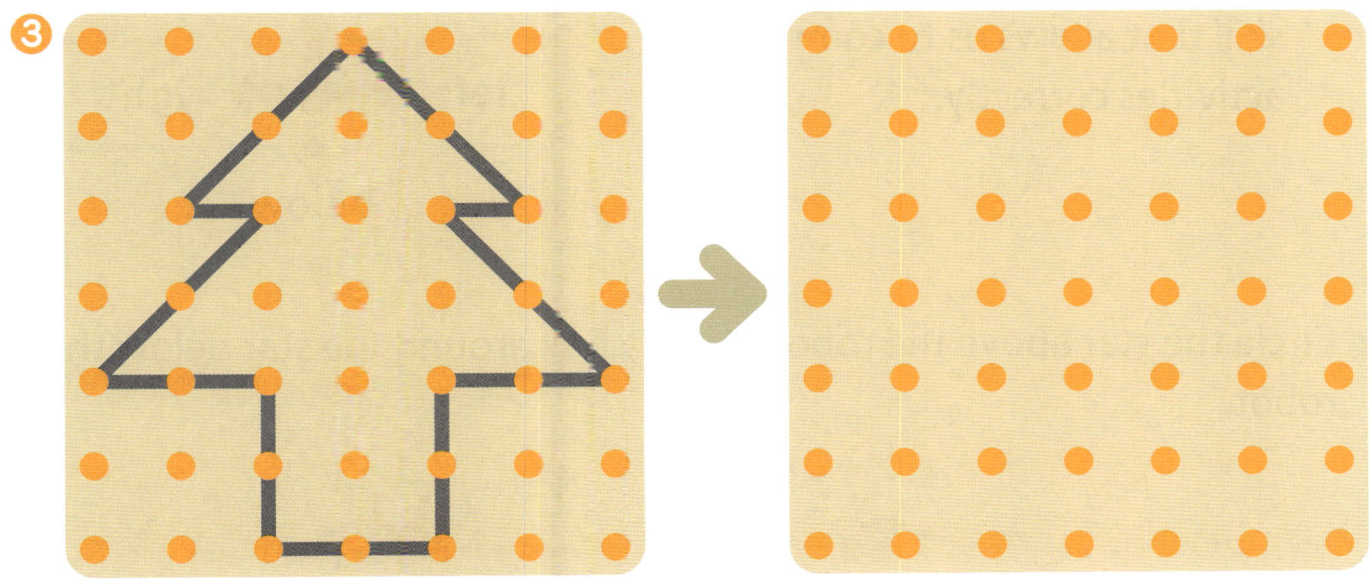

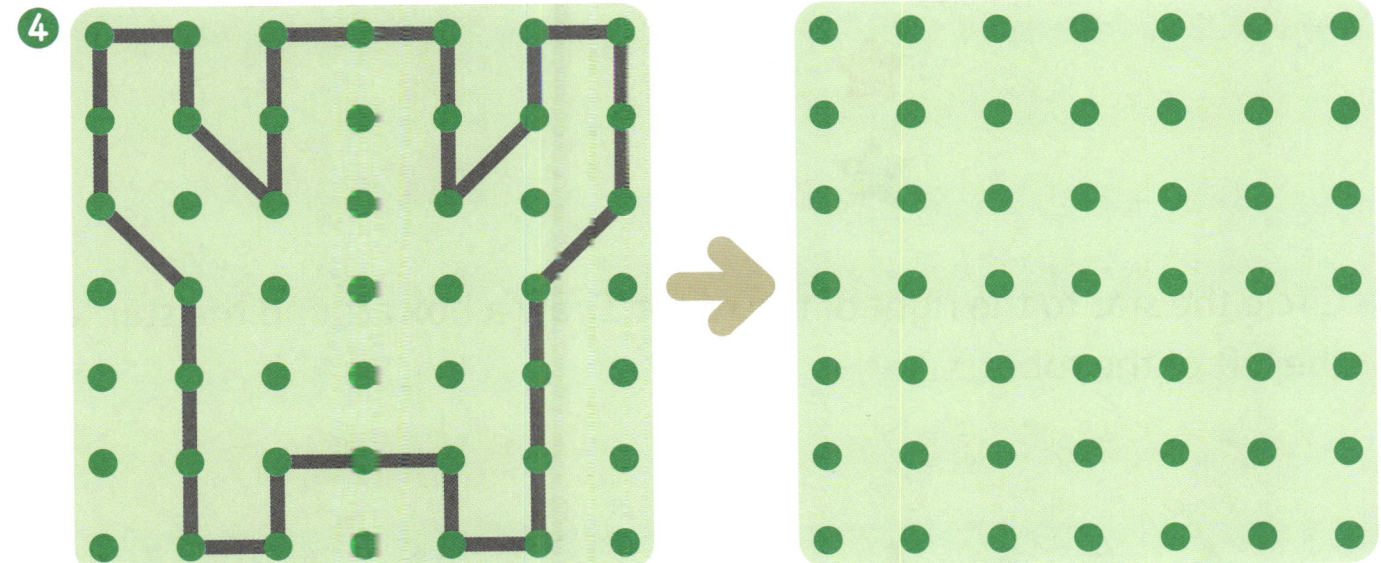

Direction Words

Following directions is an important skill that allows us to complete activities correctly.

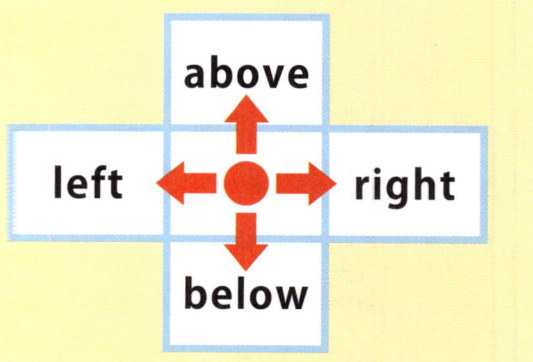

■ Circle the star above the robot. Draw a box around the star below the robot.

■ Circle the star to the right of the robot. Draw a box around the star to the left of the robot.

■ **Write a check mark (✓) on the correct answer.**

① **What is above the ♥ ?**

② **What is below the ♣ ?**

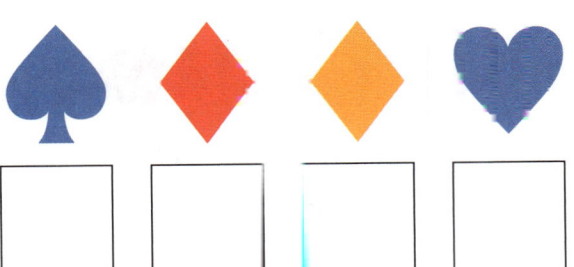

③ **What is to the right of the ◆ ?**

④ **What is to the left of the ♠ ?**

Matching

KEY POINTS

Matching is an important skill that helps us build relationships between different objects.

■ Draw a line to the matching letter.

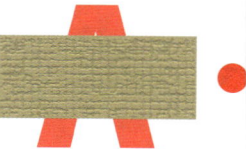

■ Draw a line to the matching number.

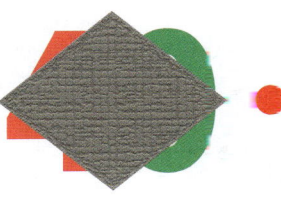 •

 •

 •

 •

• **83**

• **78**

• **57**

• **29**

• **15**

• **82**

• **40**

• **36**

Physical Education Break!

It's important to move your body and exercise!
Try this fun activity below for a study break!

■ Complete the exercise for each letter to spell your name.

Spell Your Name Exercise Game!

A-B-C	D-E-F	G-H-I
5 Jumping Jacks	15 Arm Circles	5 Lunges to the left

J-K-L	M-N-O	P-Q-R
10 High Knees	Run in place for 30 seconds	5 Lunges to the right

S-T-U	V-W-X	Y-Z
10 Toe Touches	10 Jumping Jacks	5 Sit ups

Unit **5** Table of Contents

Use this page to keep track of your progress throughout the book. Place a check mark in the box when you have completed a section.

Writing

- ☐ Opinion Writing 1 ——— 252
- ☐ Opinion Writing 2 ——— 254
- ☐ Informational Writing ——— 256
- ☐ Narrative Writing ——— 258
- Brain Break ——— 250
- Mindfulness Break! ——— 251

Reading

- ☐ Building Vocabulary ——— 252
- ☐ Reading Comprehension 1 ——— 264
- ☐ Reading Comprehension 2 ——— 266
- ☐ Narrative Writing ——— 268
- Brain Break ——— 270
- Mindfulness Break! ——— 271

Math

- ☐ Data and Graphing 1 ——— 272
- ☐ Data and Graphing 2 ——— 274
- ☐ Data and Graphing 3 ——— 276
- ☐ Word Problems 1 ——— 278
- ☐ Word Problems 2 ——— 280
- Brain Break ——— 282
- Maze Break! ——— 283

Science

- ☐ Energy and Light ——— 284
- ☐ Light and Shadow ——— 286
- ☐ Sound Energy ——— 288
- ☐ Natural or Man-made ——— 290
- Brain Break ——— 292
- Art Break! ——— 293

Social Studies

- ☐ What is an Economy? ——— 294
- ☐ Goods and Services ——— 296
- ☐ Needs and Wants ——— 298
- ☐ Jobs ——— 300
- Brain Break ——— 302
- Mindfulness Break! ——— 303

Thinking Skills

- ☐ Patterns with Rotating Blocks ——— 304
- ☐ Color and Shape Patterns ——— 306
- ☐ Identifying Objects ——— 308
- ☐ Problem Solving ——— 310
- Physical Education Break! ——— 312

Opinion Writing 1

Opinion pieces give an opinion about something.

Fact
We get homework every night.

Opinion
We shouldn't have homework.

■ Write a F next to facts. Write an O next to opinions.

① **O** Horses are the best animal.

② Ice cream is cold.

③ Her scarf is pretty.

④ Snakes don't have legs.

Opinions are supported by reasons.

We shouldn't have to do homework
because we need time to play.

■ Match the opinion and the reason.

Pizza is delicious		because you can swim.
Cats are the best pet		because it has cheese.
It's fun to go to the beach		because they make me laugh.
I like funny movies		because they clean themselves.

Opinion Writing 2

■ Write about your favorite breakfast food.

My favorite thing to eat for breakfast is

. I like it because

.

It tastes   **. Some**

people like to eat   **.**

But it is not as good because

.

■ **What is your favorite season? Why? Write an opinion piece below.**

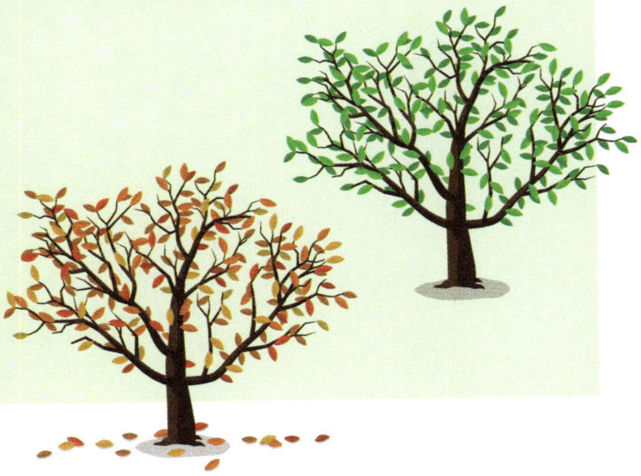

Informational Writing

Informational texts tell about a topic. They give facts about the topic.

■ Write about the weather outside.

Right now, the weather is _____ .

The sky is _____ **. I can see**

_____ **. The temperature is**

_____ **. It's a good day to**

_____ **.**

■ **Choose an animal. Write an informational text about the animal.**

Narrative Writing

KEY POINTS

Narratives tell a story. A story is made up of events.

■ Put the events in order. Write a number next to each box.

■ Tell a story using the picture on the last page. Make sure you write the events in order.

Brain Break!
Journal Entry

■ Write a journal entry.

Write about your favorite family trip!

■ Draw a place that you feel peaceful and calm.

> Think of a place that makes you feel happy and calm. You can imagine you are there whenever you feel sad or stressed.

Building Vocabulary

KEY POINTS

Some words have affixes. These are word parts that are in many words. Learning affixes can help you understand new words.

un-	(not) unhappy	**-ing**	(doing now) running
dis-	(not) dislike	**-ed**	(did already) cooked
re-	(again) redo	**-s**	(more than one) pencils

■ Circle the affixes in each word.

unclear   swimming

disagree   reread

trees   danced

■ Use what you know about affixes to write the meaning of each word.

untie

writing

painted

colors

rewrite

dishonest

Reading Comprehension 1

KEY POINTS

Words can be sorted into categories. This helps us make connections and build vocabulary.

■ Sort the words below.

bird	orange	cow	pencil	pink
book	moose	backpack	green	

Colors	Animals	School supplies

■ Underline words related to water. Circle words related to animals. Highlight words related to food.

Greta sat by the lake. She threw

out a piece of bread. She heard the

swans coming. They made a big splash.

They finished the bread and looked for

some other treats. The ducks came

over too. But they were too late.

Reading Comprehension 2

KEY POINTS

Sometimes, words fit into a catgeory together, but they still have different meanings.

Look

Glare

Peek

Stare

■ Draw your own pictures to show the difference between large, giant, and big.

Large	Giant	Big

■ Sort the words into their categories and draw a picture.

| jump | eat | baby | skip | munch |
| child | swallow | hop | toddler |

jump

eat

baby

Narrative Writing

■ Read the text. Write what the underlined words mean below.

There are many ways to get around. **Buses** drive down the street. Trains run on tracks. **Subways** run on tracks below ground. And if you have a car, **driving** isn't so bad!

Buses

Subways

Driving

■ Read the text. Write what the underlined words mean below.

Celia felt **unlucky**. It was her birthday. But everyone forgot. Then she walked into her house. "Surprise!" everyone yelled. It was a party! They had a **celebration**. They did remember after all! It was so fun that Celia wished they could **redo** it.

unlucky

celebration

redo

Brain Break
Vocabulary Word Search

■ Circle the words in the Word Search.

colors	unlucky	disrespect	rewrite
	dishonest	painted	untie

D	I	S	R	E	S	P	E	C	T
I	V	N	S	E	Q	T	J	L	P
S	C	D	X	U	N	T	I	E	X
H	D	E	Z	N	Z	U	F	U	R
O	W	T	F	L	D	Y	R	P	E
N	I	N	T	U	A	O	E	O	W
E	J	I	Y	C	G	L	D	L	R
S	U	A	U	K	A	K	S	M	I
T	H	P	R	Y	N	M	C	H	T
X	G	B	T	U	A	N	R	S	E
M	M	L	C	O	L	O	R	S	Q

Mindfulness Break!

■ Circle the mindful actions.

Leaving your jacket on the floor when you come home.

Cleaning up your room.

Giving your sibling a hug when they are sad.

Taking a toy from your sibling without asking.

Raising your hand before talking in class.

Leaving your toys all over the house.

Data and Graphing 1

■ Color a box for each item.

❶

❷

1	2	3	4	5	6	7

❸

1	2	3	4	5	6	7

❹

1	2	3	4	5	6	7

⑤

7	
6	
5	
4	
3	
2	
1	

⑦

7		
6		
5		
4		
3		
2		
1		

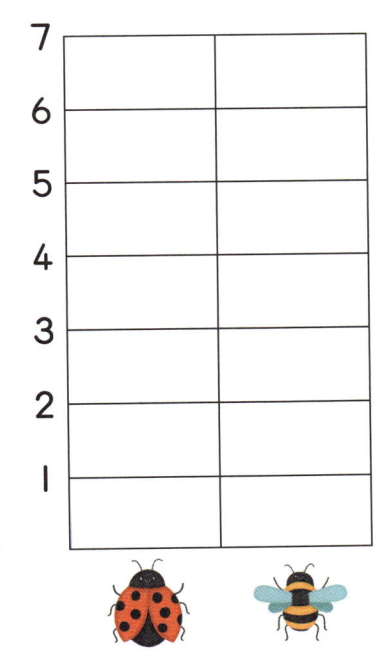

⑥

7	
6	
5	
4	
3	
2	
1	

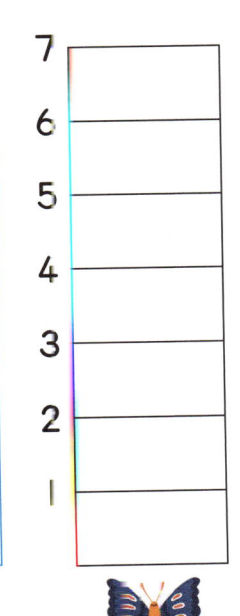

⑧

7		
6		
5		
4		
3		
2		
1		

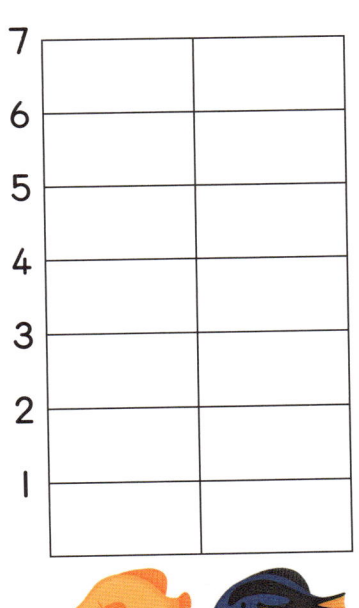

Data and Graphing 2

A bar graph is a kind of picture that shows information. Each bar represents a different group. The height of the bar shows how many are in that group.

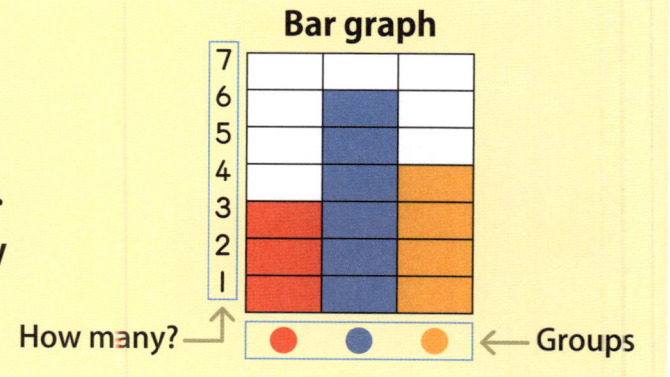

Bar graph

■ Make a bar graph. Color one box in the graph below for each candy.

■ Make a bar graph. Color one box in the graph below for each shape.

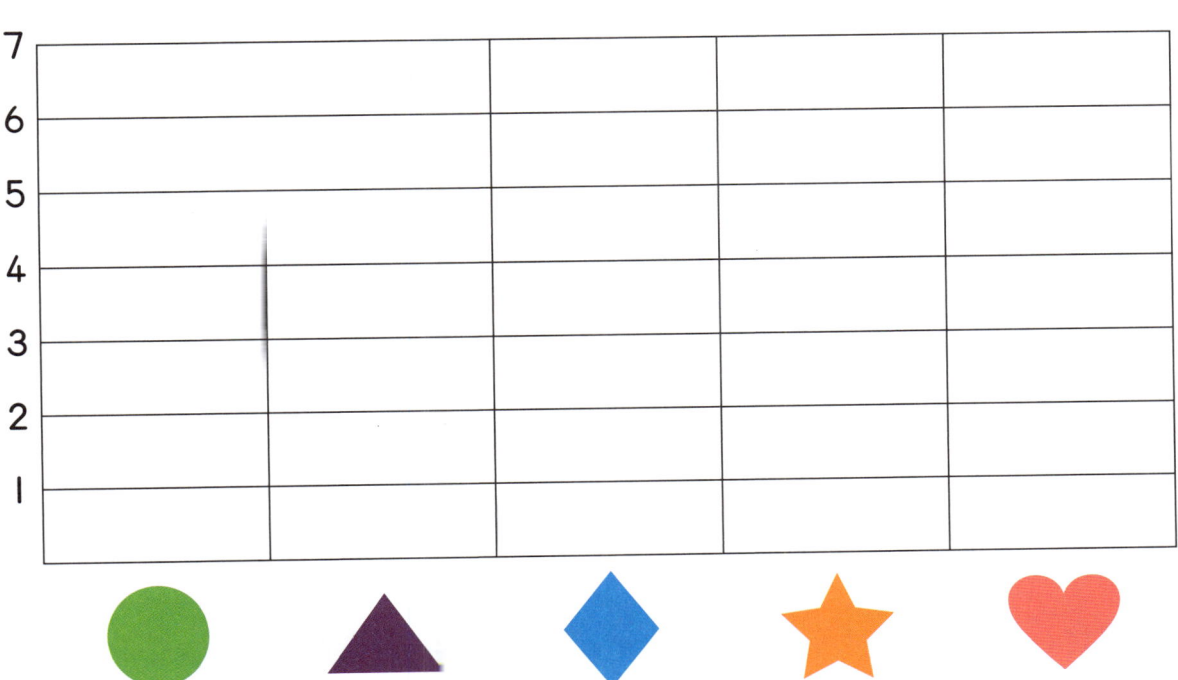

Data and Graphing 3

■ Use the bar graph to answer the questions.

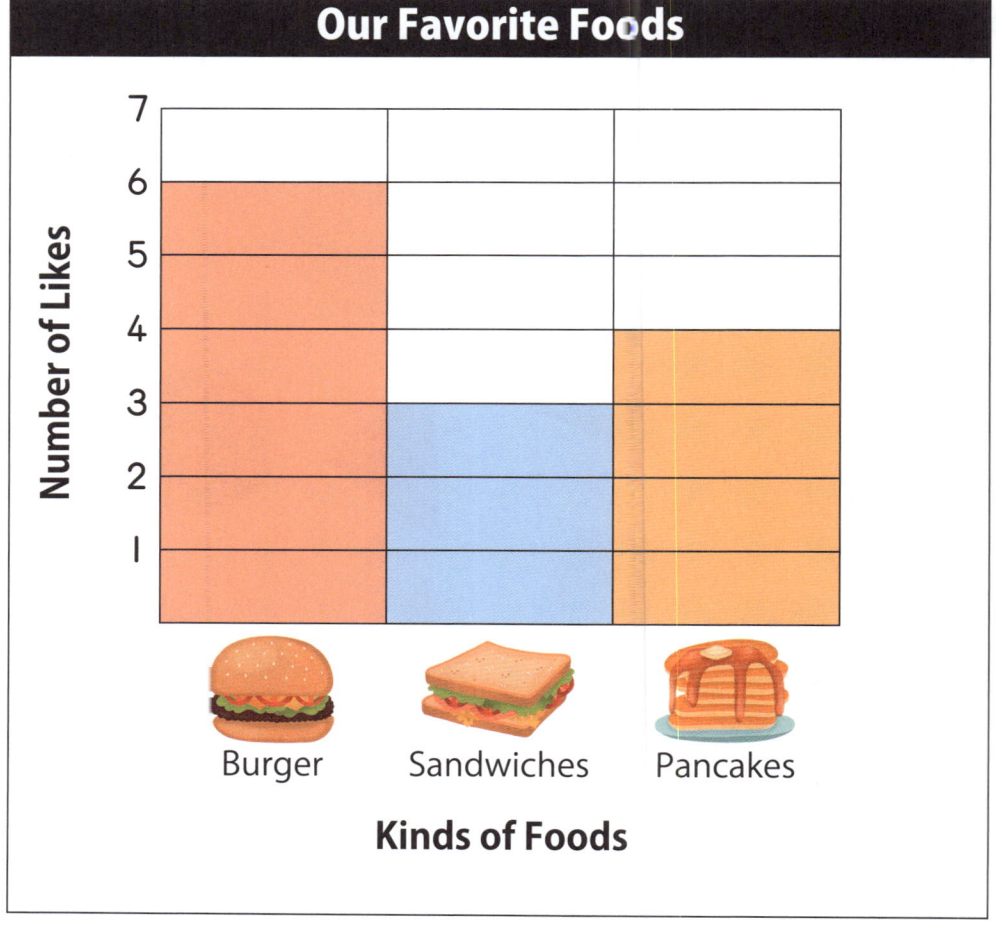

Our Favorite Foods

Number of Likes

7
6
5
4
3
2
1

Burger   Sandwiches   Pancakes

Kinds of Foods

❶ How many people like burgers best?

❷ How many people like sandwiches best?

❸ How many people like pancakes best?

❹ Which food did most people choose?

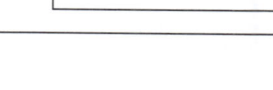

❺ Which food did the least number of people choose?

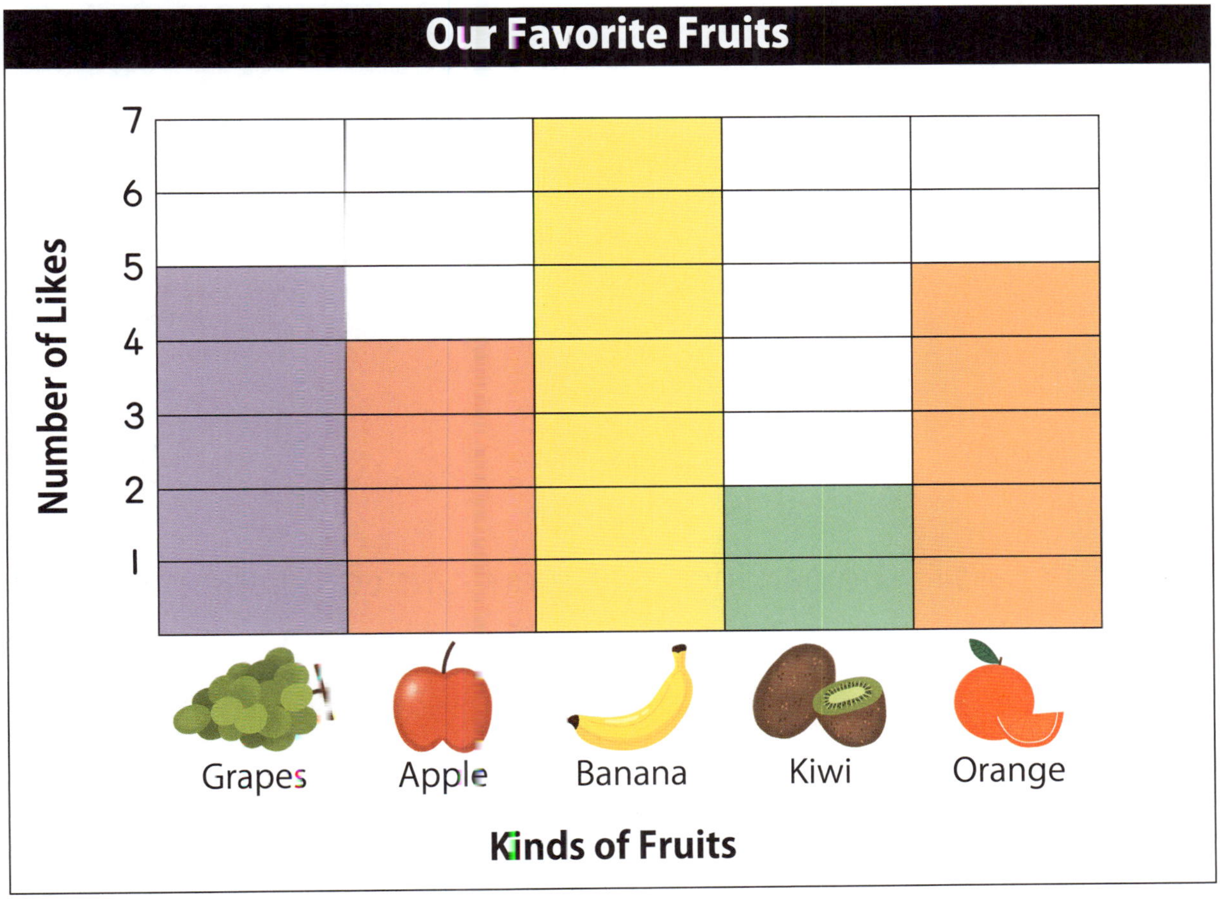

Our Favorite Fruits

Number of Likes

7
6
5
4
3
2
1

Grapes · Apple · Banana · Kiwi · Orange

Kinds of Fruits

❶ How many people like grapes best?

❷ How many people like apples best?

❸ How many people like oranges best?

❹ Which fruit did most people choose?

❺ Which fruit did the least number of people choose?

Word Problems 1

■ **Answer the following word problems.**

1 Sam has 4 balloons and Kate has 2 balloons. How many balloons are there in all?

$$4 + 2 = 6$$

Ans. _____ balloons

2 There are 9 cars in the parking lot. 3 more cars come and park. How many total cars are there?

Ans. _____ cars

3 Eli picked 12 oranges. 5 oranges are left in the tree. How many oranges are there altogether?

Ans. _____ oranges

④ Fred had 8 picture books. After he lent 4 picture books to his friend, how many did he have left?

$8 - 4 = 4$

Ans. _____ books

⑤ Rachel threw 15 balls. 7 balls went into the basket. How many balls did not go in the basket?

Ans. _____ balls

⑥ Paul's class has 10 boys and 8 girls. How many more boys than girls does his class have?

Ans. _____ boys

Word Problems 2

■ **Answer the following word problems.**

① Laura is second from the front. There are 4 children behind her in line. How many children are in the line altogether?

Ans. _____ children

② Max is sixth from the front of the line for the bus, and there are 9 people behind him. How many people are waiting for the bus?

Ans. _____ people

③ There are 7 hats on a row of hooks. Brian's hat is the third from the right. How many hats are there to the left of his hat?

Ans. _____ hats

❹3 birds were eating food. 4 birds landed, and then 3 more birds landed. How many birds are there now?

$$3 + 4 + 3 =$$

Ans. _____ birds

❺Christina had 9 candies. She gave her brother 2 candies and her sister 4 candies. How many candies does she have now?

Ans. _____ candies

❻Ken had 6 apples. His mother gave him 2 apples. Then he used 3 apples in a pie. How many apples does he have now?

Ans. _____ apples

Brain Break!
True or False Quiz

■ Read the silly questions below and check (✔) if the answer is true or false.

1 William ate 8 melons yesterday. Today he ate 11 more. He has eaten a total of 19 melons since yesterday.

True   False
☐   ☐

2 Olivia circled the globe 5 times on March 6 and 6 times on March 7 in her boat. In total, she circled the globe 13 times in these two days.

True   False
☐   ☐

3 Lucas played rock-paper-scissors with a dinosaur 10 times. He won 4 times. In other words, the dinosaur won 7 times.

True   False
☐   ☐

Unit 5

Maze Break!

■ Trace the path from start to finish!

Energy and Light

Energy is what allows you to do work. Energy is how things change and move. There are different types of energy. One type of energy is light energy. We can see light energy, and light helps us see other things, too. Light can come from nature, like the sun. It can also come from something man-made, like a light bulb.

■ **Answer the questions.**

❶ What is light energy?

_____

❷ What examples of light can you think of?

_____

■ Sort the things that make light.

| sun | lamp | lightbulb |
| starlight | flashlight | moonlight |

Natural	**Man-made**

Light and Shadow

KEY POINTS

When something blocks a light, it creates a shadow. Shadows are dark areas. Shadows can be large or small. Their shape matches the thing that blocks the light.

■ Answer the questions.

❶ What direction does light travel?

_____

❷ What are shadows shaped like?

_____

■ Circle the object that made the shadow.

1

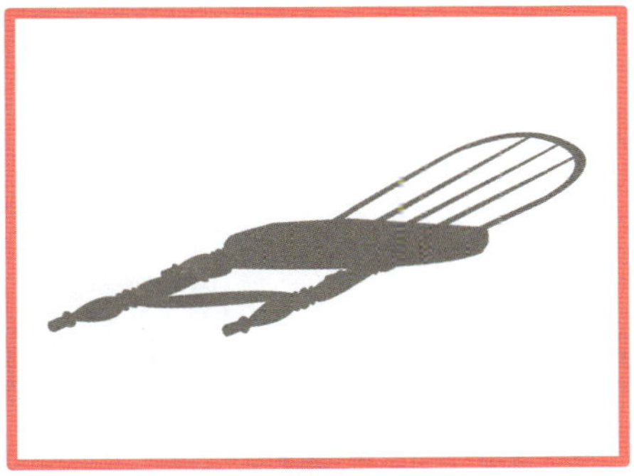

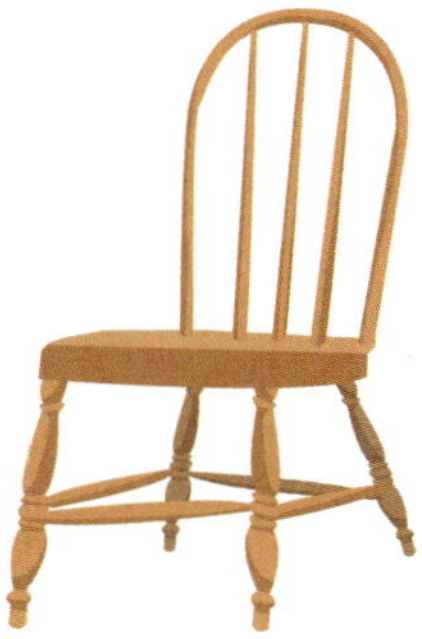

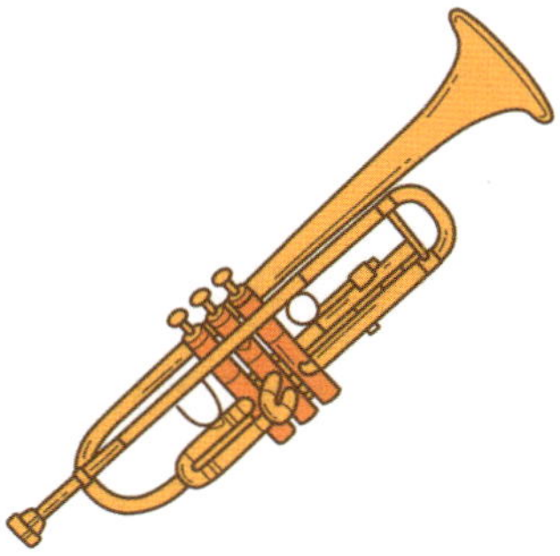

2

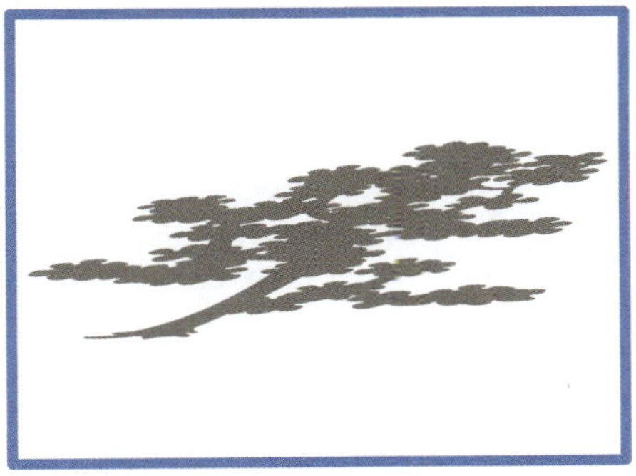

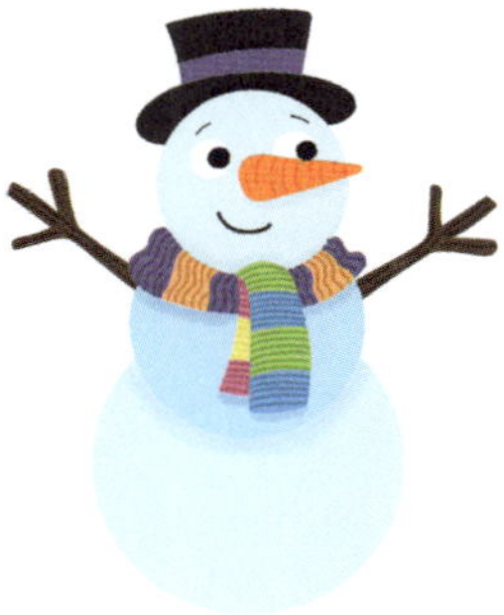

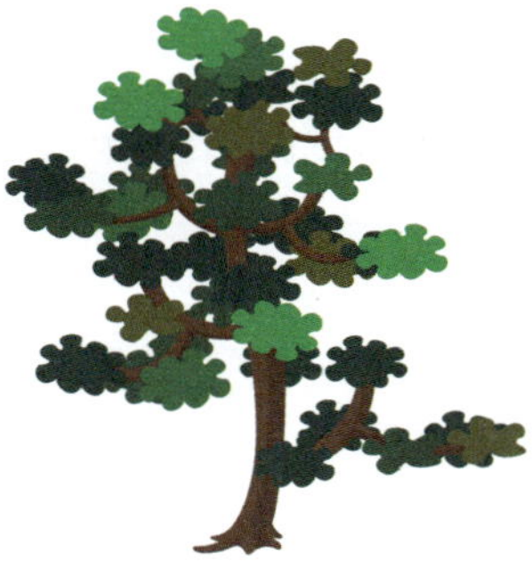

3

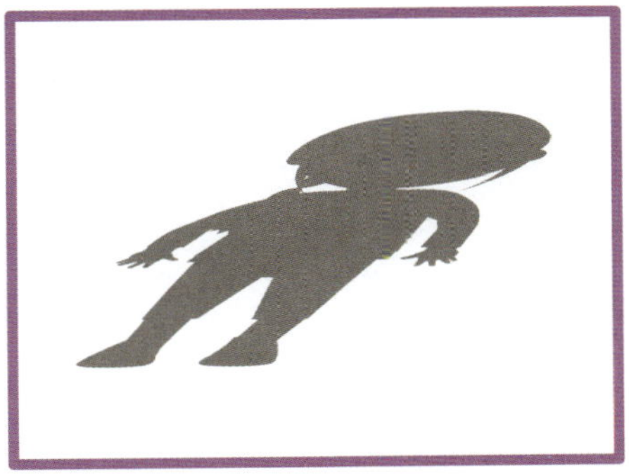

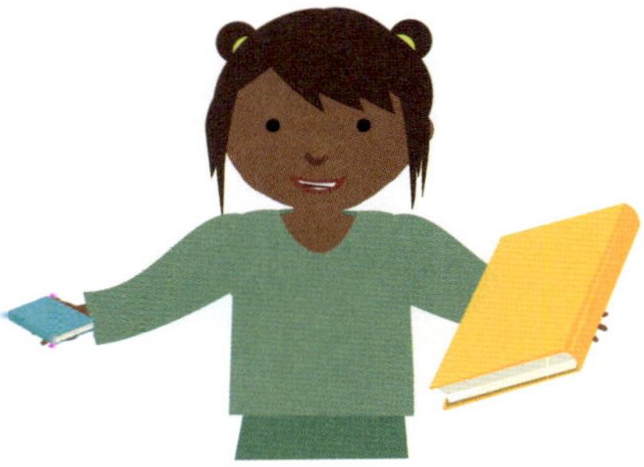

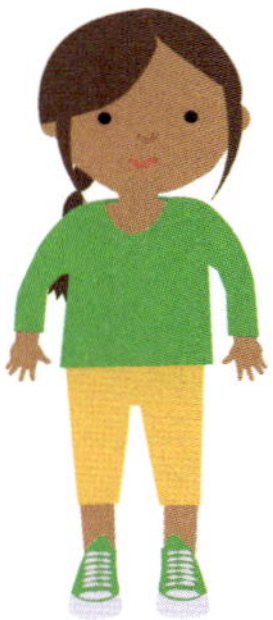

4

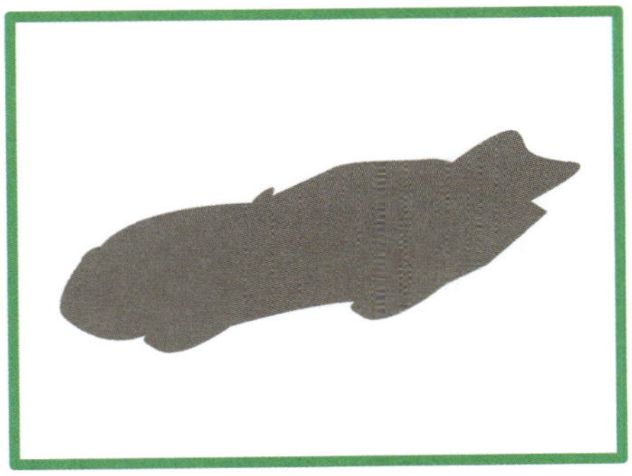

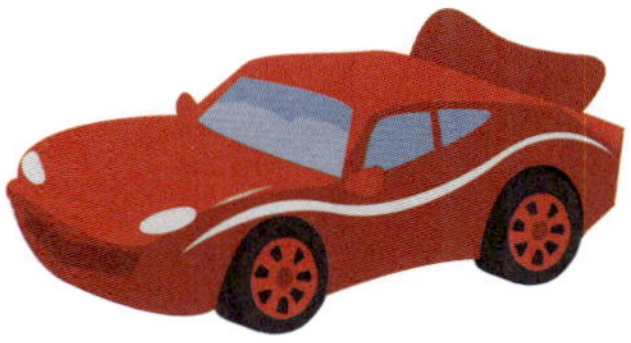

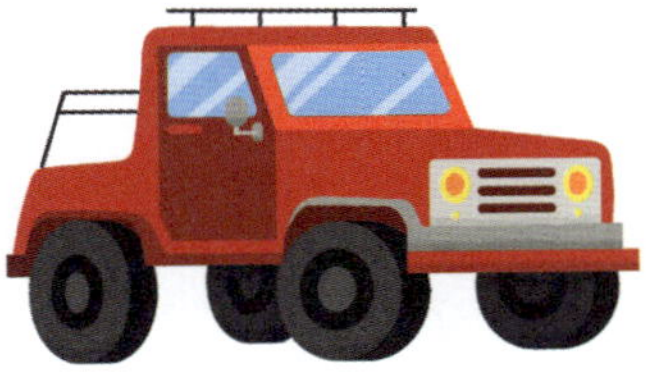

287

Sound Energy

KEY POINTS

Another type of energy is sound energy. Sound energy is something you can hear. It takes movement to hear sound. When a musician plays a guitar, they move the strings. The strings vibrate and make sound waves that move through the air. We hear it as music.

■ Answer the questions.

❶ What is sound energy?

_____

❷ How do we hear sound?

_____

■ Color the objects that make sound energy blue.
  Color the objects that make light energy yellow.

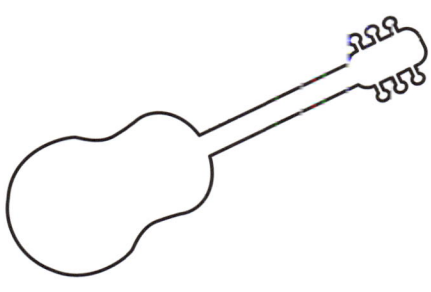

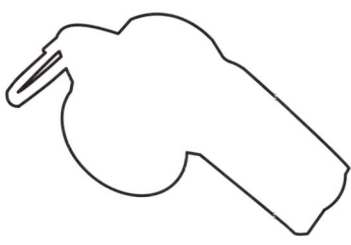

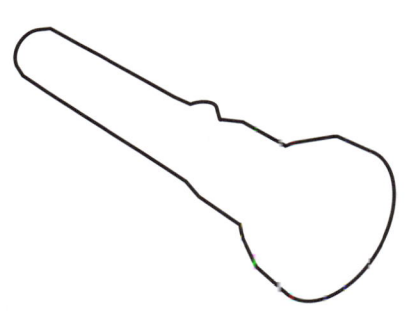

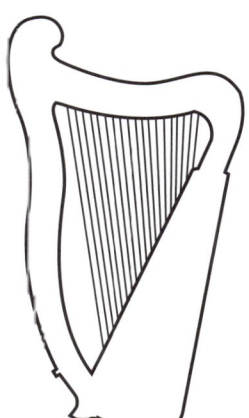

Natural or Man-made

KEY POINTS

Like light energy, sound energy can be natural or man-made. A person can strum a guitar and the string will vibrate back and forth. This movement bumps the air around it and starts sound waves. A bird singing in a tree is an example of natural sound energy. The bird's song vibrates through the air to make sound we can hear.

■ Answer the questions.

❶ How is sound energy made?

_____

❷ Write an example of man-made sound energy.

_____

■ Match the object to the sound it would make.

meow!

hello!

beep!

Brain Break
Science Journal 5

Different objects make different sounds when struck. Find some objects around your home to use like a drum. Use your hands to strike the surface. Which makes the loudest sound? Which makes the softest? Record a list below.

Object	Loud	Soft	No sound

Art Break!

■ Choose a small object from around your house. Place it on the paper and see if it makes a shadow with the overhead light or a flashlight. Trace the shadow it creates and color it black.

What is an Economy?

KEY POINTS

The way people make and spend money in a society is called an economy. An economy can be large like the economy of the United States or small like the economy of a town. Economies can be strong or weak depending on the amount of money and people they have.

■ Answer the questions.

❶ What is an economy?

_____

❷ What can make an economy strong or weak?

_____

Date

Great Job Sticker

Place a check mark (✓) under the examples of people participating in the economy.

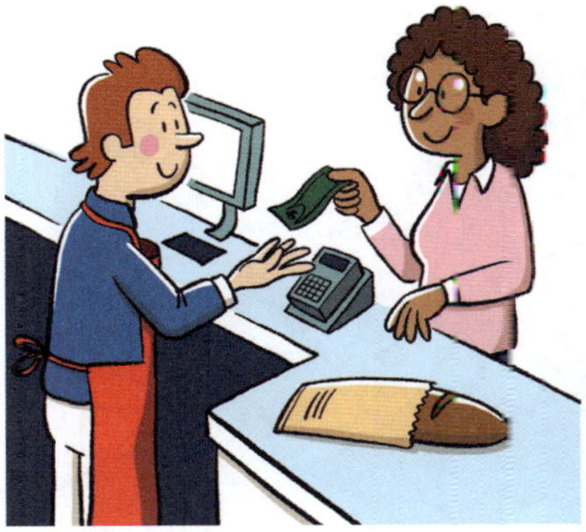

☐

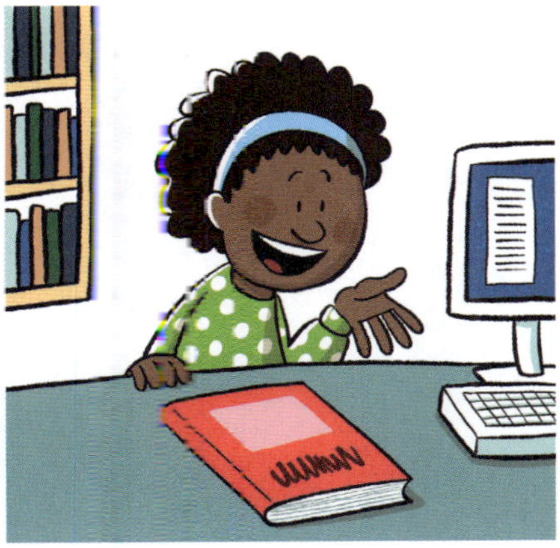

☐

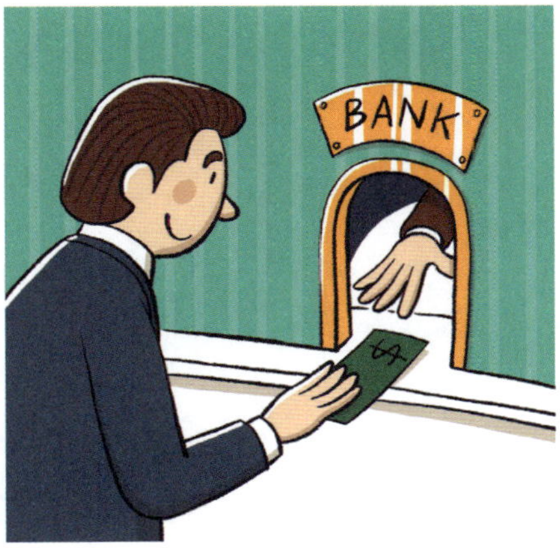

☐

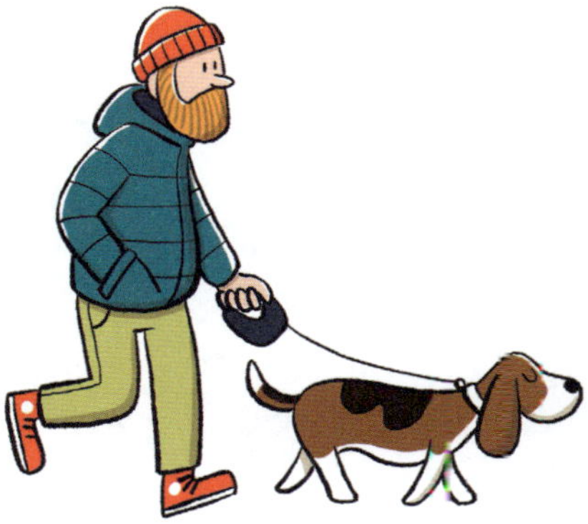

☐

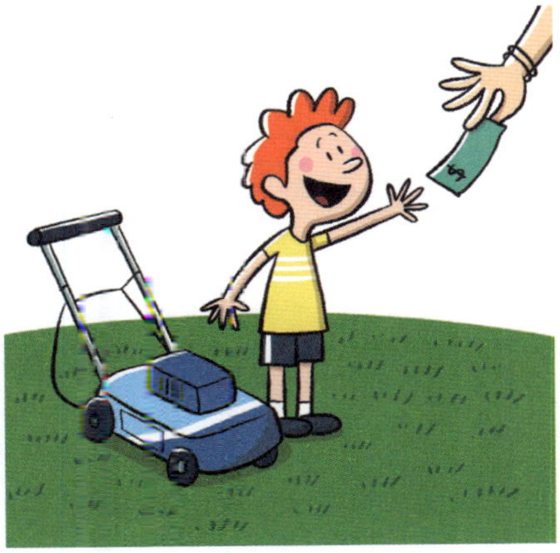

☐

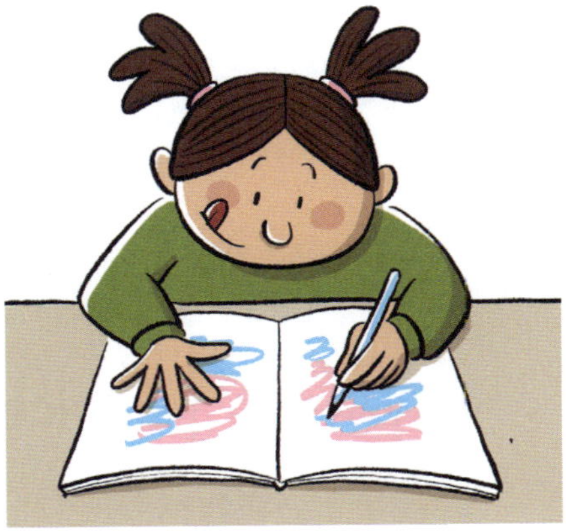

☐

Goods and Services

KEY POINTS

People spend money on goods and services. A good is an object like a carton of milk, an apple, or a computer. A service is a job someone does for another person like fixing a broken pipe or car.

■ **Answer the questions.**

❶ What is a good?

❷ What is a service?

■ Circle the goods or services in the right column.

Goods

Services

Goods

Services

Needs and Wants

Goods and services can be divided into needs and wants. Needs are things people need for their daily life, such as food and medical care. Wants are things that people like to have, such as candy and amusement parks.

■ Answer the questions.

❶ What is a need?

❷ What is a want?

■ Write or draw some of your own needs and wants in the table below.

Needs	Wants

Jobs

KEY POINTS

A job is a service people perform to earn money.
There are many different jobs. Some examples are:

| Teacher | Police Officer | Waiter | Pro-athlete |

■ **Answer the questions.**

❶ What is a job?

❷ What other examples of jobs can you name?

Date

Great Job Sticker

■ Match the job to the right tool.

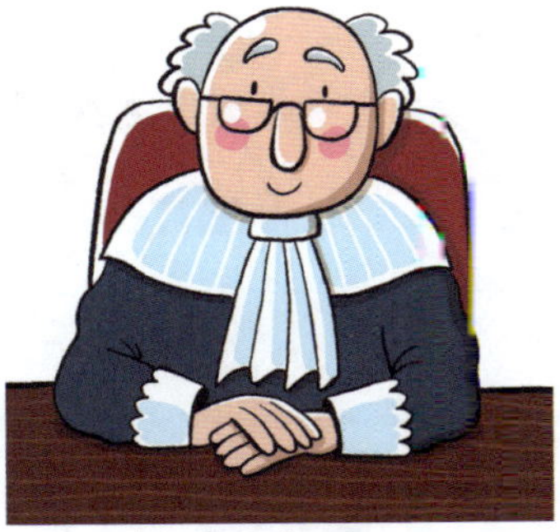

Judge

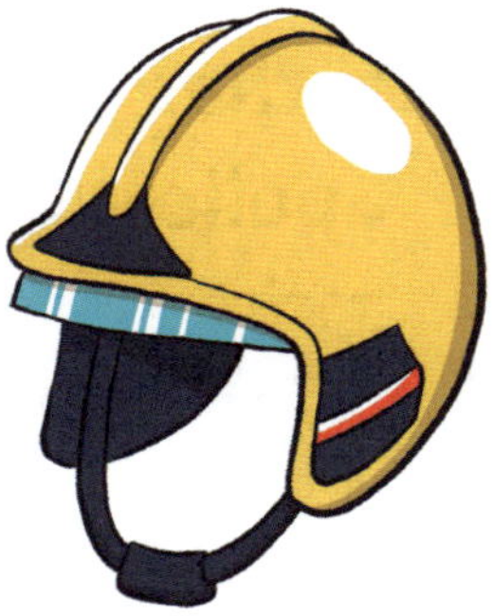

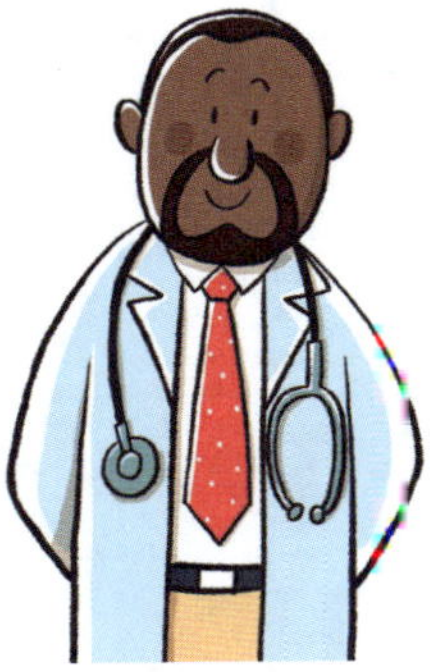

Doctor

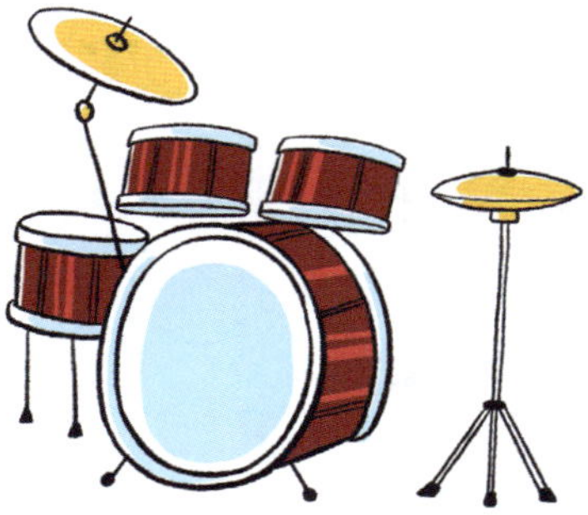

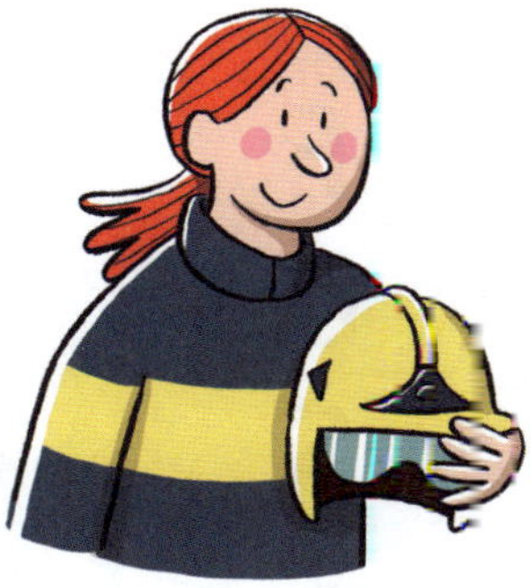

Firefighter

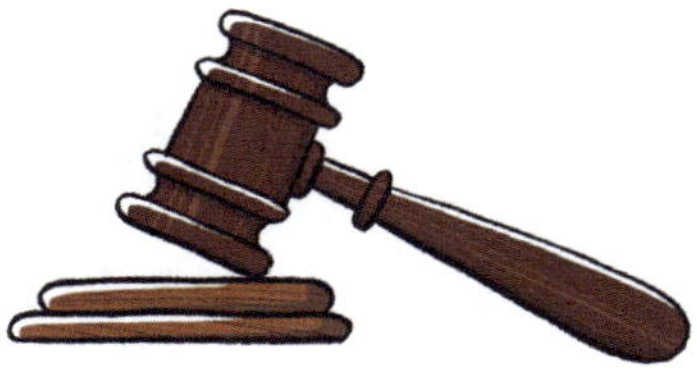

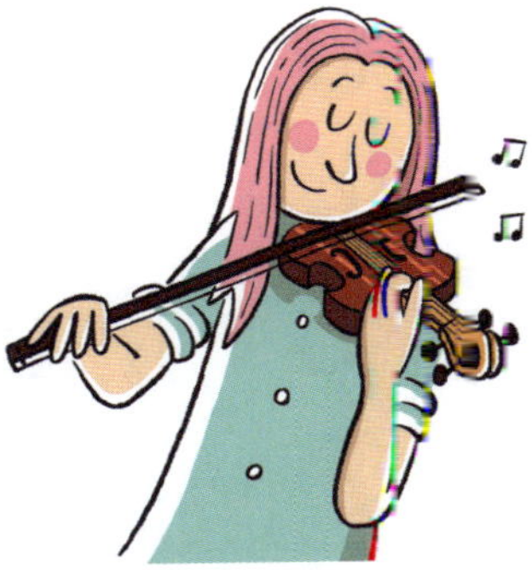

Musician

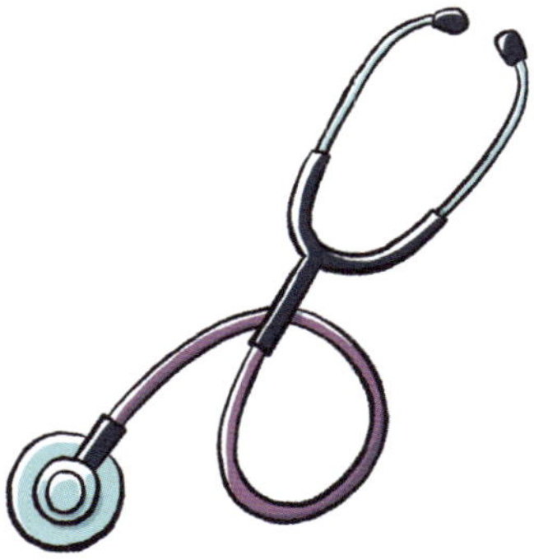

Brain Break
Word Search

■ Circle the words in the Word Search.

teacher	judge	doctor	musician	chef
police	nurse	vet	athlete	waiter

M	W	Y	C	H	E	F
U	E	T	A	I	O	X
S	T	E	S	E	V	W
I	Y	A	D	A	E	Q
C	H	C	X	T	T	H
I	V	H	Z	H	H	Y
A	B	E	C	L	G	W
N	U	R	S	E	F	A
X	N	W	M	T	D	I
J	M	U	I	E	S	T
U	P	K	L	S	A	E
D	D	O	C	T	O	R
G	I	M	P	O	L	K
E	P	O	L	I	C	E
A	R	T	U	N	P	F

Mindfulness Break!

■ Draw picture of your dream job!
What would you wear? What tools would you have?

Patterns with Rotating Blocks

KEY POINTS

Being able to follow and complete a pattern is an important critical thinking skill to practice!

■ Write a check mark (✓) below the picture that comes next in the pattern.

①

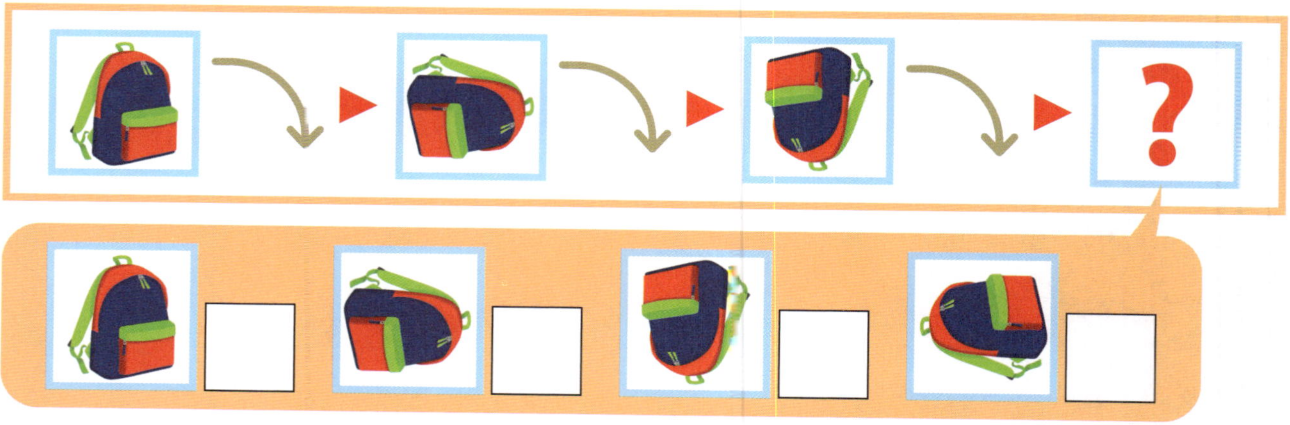

②

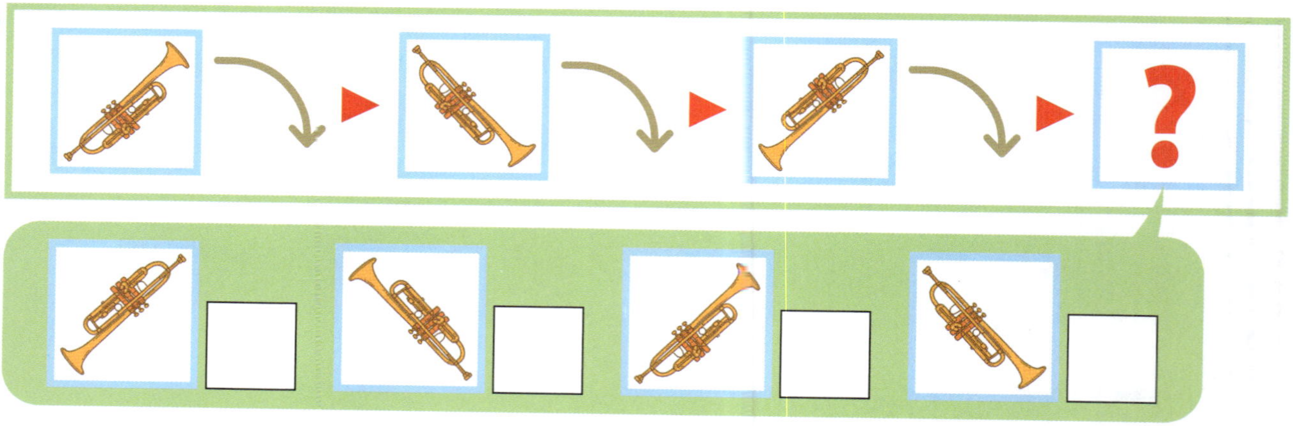

③

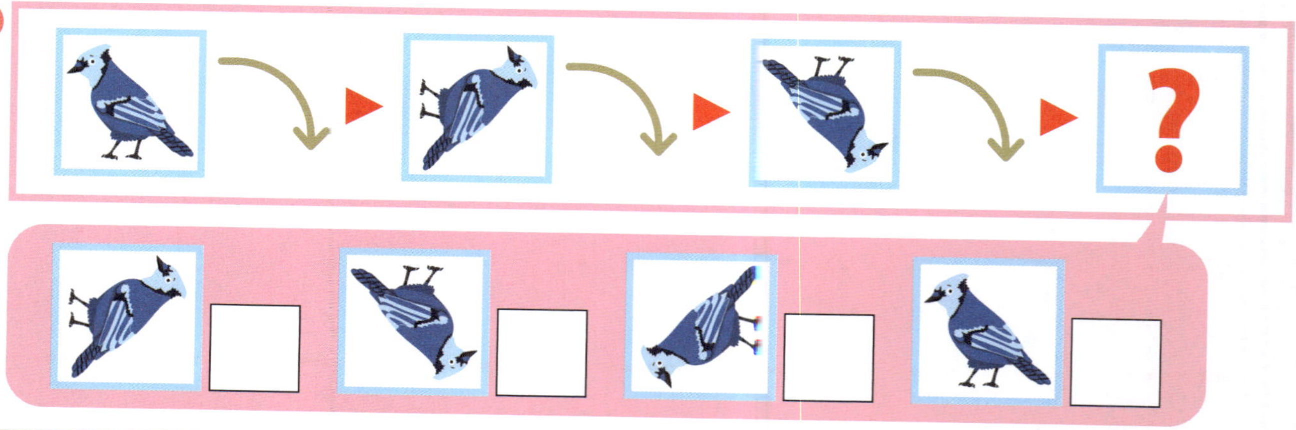

4

5

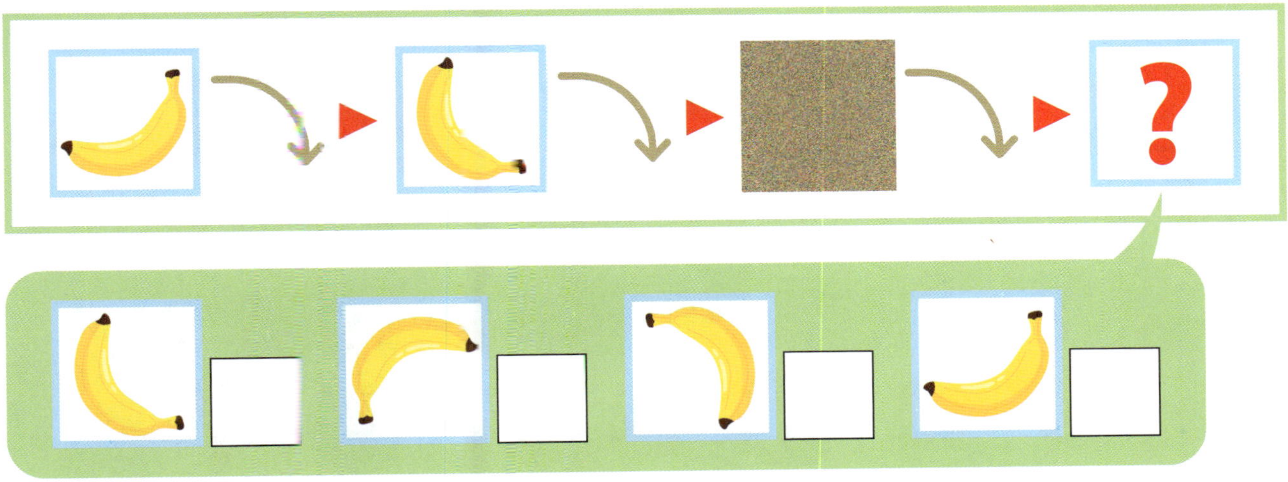

6

■ Write a check mark (✓) below the picture that comes next in the pattern.

❶

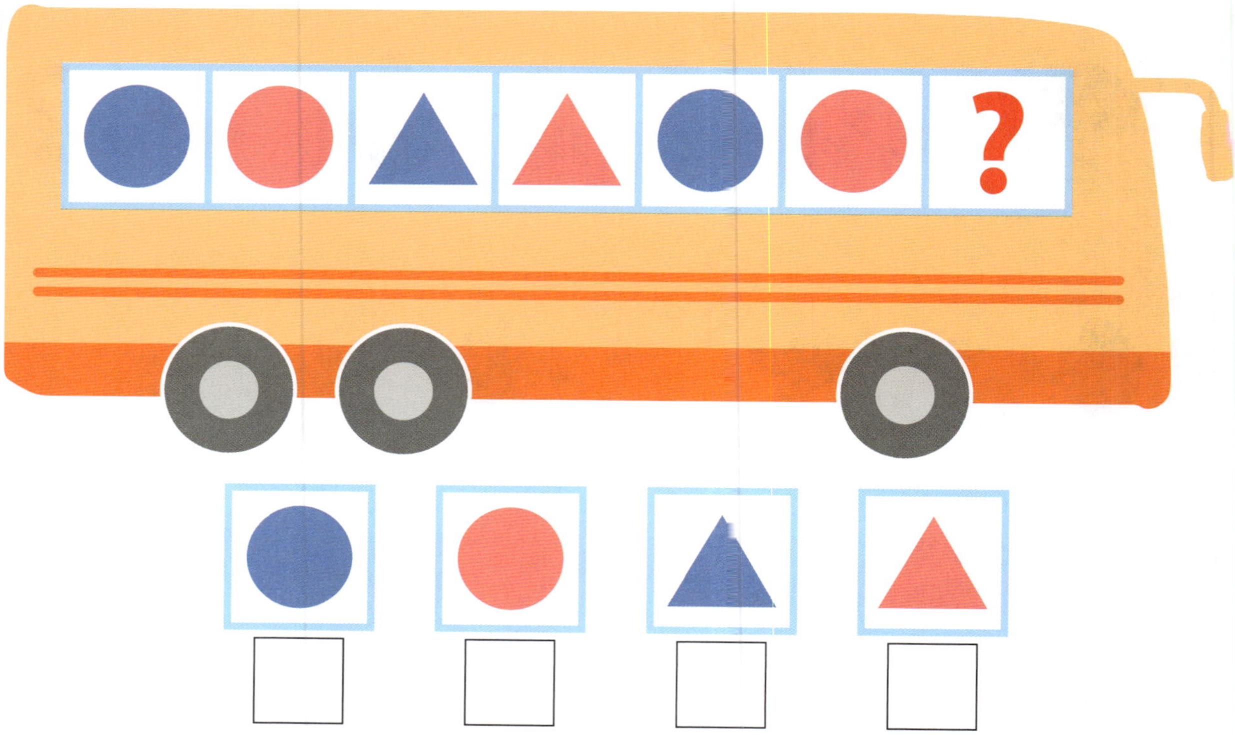

3

4

Identifying Objects

■ Find and circle one ice cream that matches each of the ice creams below.

Problem Solving

■ Help the child get across the river safely! Draw your answer.

■ Rescue the cat from the tree! How can you get it down?
Draw your answer.

Physical Education Break!

It's important to move your body and exercise!
Try this fun activity below for a study break!

- Pick 5 exercises from the list and try to do them daily!
  Record your progress in the chart!

10 jumping jacks	5 sit ups	5 squats
1 minute run in place		10 frog hops
1 minute yoga pose	30 seconds high knees	
30 seconds marching in place	10 star jumps	

Daily Exercise Plan

Exercise	❶	❷	❸	❹	❺
Monday					
Tuesday					
Wednesday					
Thursday					
Friday					
Saturday					
Sunday					

Ace First Grade
Answer Key

Unit 1 Language Arts

p. 6
① boy, bus, school
② girl, sandwich, lunch
③ teacher, book, class

p. 7
① New York, Empire State Building
② Sam, *The Cat in the Hat*
③ Ali, Sasha

p. 8
① Katie's backpack
② Tony's apple
③ computer's mouse ("mouse's computer" also acceptable)

p. 9
nouns: hand, teacher, backpack, desk, friend, school
proper nouns: Lila, Ms. Francis, Pine Grove Elementary School, Quincy
possessive nouns: dad's

p. 10
① paint ② sing ③ play

p. 11
① likes ② drives ③ ride

p. 12

S	T	Q	R	Z	W	E	R	B	U	S	T	Y	U
C	R	A	B	O	Y	C	Y	W	F	U	Y	O	B
H	F	Z	F	X	S	D	V	E	A	I	J	A	O
O	H	X	V	E	D	H	T	R	M	O	K	V	O
O	J	S	G	T	F	O	T	H	O	P	A	R	K
L	K	W	B	Y	S	N	O	J	I	R	K	C	P
S	M	G	T	U	D	E	I	C	Y	T	L	F	P
E	D	Y	O	F	S	U	V	B	N	M	G	O
F	E	R	U	L	G	T	H	I	R	S	T	H	I
G	R	L	J	K	H	Y	N	E	C	V	B	J	K
H	T	H	M	K	U	S	D	V	T	Y	U	I	O
U	I	L	K	N	M	C	T	E	A	C	H	E	R
A	N	G	E	R	B	N	M	R	E	W	Q	A	S

Unit 1 Reading

p. 14
sing, lot, bun, well, rat

p. 15

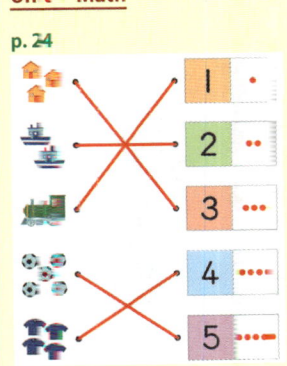

p. 16
sale, bone, root, bean, fire

---

p. 17

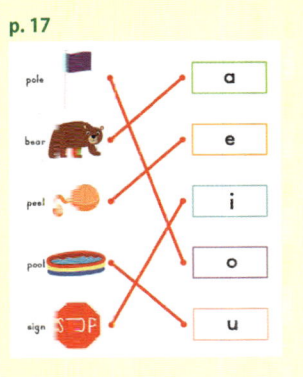

p. 18
break, spot, greet, flame, plop, cap

p. 19

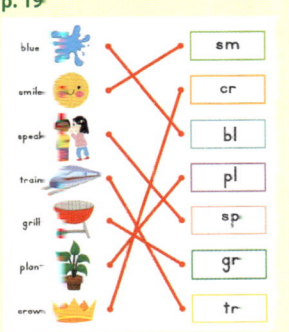

p. 20
chin, shine, phone, this

p. 21
chips, tooth, shore, splash, cheer, cheese

p. 22

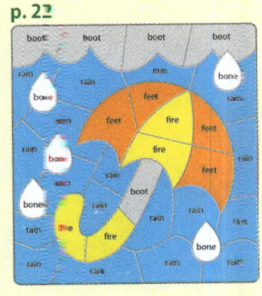

Unit 1 Math

p. 24

---

p. 25

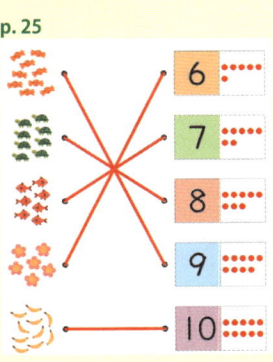

p. 30
① 18 ② 23 ③ 40

p. 31
① 17 ③ 45 ⑤ 96
② 21 ④ 33 ⑥ 52

p. 32
① > ③ < ⑤ >
② < ④ = ⑥ =

p. 33
① < ③ < ⑤ > ⑦ >
② > ④ = ⑥ = ⑧ <

p. 34

Unit 1 Science

p. 36
① All living things take in food and water, grow, breathe, move, and reproduce.
② Plants make their own food.
③ Plants take in water through their roots and leaves.

p. 37

p. 39
① leaves ③ stem
② flowers ④ roots

---

p. 41

p. 43
① protection ③ reproduce
② sunlight

p. 44
(Answers will vary.)

Unit 1 Social Studies

p. 47
(Answers will vary.)

p. 49
① George Washington
② Clara Barton
③ Frederick Douglass
④ (Answers will vary.)

p. 51
① July 4th celebrates the adoption of the Declaration of Independence.
② Former presidents of the United States.
③ The end of slavery in the United States.
④ The American people who have died in military service.

p. 53
① The Statue of Liberty stands for freedom.
② Four presidents
③ Washington, D.C

p. 54
Across
① Douglass
③ flag
⑤ United States
⑦ Juneteenth
⑨ monument
Down
② July
④ Memorial
⑥ Washington

Unit 1 Technology

p. 56
① Calculator ④ Refrigerator
② TV ⑤ Cell phone
③ Washing machine ⑥ Airplane

p. 57

p. 58

Printer
Mouse
Screen
Keyboard

p. 59
❶Web camera ❸Speaker
❷Printer ❹Headphones

p. 60

p. 61
❶Shift ❹Backspace
❷Space ❺Enter
❸Period

p. 62
❶dog ❷pie ❸lion ❹apple

p. 63

wheel
white
water

Unit 2 Language Arts

p. 66
❶She ❷They ❸me

p. 67
❶their ❷my ❸your

p. 68
❶draws ❷builds ❸reads

p. 69
❶wrote ❷ate ❸kicked

p. 70

☑ She will eat fish for dinner.
☐ They drive to work.
☑ She will do her homework.
☐ He played the guitar.

p. 71
past tense: watched, played, liked, taught
present tense: know, stand
future tense: will show, will pass

p. 72
❶yellow ❸round
❷green ❹sweet

p. 73
(Answers will vary.)
❶black ❹small
❷brown ❺happy
❸stinky

p. 74
(Answers will vary.)

Unit 2 Reading

p. 76

☐ Will is running.
☐ Will is late for school.
☑ Will is afraid.

p. 77
helpful, hungry

p. 78
a library, a park, a school

p. 79

☑ Stephanie is in the park.
☐ It's warm out.
☑ The trees have colorful leaves.

p. 80

☐ Xavier is a boy.
☑ Xavier rushed out of bed.
☐ The school was big and full of people.
☑ Xavier made it to school on time.

p. 81

2 Sam's parents said no.
4 Sam's parents agreed to get a dog.
1 Sam wanted a dog.
3 Sam took care of Spot.

p. 82
Main idea: I went to the beach.
Details: The water was scary. The waves were big. I saw a jellyfish in the water. I wondered if there were sharks.

p. 83
❶T ❷D ❸D ❹D ❺D

p. 84
(Answers will vary.)

Unit 2 Math

p. 86
❶2+3=5 ❸3+1=4
❷5+2=7 ❹4+2=6

p. 87
7➡4➡9➡8➡10

p. 88
❶6 ❷3 ❸1 ❹8 ❺5 ❻7

p. 89

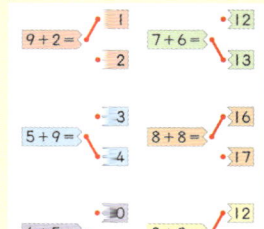

9 + 2 = 11
7 + 6 = 13
5 + 9 = 14
8 + 8 = 16
6 + 5 = 11
3 + 9 = 12

p. 90
❶15+1=16 ❸14+3=17
❷12+7=19 ❹10+10=20

p. 91

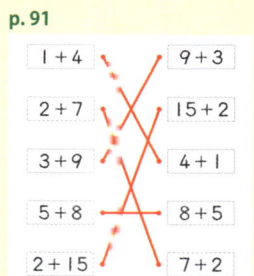

1 + 4   9 + 3
2 + 7   15 + 2
3 + 9   4 + 1
5 + 8   8 + 5
2 + 15   7 + 2

p. 92
❶2 ❷4 ❸5 ❹6 ❺1 ❻3

p. 93
3➡1➡8➡2➡4

p. 94
❶2 ❷5 ❸6 ❹9

p. 95

11 − 2   15 − 9
12 − 4   17 − 8
14 − 5   13 − 9

p. 96

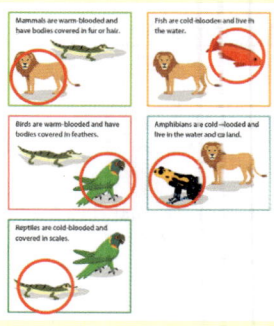

Unit 2 Science

p. 98
❶There are five types of animals.
❷They need food and water to live.

p. 99

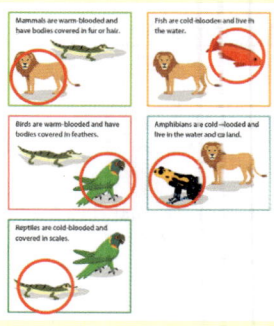

p. 101

Desert
Arctic
Rainforest

p. 103

p. 105
(Answers will vary.)

p. 106
(Answers will vary.)

Unit 2 Social Studies

p. 108
❶A community is a group of people who live and work together in the same area.
❷A citizen is a member of a community.
❸Following laws, being a good neighbor, and helping solve community problems.

p. 109
(Answers will vary.)

p. 110
❶A rule is something people follow.
❷A law is a rule created by a country's government.

p. 111
❶Rule ❸Law ❺Rule
❷Law ❹Rule

p. 113

p. 114
❶A community is an area where different people live, work, and spend their time together.
❷People in the community need to follow rules and laws.

p. 115

p. 116

Unit 2 Technology

pp. 118–119

pp. 120–121

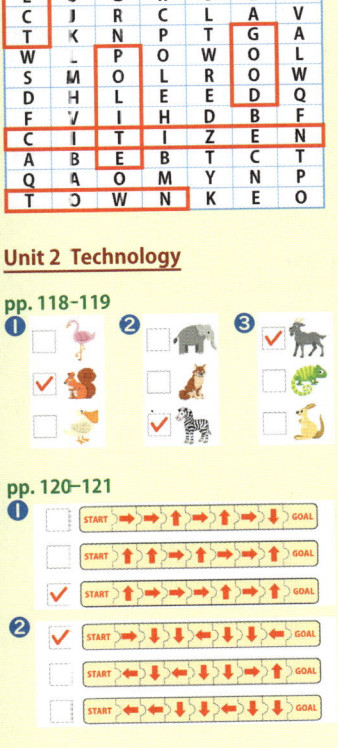

p. 122
❶4 ❷3 ❸6

p. 123
❶ ❷✓

p. 124

p. 125

Unit 3 Language Arts

p. 128
❶on ❸before
❷outside ❹down

p. 129
❶in ❸over ❺on
❷on ❹at

p. 130
❶Bil ❹Uncle Joe
❷Mr Gordon ❺Mia Thomas
❸Ms. Eden ❻Grandma Nina

p. 131
❶Tuesday, May 7
❷Friday, October 19
❸Sunday, February 26
❹Thursday, July 1

p. 132
❶. ❷? ❸! ❹?

p. 133
.?.../!/../!/?

p. 134
We started school on August 28, 2023.
My favorite animals are monkeys, cows, and snakes.
I was born on June 11, 2018.
I like to sing, dance, and play piano.

p. 135
❶✗
I have a green, yellow, and blue backpack.
❷✓
❸✗
I have three cats, two dogs, and a frog.
❹✓
❺✗
Our last day of school is May 29, 2024.
❻✗
At the park we saw a squirrel, a deer, and a raccoon.

p. 136
Samson was a bunny who lived to eat carrots. One day he found a garden that had carrots, tomatoes, and corn. He ate so many carrots. He got a tummy ache! He lay down in a flower bed to sleep. Samson woke up and felt much better. The end.

Unit 3 Reading

p. 138
☐ Sasha looked in the closet.
✓ Sasha searched under the bed.
☐ Sasha sat down at her desk.

p. 139
(Answers will vary.)
❶Spencer felt sad.
❷His friend was away.
❸He decided to write her a letter.

p. 140
Studying can help you do well on tests.

p. 141
(Answers will vary.)

p. 142
☐ It is daytime.
✓ Lola made a noise outside his door.
☐ Mateo is being noisy.

p. 143
Sophie: loves her grandmother's chocolate cake
Sophie's grandmother: teaches her to bake
The setting: kitchen

p. 144
sour — taste
soft — touch
stinky — smell
bright — hearing
loud — sight

p. 145
hot, sticky, salty, crashed, loudly, cool, pinch, tiny

p. 146
promise

Unit 3 Math

p. 148
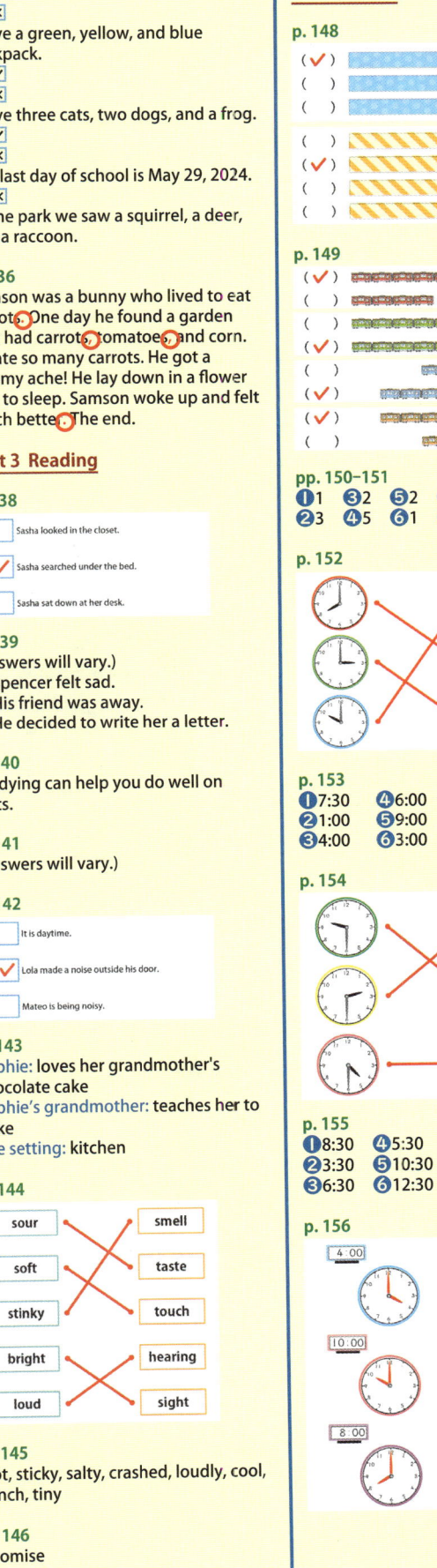

p. 149

pp. 150–151
❶1 ❸2 ❺2 ❼5
❷3 ❹5 ❻1 ❽3

p. 152

p. 153
❶7:30 ❹6:00 ❼2:00
❷1:00 ❺9:00 ❽5:00
❸4:00 ❻3:00 ❾11:00

p. 154

p. 155
❶8:30 ❹5:30 ❼7:30
❷3:30 ❺10:30 ❽11:30
❸6:30 ❻12:30 ❾1:30

p. 156

p. 157

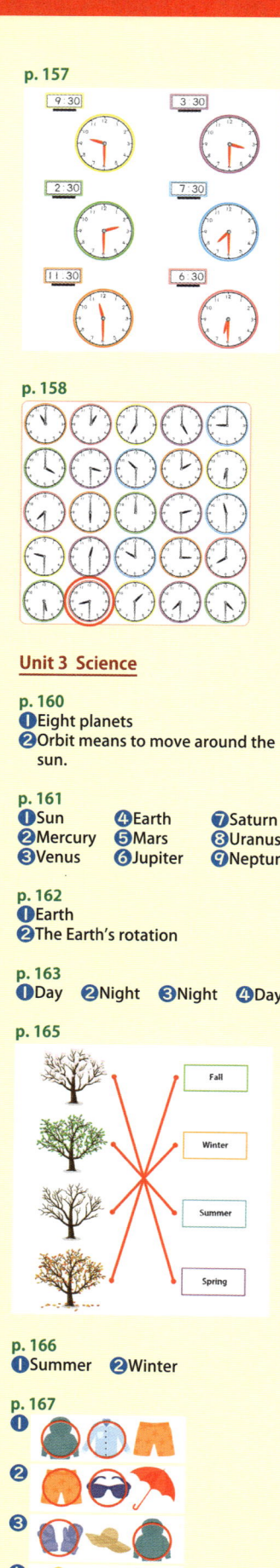

p. 158

Unit 3 Science

p. 160
❶Eight planets
❷Orbit means to move around the sun.

p. 161
❶Sun ❹Earth ❼Saturn
❷Mercury ❺Mars ❽Uranus
❸Venus ❻Jupiter ❾Neptune

p. 162
❶Earth
❷The Earth's rotation

p. 163
❶Day ❷Night ❸Night ❹Day

p. 165

Fall
Winter
Summer
Spring

p. 166
❶Summer ❷Winter

p. 167

p. 168
(Answers will vary.)

Unit 3 Social Studies

p. 170
❶A map is used to help people find places.
❷Maps show countries, landforms, places, buildings, etc.

p. 171
❶B (Town map)
❷A (Country map)
❸C(Store map)

p. 172
❶A compass rose shows direction on a map.
❷East, west, north, and south.

p. 173
❶West ❷West ❸East ❹South

p. 174
❶They are natural features like mountains, rivers, and others.
❷Man-made

p. 175

Man-made
Natural
Man-made

p. 176
❶Map symbols are used to show natural or man-made features on a map.
❷A legend is a list of map symbols.

p. 177

cave
tree
mountain
river

Unit 3 Personal Finance

p. 180

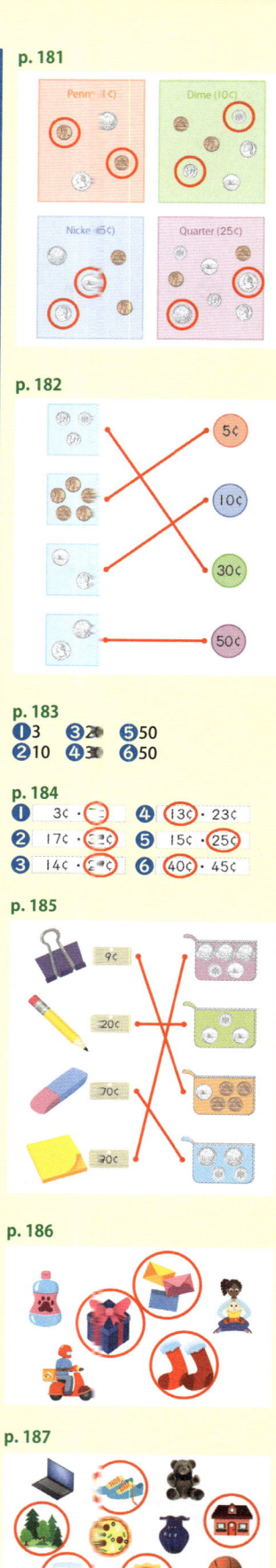

p. 181

Penny (1¢)   Dime (10¢)
Nickel (5¢)   Quarter (25¢)

p. 182

5¢
10¢
30¢
50¢

p. 183
❶3 ❸2 ❺50
❷10 ❹3 ❻50

p. 184
❶ 3¢ · 7¢ ❹ 13¢ · 23¢
❷ 17¢ · 75¢ ❺ 15¢ · 25¢
❸ 14¢ · 41¢ ❻ 40¢ · 45¢

p. 185

9¢
20¢
70¢
30¢

p. 186

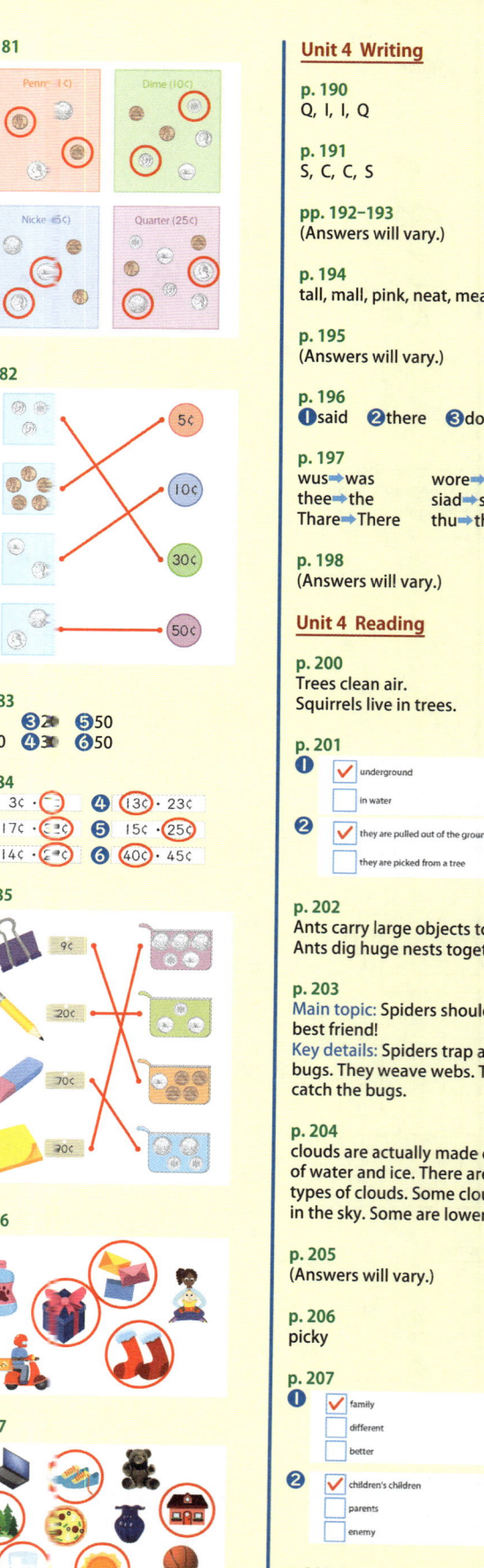

p. 187

Unit 4 Writing

p. 190
Q, I, I, Q

p. 191
S, C, C, S

pp. 192–193
(Answers will vary.)

p. 194
tall, mall, pink, neat, meat

p. 195
(Answers will vary.)

p. 196
❶said ❷there ❸do ❹You

p. 197
wus➡was   wore➡were
thee➡the   siad➡sad
Thare➡There thu➡the

p. 198
(Answers will vary.)

Unit 4 Reading

p. 200
Trees clean air.
Squirrels live in trees.

p. 201
❶
✓ underground
☐ in water
❷
✓ they are pulled out of the ground
☐ they are picked from a tree

p. 202
Ants carry large objects together.
Ants dig huge nests together.

p. 203
Main topic: Spiders should be man's best friend!
Key details: Spiders trap and eat other bugs. They weave webs. The webs catch the bugs.

p. 204
clouds are actually made of tiny drops of water and ice. There are different types of clouds. Some clouds are high in the sky. Some are lower.

p. 205
(Answers will vary.)

p. 206
picky

p. 207
❶
✓ family
☐ different
☐ better
❷
✓ children's children
☐ parents
☐ enemy

p. 208
(Answers will vary.)

Unit 4 Math

p. 210

p. 211

p. 212

p. 213
1. 2 1
2. 2 2
3. 2 1 1
4. 4 1 2

p. 214

p. 215

p. 216

Triangle
Rectangle
Square
Diamond
Circle
Oval

p. 217
1. 2
2. 2
3. 1 3
4. 3 4

p. 218
(Answers will vary.)

p. 219

p. 220
(Answers will vary.)
1. 2. 3.

Unit 4 Science

p. 222
1. All things are made of matter.
2. There are 3 states of matter.

p. 223

Solid
Gas
Liquid

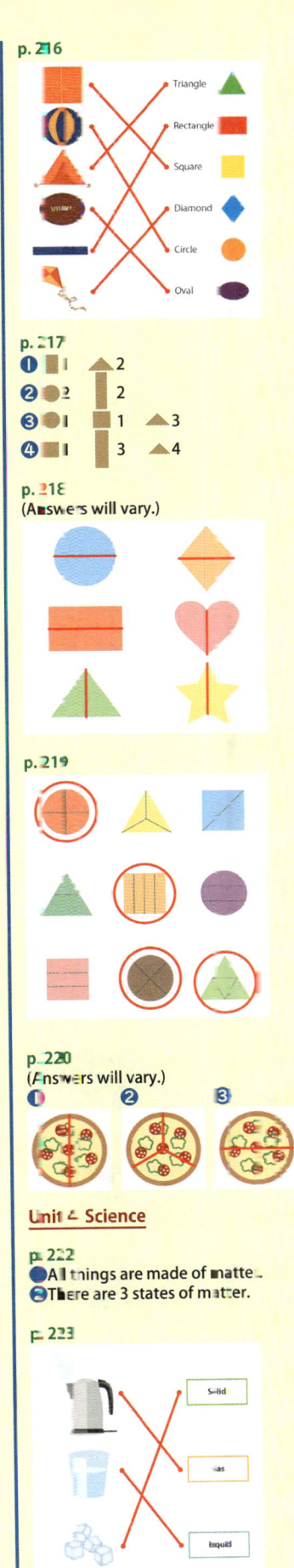

p. 225
1. gas
2. solid
3. liquid
4. solid
5. liquid
6. gas

p. 227
1. ☑ heated ☐ cooled
2. ☑ heated ☐ cooled
3. ☐ heated ☑ cooled

p. 229
(Answers will vary.)
1. bumpy, orange, bouncy
2. blue, smooth, delicate
3. soft, fuzzy, small
4. soft, squishy, yellow

p. 230
(Answers will vary.)

Unit 4 Social Studies

p. 232
1. Celebrations, food, language, and art that are shared by communities.
2. 3. (Answers will vary.)

p. 233
(Answers will vary.)

p. 235
(Answers will vary.)
1. 2. 3.

p. 236
1. Language is a way people communicate.
2. Language is important because people use it to communicate and share ideas.

p. 237
(Answers will vary.)

pp. 238–239
(Answers will vary.)

p. 240
Across
1. Language
3. Community
5. Holiday
Down
2. Tradition
4. People
6. Culture
8. Food

Unit 4 Thinking Skills

pp. 242–243
1. 2. 3. 4.

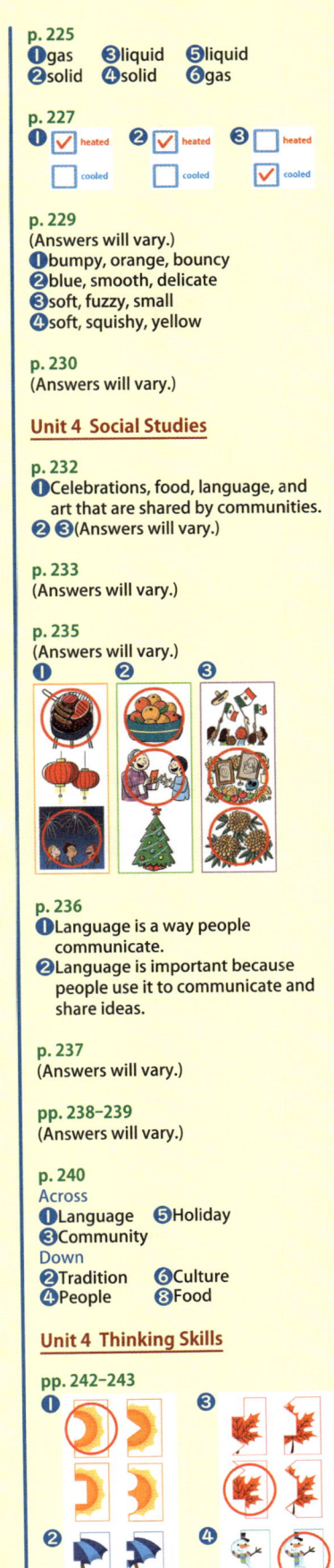

pp. 244–245
1. 2. 3. 4.

p. 246

p. 247
1. 2. 3. 4.

p. 248
Q
X
S
V
O
C
W
A

p. 249
83
78
57
29
15
82
40
36

Unit 5 Writing

p. 252
1. O 2. F 3. O 4. F

p. 253
Pizza is delicious — because you can swim.
Cats are the best pet — because it has cheese.
It's fun to go to the beach — because they make me laugh.
I like funny movies — because they clean themselves.

pp. 254–255
(Answers will vary.)

pp. 256–257
(Answers will vary.)

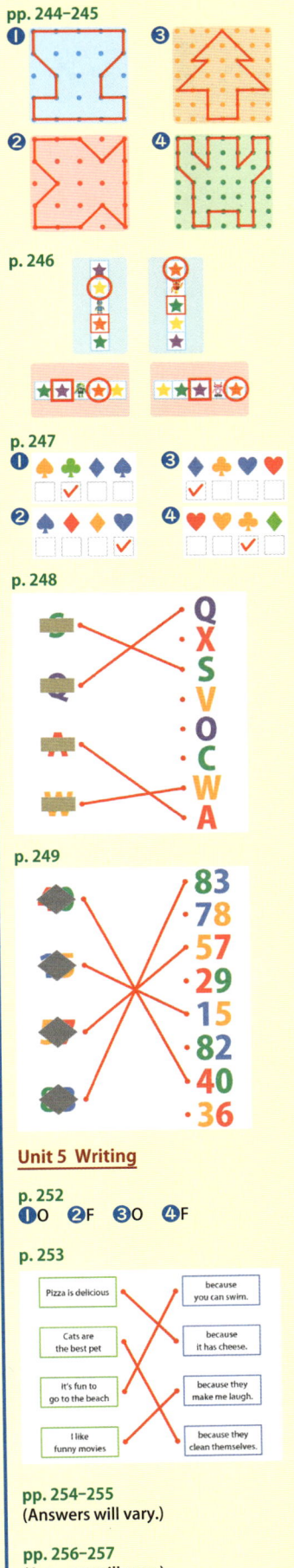

p. 258

4   1   3
5   2

p. 259

(Answers will vary.)

pp. 260–261

(Answers will vary.)

Unit 5 Reading

p. 262

unclear, swimming, disagree, reread, trees, danced

p. 263

untie: undo a knot or tie
writing: to write right now
painted: paint, in the past
colors: more than one color
rewrite: write again
dishonest: not honest

p. 264

Colors: orange, pink, green
Animals: bird, cow, moose
School supplies: pencil, book, backpack

p. 265

water: lake, splash
animals: swans, ducks
food: bread, treats

p. 266

(Answers will vary.)

p. 267

jump, skip, hop

eat, munch, swallow

baby, child, toddler

p. 268

Buses: big vehicles that drive on roads
Subways: trains that go underground.
Driving: being in a car

p. 269

unlucky: not lucky
celebration: party
redo: do it again

p. 270

D	I	S	R	E	S	P	E	C	T
I	V	N	S	E	Q	T	J	L	P
S	C	D	X	U	N	T	I	E	X
H	D	E	Z	N	Z	U	F	U	R
O	W	T	F	L	Y	R	P	E	E
N	I	I	L	U	A	O	E	O	W
E	J	U	C	G	L	D	L	L	R
S	U	A	U	K	Y	A	K	S	I
T	H	P	R	Y	N	M	C	H	T
X	G	B	T	U	A	N	R	S	E
M	M	L	C	O	L	O	R	S	Q

Unit 5 Math

pp. 272–273

p. 274

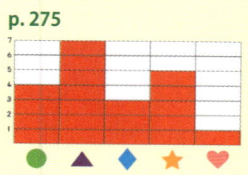

p. 275

● ▲ ◆ ★ ♥

p. 276

❶ 6   ❸ 4   ❺ Sandwiches
❷ 3   ❹ Burger

p. 277

❶ 5   ❷ 4   ❸ 5   ❹ Banana   ❺ Kiwi

pp. 278–279

❶ 4+2=6   Ans. 6 balloons
❷ 9+3=12   Ans. 12 cars
❸ 12+5=17 Ans. 17 oranges
❹ 8−4=4   Ans. 4 books
❺ 15−7=8   Ans. 8 balls
❻ 10−8=2   Ans. 2 boys

p. 280–281

❶ 2+4=6   Ans. 6 children
❷ 6+9=15   Ans. 15 people
❸ 7−3=4   Ans. 4 hats
❹ 3+4+3=10 Ans. 10 birds
❺ 9−2−4=3   Ans. 3 candies
❻ 6+2−3=5   Ans. 5 apples

p. 282

❶ True   ❷ False   ❸ False

Unit 5 Science

p. 284

❶ Light energy is energy we can see and that helps us see things.
❷ (Answers will vary.)

p. 285

Natural: sun, starlight, moonlight
Man-made: lamp, lightbulb, flashlight

p. 286

❶ Light travels in a straight line.
❷ Shadows are shaped like the objects that block the light.

p. 287

p. 288

❶ Sound energy is a type of energy you can hear.
❷ We hear sound when vibrations move through the air and bounce off our eardrums.

p. 289

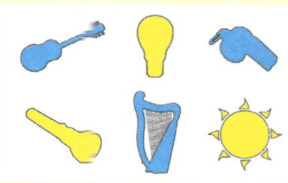

p. 290

❶ Sound energy is made when sound makes vibrations through the air which come back to our eardrums.
❷ (Answers will vary.)

p. 291

p. 292

(Answers will vary.)

Unit 5 Social Studies

p. 294

❶ An economy is the way people make and spend money in a society.
❷ An economy can be strong or weak based on the amount of money people make and spend.

p. 295

p. 296

❶ A good is an object like a carton of milk or a computer.
❷ A service is a job that a person performs like fixing a car.

p. 297

p. 298

❶ A need is something a person must have to live.
❷ A want is something people would like to have, but don't need.

p. 299

(Answers will vary.)

p. 300

❶ A job is a service people perform to earn money.
❷ (Answers will vary.)

p. 301

p. 302

M	W	Y	C	H	E	F
U	E	T	A	I	O	X
S	I	E	S	E	V	W
I	Y	A	D	A	E	Q
C	H	C	X	T	T	H
I	V	H	Z	H	E	Y
A	B	E	C	L	G	W
N	U	R	S	E	F	A
X	N	W	M	T	D	I
J	M	U	I	E	S	T
U	P	K	L	S	A	E
D	D	O	C	T	O	R
G	I	M	P	O	L	K
E	P	O	L	I	C	E
A	R	T	U	N	P	F

Unit 5 Thinking Skills

pp. 304–305

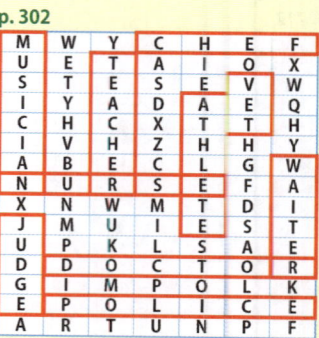

pp. 306–307

pp. 308–309

pp. 310–311

(Answers will vary.)

KUMON Ace First Grade

Unit 1

COMPLETED!

Unit 2

COMPLETED!

Unit 3

COMPLETED!

Unit 4

COMPLETED!

Unit 5

COMPLETED!

All Pages Completed!

Excellent Work!

CERTIFICATE
OF ACHIEVEMENT

is hereby congratulated on completing

Kumon Ace First Grade

_____   _____
Date   Parent or Guardian

ADDITION

+1

1 + 1 = 2
2 + 1 = 3
3 + 1 = 4
4 + 1 = 5
5 + 1 = 6
6 + 1 = 7
7 + 1 = 8
8 + 1 = 9
9 + 1 = 10
10 + 1 = 11

+2

1 + 2 = 3
2 + 2 = 4
3 + 2 = 5
4 + 2 = 6
5 + 2 = 7
6 + 2 = 8
7 + 2 = 9
8 + 2 = 10
9 + 2 = 11
10 + 2 = 12

+3

1 + 3 = 4
2 + 3 = 5
3 + 3 = 6
4 + 3 = 7
5 + 3 = 8
6 + 3 = 9
7 + 3 = 10
8 + 3 = 11
9 + 3 = 12
10 + 3 = 13

+4

1 + 4 = 5
2 + 4 = 6
3 + 4 = 7
4 + 4 = 8
5 + 4 = 9
6 + 4 = 10
7 + 4 = 11
8 + 4 = 12
9 + 4 = 13
10 + 4 = 14

+5

1 + 5 = 6
2 + 5 = 7
3 + 5 = 8
4 + 5 = 9
5 + 5 = 10
6 + 5 = 11
7 + 5 = 12
8 + 5 = 13
9 + 5 = 14
10 + 5 = 15

+6

1 + 6 = 7
2 + 6 = 8
3 + 6 = 9
4 + 6 = 10
5 + 6 = 11
6 + 6 = 12
7 + 6 = 13
8 + 6 = 14
9 + 6 = 15
10 + 6 = 16

+7

1 + 7 = 8
2 + 7 = 9
3 + 7 = 10
4 + 7 = 11
5 + 7 = 12
6 + 7 = 13
7 + 7 = 14
8 + 7 = 15
9 + 7 = 16
10 + 7 = 17

+8

1 + 8 = 9
2 + 8 = 10
3 + 8 = 11
4 + 8 = 12
5 + 8 = 13
6 + 8 = 14
7 + 8 = 15
8 + 8 = 16
9 + 8 = 17
10 + 8 = 18

+9

1 + 9 = 10
2 + 9 = 11
3 + 9 = 12
4 + 9 = 13
5 + 9 = 14
6 + 9 = 15
7 + 9 = 16
8 + 9 = 17
9 + 9 = 18
10 + 9 = 19

+10

1 + 10 = 11
2 + 10 = 12
3 + 10 = 13
4 + 10 = 14
5 + 10 = 15
6 + 10 = 16
7 + 10 = 17
8 + 10 = 18
9 + 10 = 19
10 + 10 = 20

SUBTRACTION

 **−1**

$1 - 1 = 0$
$2 - 1 = 1$
$3 - 1 = 2$
$4 - 1 = 3$
$5 - 1 = 4$
$6 - 1 = 5$
$7 - 1 = 6$
$8 - 1 = 7$
$9 - 1 = 8$
$10 - 1 = 9$

 **−2**

$2 - 2 = 0$
$3 - 2 = 1$
$4 - 2 = 2$
$5 - 2 = 3$
$6 - 2 = 4$
$7 - 2 = 5$
$8 - 2 = 6$
$9 - 2 = 7$
$10 - 2 = 8$
$11 - 2 = 9$

 **−3**

$3 - 3 = 0$
$4 - 3 = 1$
$5 - 3 = 2$
$6 - 3 = 3$
$7 - 3 = 4$
$8 - 3 = 5$
$9 - 3 = 6$
$10 - 3 = 7$
$11 - 3 = 8$
$12 - 3 = 9$

 **−4**

$4 - 4 = 0$
$5 - 4 = 1$
$6 - 4 = 2$
$7 - 4 = 3$
$8 - 4 = 4$
$9 - 4 = 5$
$10 - 4 = 6$
$11 - 4 = 7$
$12 - 4 = 8$
$13 - 4 = 9$

 **−5**

$5 - 5 = 0$
$6 - 5 = 1$
$7 - 5 = 2$
$8 - 5 = 3$
$9 - 5 = 4$
$10 - 5 = 5$
$11 - 5 = 6$
$12 - 5 = 7$
$13 - 5 = 8$
$14 - 5 = 9$

 **−6**

$6 - 6 = 0$
$7 - 6 = 1$
$8 - 6 = 2$
$9 - 6 = 3$
$10 - 6 = 4$
$11 - 6 = 5$
$12 - 6 = 6$
$13 - 6 = 7$
$14 - 6 = 8$
$15 - 6 = 9$

 **−7**

$7 - 7 = 0$
$8 - 7 = 1$
$9 - 7 = 2$
$10 - 7 = 3$
$11 - 7 = 4$
$12 - 7 = 5$
$13 - 7 = 6$
$14 - 7 = 7$
$15 - 7 = 8$
$16 - 7 = 9$

 **−8**

$8 - 8 = 0$
$9 - 8 = 1$
$10 - 8 = 2$
$11 - 8 = 3$
$12 - 8 = 4$
$13 - 8 = 5$
$14 - 8 = 6$
$15 - 8 = 7$
$16 - 8 = 8$
$17 - 8 = 9$

 **−9**

$9 - 9 = 0$
$10 - 9 = 1$
$11 - 9 = 2$
$12 - 9 = 3$
$13 - 9 = 4$
$14 - 9 = 5$
$15 - 9 = 6$
$16 - 9 = 7$
$17 - 9 = 8$
$18 - 9 = 9$

−10

$10 - 10 = 0$
$11 - 10 = 1$
$12 - 10 = 2$
$13 - 10 = 3$
$14 - 10 = 4$
$15 - 10 = 5$
$16 - 10 = 6$
$17 - 10 = 7$
$18 - 10 = 8$
$19 - 10 = 9$